The Angel of
Grozny

Other Books by Åsne Seierstad

With Their Backs to the World: Portraits from Serbia
Bookseller of Kabul
A Hundred and One Days"A Baghdad Journal

The Angel of Grozny

Orphans of a Forgotten War

Åsne Seierstad

Translated by
Nadia Christensen

BASIC
BOOKS

A Member of the Perseus Books Group
New York

Books published by Basic Books are available at special discounts
for bulk purchases in the United States by corporations, institutions,
and other organizations. For more information, please contact the Special
Markets Department at the Perseus Books Group, 2300 Chestnut Street,
Suite 200, Philadelphia, PA 19103, or call (800) 810-4145, ext. 5000,
or e-mail special.markets@perseusbooks.com.

A CIP catalog record for this book is available from the Library of Congress.
ISBN-13: 978-0-465-01122-3
Library of Congress Control Number: 2008925222

British ISBN: 978-1-84408-395-4
10 9 8 7 6 5 4 3 2 1

Contents

1

The Little Wolf

The blood flows into the mud, where it carves thin red paths. The slope is dark with mould and decay, and soon the blood will be absorbed and will disappear. The skull is crushed, the limbs lifeless. Not so much as a whimper is heard.

Red drops have splashed his trousers, but he can rinse them off in the water that flows in the flat riverbed below. With the brick still in his hand he feels strong, invincible and calm. He stands looking at the lifeless eyes. Blood still trickles out and is sucked into the sediment. He kicks the corpse and walks down to the river. The scrawny mongrel will soon be food for new stray dogs, and later for flies and maggots and other crawling things.

Once, he drowned a cat in a sewage ditch, but it didn't give him the same feeling as killing dogs. Now he mostly kills dogs. And pigeons. They perch by the dozen up in the tall apartment buildings. He sends them scattering in fright from the kitchen to the living room to the bedroom and lavatory, right through holes in damaged walls where the concrete dangles in huge chunks. The apartments are like half-crushed shells; rows of rooms are no more than piles of masonry and dust. Everything usable that wasn't destroyed in the attacks is stolen, devoured. A few dilapidated things remain: a warped stool, a broken shelf.

The buildings were left standing as walls of defence on the flat landscape when the first rockets were aimed at the city. Here the city's defenders barricaded themselves; here, they thought, they would stop the invasion. Throughout an unyielding, bone-chilling winter the battles raged from neighbourhood to neighbourhood, from street to street, from house to house. The resistance fighters had to keep withdrawing further out of the city, surrendering the rows of deserted apartment blocks like eerie shooting targets for the Russians' rockets. In some of the buildings you can still read the rebels' graffiti on the walls — *Svoboda ili Smert* — Freedom or Death!

On stairways without banisters, on ledges where one false step means you plummet to the bottom, in rooms where at any moment the ceiling can collapse on top of him or the floor give way under him — this is where Timur lives. From the top of the concrete skeletons he can peer out through holes in a wall at the people below. When he gets hungry he startles the pigeons, which flutter away in confusion. He chases them into a corner and chooses his victim. The fattest. Grasping it tightly between his legs, he breaks its neck with a practised grip. He twists off the head, quickly turns the bird upside down, and holds it like that until all the blood flows out. Then he plucks it, thrusts a stick through its body and roasts it over a fire he's lighted on the top floor whose roof has been blasted off. Sometimes he roasts two.

In the rubbish dump on the hillside below he ferrets out half-rotten tomatoes, partially eaten fruit, a crust of bread. He searches in the top layers because the refuse quickly becomes covered with dust and muck and, when the rain comes, gets mixed with bits of glass, metal and old plastic bags. The dump is a lifeless place. Only up on the asphalt strip at the top of the steep hill is there movement. People, cars, sounds. When he's down here, amid the rotting earth, he's hidden from the life up there, the street life, the human life. Just as on a top floor, almost in the sky, he's hidden from the life below.

Quick as a squirrel, slippery as an eel, lithe as a fox, with the eyes of a raven and the heart of a wolf, he crushes everything he comes upon. His bones protrude from his body, he's strong and wiry, and always hungry. A mop of dirty blond hair hangs over two green eyes. His face, with its winsome, watchful expression, is unsettled by these eyes that flit restlessly to and fro. But they can also take aim like arrows and penetrate whatever they see. Put to flight, in flight. Ready for battle.

He knows how to kick well. His best kick he does backwards: advancing as if to attack with his fists, he suddenly spins round and thrusts out a leg with a quick movement, striking high and hard with a flat foot. He practises up in the apartment building, kicking and hitting an imaginary enemy. In his belt he carries a knife; this and the bricks are Timur's weapons. His life is a battle with no rules.

He is too much of a coward to be a good pickpocket. There's one thing in particular he's afraid of – a beating. So he steals only from those smaller than himself. When it starts to get dark he waylays the youngest children who beg at the bazaar or by the bridge across the Sunzha and intimidates them into handing over the coins they collected during the day. He beats up those who object or try to evade him, and he hits hard. The unfortunate victims are left in tears. The young predator slinks away.

Summer is coming, and the little wolf will soon be twelve years old.

When he was only a few months old, towards the end of 1994, he heard the first bomb blasts. That first winter of war he lay wrapped in a blanket on his mother's lap in a dark cellar while the sounds assaulting his ears formed his first memories. Before he could walk he saw people stagger, fall and remain lying on the ground. His father joined the resistance and was killed in a rocket attack on Bamut in the foothills of the southwestern mountains when Timur was one year old. His widowed mother then carried the boy in a shawl to the home of her husband's parents. A couple of years later, she, too, was gone.

Timur spent his early childhood with his grandparents in a

small village. Life was quite peaceful for a few years, until war broke out again, this time fiercer, bloodier than before. Timur was five then. After the first year of this second war he started school, but the classes were interrupted by Russian attacks, and for months they lived in the cellar because of the constant barrage of rockets. One spring evening as they sat in the damp darkness under ground, the neighbouring house was hit. When things quietened down, Timur peered outside and saw something roll past the door: the neighbour's head, thudding steadily down the road.

Timur's grandparents died when he was seven. At the second funeral it was decided that he should go to live with his father's brother, Omar, a young man in his mid-twenties. Liana, who was one year older than Timur, would go there, too. The two children had the same father, different mothers, and had not known about each other before.

They moved into the uncle's one-room flat in a bombed-out building in the Zavodskoi district of Grozny. Towards evening Omar sat down with a bottle of booze and told the children, aged seven and eight, to go to sleep on the dirty kitchen floor. They lay next to each other listening to the sounds in the ravaged apartment building.

The next morning the uncle ordered them out into the street. If they didn't come home with money – enough money – they would get a beating.

That's what invariably happened. The uncle used an electric cable that had been stripped of its plastic insulation. Only a small piece of plastic remained at one end, the part he gripped when he hit them. He held the metal over the stove until it glowed and whipped it across their naked backs again and again as they lay together on the floor with their knees curled up under them.

They learned quickly.

Liana practised the art of interpreting people's intentions and movements to detect their unguarded moments. Then her small hands stole into pockets and handbags. She roamed the streets and marketplaces with an angelic look on her face. Like her half-brother, she had pale, almost translucent, skin and luminous green eyes that could penetrate people's necks and backs, pockets and bags. But her look was veiled, detached. It didn't grab hold as Timur's did.

The siblings adapted to street life, but living in the gutter affected their appearance in different ways. The more devilish a thief she became the more angelic Liana appeared – people saw only two large childish eyes and an emaciated body – whereas Timur became more stooped and scowling. He looked like a petty crook, in fact, but preferred to gather bricks from tumbledown buildings rather than risk being caught stealing. He was paid two roubles for the bricks – about four pence – at building sites. It was hard work because the bricks weren't scattered individually; they might form part of a wall, a doorway, a brick edging. You had to hack away pieces with a sledgehammer before you could scrape off the plaster, concrete or cement. Only then would you get anything for them. He had to fight for the best locations because there were many who tried to earn money this way, adults with families to feed as well as children like him. To deal with the larger pieces of masonry the young boys preferred to work in groups, where the youngest children, who cleaned off the plaster, were only six or seven years old. Timur stood hunched over as he hacked with his hammer; sometimes he got so tired he had to sit back on his haunches. He was so thin that when he squatted to clean the bricks his bones stuck out like two points from the seat of his trousers.

Zavodskoi – 'Factory Town' – was the site of big production plants. Its oil refineries had been among the largest in the Soviet Union. Now they lay like leaking chemical disasters. Mines had been laid in many of them, too. Timur learned to watch out for mines and explosives that had not detonated. To risk a mine exploding was better than getting another round of blows on his back from the glowing copper. Besides gathering bricks, he collected all the metal, iron reinforcing rods, aluminium and wires he could find. For that he got two roubles a kilo. One morning a heavy metal plate fell on to his foot. A deep open wound, infected and full of pus, eventually became an aching, crooked scar. All summer he limped around with sledgehammer in hand and a knife in his belt and developed an even more dangerous look.

But when he lay next to his half-sister on the cold kitchen floor hearing his uncle snoring in the other room, he felt knotted up. He thought about a life in which he wouldn't have to be afraid. The thought occurred to him that Omar, lying there in a drunken stupor, was an easy target. A brick hidden in Timur's hand: *bam*, on his uncle's head; a knife, *swish*, across his throat, and . . . But the thought always ended in a nightmare: the uncle woke up, grabbed the hand holding the knife and turned it on Timur.

In the neighbouring flat lived another man with young relations who had lost their parents. The neighbour and the uncle often drank together, and sometimes they brought in Timur and the neighbour's nephew, Naid, who was two years younger, and ordered them to fight. Whoever lost would get a beating. The two drunkards cheered and shouted. Naid was smaller and even thinner than Timur, so usually he was the one who got a good thrashing from the two men as punishment for losing the fight. Like Timur, the boy next door also grew up with burn scars across his back and on the backs of his legs. Sometimes a neighbour came in and scolded the men for making such a racket and threatened to report them to the police. Timur hoped she would carry out her threats, but she never did.

At that time, Grozny lay in ruins. There were fighter planes in the sky, tanks in the streets, bursts of gunfire at night. Many of the inhabitants had fled; those who could leave, did. Others hung on, had no place to go, and struggled to cope somehow in the chaos. Few paid any attention to the children.

As Timur gradually became more adept with the sledgehammer he managed to put aside a few roubles. When he was ten years old he bought beer and a packet of cigarettes for the first time. He thought that if he drank he'd get stronger, because his uncle hit hardest when he was drunk. Timur drank some beer and wanted to find someone to beat up. But he only became dizzy. He didn't grow strong; he just felt more miserable and more lonely.

Dusk was the worst. Every afternoon, just before it got dark, he was ordered to leave while his sister had to stay at home. Timur wasn't allowed to come back before the last rays of sunlight had disappeared.

One afternoon when the door had been locked behind him, he drifted down to the river and began throwing small stones into the water. The sun was setting and a rosy glow that had settled over the rooftops struck his eyes. One pebble after another created rings on the surface until they disappeared in the current as the river passed on under the bridge. His eyes followed the patterns until he began to shiver. The warm light was suddenly gone, the city looked bleak again. A couple of dogs limped around in the rubbish along the water's edge. He looked around, picked up a large stone from the rubbish, and whistled to one of the dogs. He leaned down, clucked and beckoned as if he had something to offer. When the animal approached him, he raised his right hand, the one holding the rock, and brought it down on the creature's head with all his strength. The dog howled and sank to the ground. Then Timur took the sharp stone in both hands and struck again. They were such wretched creatures, these mutts — scrawny, weak and trembling. Hungry dogs weren't dangerous. It was the satiated, the well-fed ones, that bit you.

He sat by the river for a while. The rocks were ice-cold. The air was raw and the damp seeped into his clothing. He started to get up to go home, but then sat down again. He couldn't bear the thought of his uncle, the foul-smelling apartment, his sister's sobs. He decided he'd never go home again.

When it got dark, he lay down in some large pipes a little further along the riverbank. They provided a little shelter, but all night he lay cold and frightened, listening to the wild dogs howling. The dogs that were so easy to kill during the day became slavering wolves in the darkness.

At night they were the strongest ones.

The little dog killer lives in Russia. He was born in Russia, he speaks Russian, he looks like a Russian, with pale eyes and blond hair. During the few days he attended school he learned the same Cyrillic alphabet as the children in Siberia, had the same history lessons as students along the Volga, and he memorised the same poems by Pushkin as the children in St Petersburg. He is one person among Russia's declining population, one of barely 150 million citizens. If a proper census were taken across the nation, and if someone had found him down there by the muddy river-bed, he would have counted as but one citizen in the far-flung realm. But at no time in his life has any state wanted to count him in. Let alone wanted to look after him. Or cared about what he's lost: his parents, his childhood, his schooling. Or what he's never had: care, upbringing, security – because of a war that this same government started.

Timur is not among those whom most Russians would call 'one of us'. On the contrary, boys like him are a problem. A threat against the true citizens. The true Russians. There are two words for being a Russian. There's *rossianin*, which means a Russian national, and then there's *russky*, which refers to ethnicity. Only Slavs are *russky*, 'one of us'. When President Vladimir Putin speaks to the people of Russia, he will of course, rightly and properly, use the word *rossianin* which includes all citizens, be they Orthodox Christians, Muslims, Buddhists or Jews. Timur is *rossianin* but not *russky*. He's a citizen of Russia, but not a Russian. Timur is Chechen. In addition to Russian, he speaks his mother tongue, Chechen, but he's never learned to write it. He knows his culture through myths and legends, but has never learned his history. He knows he's a Muslim, but has never learned to pray. He tries to be proud, but doesn't really know what he's proud of. He knows he wants to fight, and he knows against whom.

A census would have revealed many things. Soviet figures from 1989 showed that the number of Chechens had just reached one million. Since the wars started, five years after that, around one hundred thousand Chechens have been killed.

Among the dead are thousands of children. They could hardly be called bandits or terrorists, as the authorities label those who resist. Not yet, anyway. But if you ask Timur what he wants to be when he grows up, he answers that he wants to be a resistance fighter. He wants to trade his knife for a Kalashnikov. He wants to fight, to fight back. He wants to exchange the dogs for Russians. He wants people to be afraid of him. That's what he wants most of all.

You can try to count the dead. You can argue about the numbers. You can count the maimed. You can argue about those numbers, too. What does it matter to lose a leg. An arm. To become crippled. To become blind. To have your hearing blasted away.

Where in the statistics do you find a violated childhood?

UNICEF reports that since 1994 up to the present day twenty-five thousand children in Chechnya have lost one or both parents. Some of them live in cardboard boxes, in bombed-out apartment buildings or in pipes by a riverbank.

A blanket of pitch-black darkness wraps itself icily around him. The night is bitterly cold. Is it wolves or dogs that are howling? Or jackals maybe? Huddled inside the pipe he tries to stay awake, because he's afraid the wild animals will attack him while he's asleep. And when the first streaks of light filter through his eyelids he creeps out, trembling with cold, and begins gathering pieces of wood and cardboard to make a hut. Before the sun is up he has built himself a small shelter out of the concrete pipe on the riverbank. It doesn't protect him against the cold night air but he hopes it will help against the dogs.

He tries to imagine that he's a wolf, a merciless wolf, a swift creature with teeth sharp as an awl. But the game doesn't warm him up and he has to abandon it.

After a while Timur moves in with gypsies. He pays them a few roubles to be allowed to sleep in their huts and sit by their fires, while he dreams of belonging to the real wolf pack. The resistance fighters, the heroes who attack the Russians from bases in the mountains, who blow up armoured vehicles. Up there, in the snow-covered mountains, that's where he wants to go. He wants to fight, as the wolves before him have fought for three hundred years according to his grandfather.

Even if he hardens himself, he still harbours painful thoughts. He has left his half-sister in a helpless situation. Alone with his uncle. He fantasises how he will rescue her. How he will break in when the uncle is lying in a drunken stupor, how he will threaten the man with a knife and save his sister.

He kills a dog instead. Kicks yet another corpse. Dopes himself up, sniffs glue. He ends up in a fight with the gypsy boys and is thrown out of the roving pack.

Once again he sleeps alone down by the riverbank with the dogs around him. Dogs that he can kill at any time. They're so weak, so cowardly, he snorts. They've forgotten they're actually wolves.

2

. . . *sharpens his* kinzhal

I can't remember the first time I heard about Chechnya. But I remember the first time I had to spell it.

Russian television, the first days of January 1995: streets filled with distorted bodies. Charred, black fragments that had once been human beings. Children's corpses frozen into the ground. Dark bloodstains in the snow. Panic in a frozen city. In the midst of this, a burned-out army tank with a star-shaped figure on its roof like a blackened copper statue – a Russian soldier with one hand on the gun barrel, the other outstretched. He'd been fused to the metal by the intense heat as the tank he commanded became an inferno. He died in that position, caught in flight.

All across Russia people sat mesmerised in front of their television sets.

For the military leadership, it was the morning after.

What had gone wrong?

On 10 December 1994, Boris Yeltsin had been admitted to hospital for a nose operation. The next day forty thousand Russian troops rolled across the snow-covered plains and crossed the border into Chechnya, a republic that had declared its independence from Russia three years earlier. The president lay on the operating table, and was therefore neither seen nor heard, but the day before the operation he had persuaded the Russian Security

Council to approve 'disarmament of all illegal armed groups'. Then he disappeared under general anaesthetic, and his minister of defence, Pavel Grachev, took command of reality.

For several weeks Russian forces launched sporadic attacks in order to make Chechnya's president, former Soviet general Jokhar Dudayev, change course. But the attacks only made the president more intransigent, and in the morning hours of New Year's Eve 1994 the assault on Grozny began. Pavel Grachev, who had celebrated his forty-fourth birthday the evening before, had declared 'a single paratroop regiment can solve all the problems within two hours'. After the first twenty-four hours, a thousand Russian soldiers had been killed.

Calmly, without firing a shot, the tanks rumbled forward on huge caterpillar treads. They did not have orders to attack, just to 'occupy the city'. They passed through the suburbs without encountering any resistance. The same was true of the apartment blocks on the outskirts of Grozny. The heavy columns rolled on until they reached the inner city. There they met the counter-attack. The Chechens stood ready in Grozny's forest of tall buildings. Tanks were set ablaze. The soldiers inside fled from the flames, only to be shot down, one by one, as they leaped out. Those who sought refuge in the buildings were attacked in the entrances, where the city's defenders stood ready with knives, swords and *kinzhals* – daggers.

How could the Russian army allow itself to be so humiliated? What kind of intelligence information was this? The minister of defence had himself said that bandits in the republic numbered in the tens of thousands. Bandits – that's what he called the separatists. Had he imagined they would run away when they saw the tanks?

According to highly placed military sources, it gradually came out that Grachev's order to storm Grozny on New Year's Eve was given almost on a whim during a drunken party at the military base in Mozdok. 'A birthday blitz', the idea was called.

The troops had been sent in without maps, without firm

orders, without knowing where they should go. The tank drivers had merely been told 'Follow the tank ahead of you'. Many of the soldiers had never handled a weapon, and those who had had generally lain flat on the ground and fired at a target. None of them had received any training for urban warfare – the most difficult of all battlefields. The army had not yet adjusted from a Cold War strategy based on nuclear warfare. Most of the tanks were old and lacked communications equipment as well as protective armour. The Chechens could toss grenades from high-rise buildings and let the ammunition and fuel that exploded inside the vehicle do the rest.

As the fighting raged, television stations broadcast a taped recording of the president's traditional New Year speech. In front of the Russian flag, Boris Yeltsin delivered his greetings; when he got to the armed forces, he lethargically intoned: 'When you risk your lives, even on New Year's Eve, remember that you are serving Russia, you are defending Russia and the Russians.'

The soldiers he addressed never got to hear those words.

I sat in shock in front of the television, together with my Russian hosts, Ludmila and Alexander, in their apartment near Belorussky Station in Moscow. We were witness to a humiliating catastrophe for the Russian army. A catastrophe that flashed on to the screen in all its horror. This was during the short period in the nineties when the Russian media were actually free to edit their own broadcasts. The TV pictures showed burning tanks every ten metres, charred, rigid corpses and body parts hanging in the trees.

How could the world's biggest army have made such an elementary mistake? Tanks, with no infantry support, inside a city where snipers swarmed over each other. 'Tanks can rule in a field, but in a city they are blind,' Grachev himself had said.

The disastrous attack might have been taken directly from the books of John F. Baddeley, who described the Caucasian wars of the eighteenth and nineteenth centuries:

The result was as expected. The troops in the centre got separated from those in the front and those in the rear, and the enemy swarmed in between, shooting from all positions, from behind every tree trunk – and even from the branches, because the huge beech trees sheltered large numbers of Chechen sharpshooters – and wherever there was confusion, they streamed forth to finish the task with a sword or *kinzhal*.

I was twenty-four years old and on my first assignment as a journalist. I had rented a small room with a window in the home of a family with three children in Moscow. Anything else was out of the question on my freelancer's budget. To cover expenses I took jobs as an interpreter. For one fumbling year I had written newspaper articles for *Arbeiderbladet*, articles without head or tail which were patched together by an understanding foreign editor. Fortunately for me, Øyvind Johnsen believed it was easier for someone who knows Russian to learn to be a journalist than for a journalist to learn Russian. He threw himself into the task body and soul, and eventually I could supply articles with lead paragraphs, headlines and subtitles. I knocked about in Moscow's streets, squares and alleys, or caught trains across the Russian steppes.

But now an old black and white TV that needed to be thumped in order to get a clear picture was my only source of information about the war. I was at a loss. I was supposed to report about hell from a place I could barely spell.

First *Che*, then *ch*, and then *nya*.

Little by little my fingers got used to the word. More and more frequently that winter I had to write about this place that I'd never been to or had any desire to visit. I took notes frantically from the television there in mouldy apartment seven, building fourteen, on Leningrad Prospect. One evening after the broadcast Ludmila started reciting a poem:

> *The Terek streams over boulders*
> *The murky waves splash*
> *A wicked Chechen crawls on to the bank*

I broke in:

> *And sharpens his kinzhal.*

I knew that poem well. The verses were fixed in my mind from the days when I used to memorise Russian poems in the Blindern student housing complex in Oslo. It was by Mikhail Lermontov, the *enfant terrible* sent to serve in the Caucasus during the 1830s after writing a poem about Alexander Pushkin's death that criticised Tsar Nicholas. The poem – like Lermontov's main work, *A Hero of Our Time* – was inspired by the Caucasus and told of Cossack mothers who rocked their infants to sleep with horror stories about the evil Chechens. 'Be prepared, little baby,' they warned.

In the same way, Chechen mothers instilled ideas of the enemy's wickedness and taught their children to become warriors. 'Take up arms, little one.' Unfortunately, some of the hypnotic rhythm gets lost in translation:

> *Papa is always a soldier*
> *Hardened in battle is he*
> *Sleep, little boy, go to sleep*
> *Sleep, go to sleep now in peace*
>
> *Soon we will come to the time*
> *You too must go off to war*
> *Valiantly fasten your stirrup*
> *Take up your weapon and fight*

'History repeats itself,' Ludmila said with a deep sigh. 'Alas, alas,' she lamented, feeling just as sorry for the Chechen children and their mothers as for the poor teenage soldiers from the Russian *glubinka* – the depths of Russia – who were sent straight to their deaths. 'Yeltsin, that drunken sot!' she cursed.

The international desk at *Arbeiderbladet* telephoned and asked me to explain the background to the conflict in the Caucasus. The mountain people that never surrendered. *Papa is always a soldier.* Three hundred years of fighting against the Russian empire. *You too must go off to war.* Fighting for their own traditions. *Sharpens his kinzhal.* New uprisings. *Take up your weapon and fight.*

The information in the media differed more and more. On Channel 1 the Russians emerged victorious from every battle and made great gains, while the independent channel NTV showed the atrocities of the war from both sides. The newspapers contradicted each other, and so did the politicians. As a freelance journalist for a newspaper with a limited budget I didn't have access to the international news bureaux. This was before you could just log on to the Internet and read. I fumbled around blindly, qualified numerous points in my articles and felt inadequate. It was utterly beyond my powers to report accurately about the war, and an uneasy thought was born.

'Do you have a seat on a plane to Grozny?'

In front of me stands a fat man in a green uniform, a sheen of perspiration on his face and neck. His sceptical eyes scrutinise me from beneath bushy blond eyebrows.

'So you want to go to war?'

The man is not exactly friendly, but not exactly unfriendly either.

'I'd like to see for myself.'

The somewhat sleepy officer considers this and asks: 'Are you sure that's right for you?'

Above the uniformed man hangs a chandelier with only a couple of bulbs lit. They are superfluous, in any case; the sun casts long rays through the dusty windows. The room's thick cement walls are painted the yellowish beige typical of Russian government ministries. It is early May, but already a sudden heatwave has enveloped the Russian capital, sweetening the city with the intoxicating fragrance of flowers and turning the trees a soft green overnight. I draw a deep breath, seeking some fresh air, but here in the corridor the air is as cloying as the colour of the walls.

'Well . . . I guess I'll find out.'

We're standing in a large carpeted room in the Ministry of Defence. The officer gives me a distant, tolerant look, and what he says next is uttered almost without thinking.

'War is not for young ladies. Why don't you write about something womanly instead – clothes, spring fashions?'

'Clothes don't interest me much.'

The officer wipes his forehead with the sweaty back of his hand and sighs. It's almost lunchtime.

'I advise you not to go.'

He looks at the clock.

'You've been warned.'

He disappears down the corridor. I stay where I am, feeling uneasy, a little beyond myself.

One morning it just hit me. I have to go. I have to see for myself. Just as quickly, I pushed the thought aside. I couldn't imagine myself in a war. Who could?

War is somewhere else, not where you are. Not where you're supposed to be. But Moscow had become a fog in which it was impossible to find your way. And when *should, should not, should, should not* became *should,* the next question presented itself: How do you go to a war? It's not just a matter of travelling there. Civilian planes are cancelled, the trains no longer run, the roads are blocked. In my dank basement existence with Ludmila and Alexander on Leningrad Prospect, I had nobody to ask. But some certainly take aeroplanes. Those who have to go to the war. The soldiers, the officers, the generals. Maybe they could take me along?

The green-uniformed man reappears in the corridor. He has a piece of paper in his hand. Some numbers scribbled with a blunt pencil on grey notepaper. A note of the planes that transport the army to Grozny.

'You can come to the military airbase at Domodedovo at five o'clock on Wednesday morning.'

He wipes the sweat from his brow again, turns round and walks away. After a couple of steps he looks back at me.

'But I'd rather the plane left without you.'

Two days later a light night turned into a brilliant sunrise some-where on the road to Domodedovo. The seductive heavenly spectacle was spoiled only by the driver who fussed and complained.

'The war? What can you do about it anyway? What does it have to do with you? Is it worth risking your life for?'

I stepped out of the car into a crystal-clear summer morning. The airport lay in the middle of a birch forest. From the area in front of the building a path led along a stream, and the ground was covered, idyllically, with a blanket of wood anemones that extended to an uneven row of low wooden fences. At a counter inside I received confirmation that I was in fact listed as a passenger on the military plane. Who said Russia was bureaucratic? I was directed to a bench by the wall, but chose instead to go outside and follow the narrow path along the stream. Beyond the building's warped doors, half-hidden behind pale green foliage, stood small wooden houses with carved window frames and decorated rooftops. Lace curtains fluttered in the windows and you could already see cabbages and carrots sprouting in the gardens. The houses were faded and peeling, revealing all the nuances of the colours they had been painted over the years. As in most villages in Russia, the inhabitants were elderly. Hunchbacked women hoed the soil; grey-haired men peered through the tiny windows. Peasant women on a bench, their hands on their canes, the budding birches, the white trunks, the murmuring brook, and the keen sense of anticipation that the scent of anemones always gives me – this was the last memory I took from Moscow.

We carried our bags on to the plane, the soldiers and I. When Ludmila realised that she couldn't change my mind about going – *Am I going to have yet another thing to worry about? They shoot anything that moves!* – she had packed a huge lunch of black bread – *sourdough lasts the longest* – a jar of tomatoes – *you need vitamins* – water – *it might be polluted down there* – a Thermos of tea and warm clothes.

'*It's summer, Luda!*' Another floral-patterned scarf.

'*You're going to the high mountains, Åsnitska!*'

I found a seat among the soldiers and when I turned round I looked into hundreds of young faces, very young faces – eighteen-year-olds on their first tour of duty. Only a few of them had ever flown in an aeroplane before. Those in window seats sat with faces pressed against the glass, while those in the middle stretched across their comrades or stared straight ahead. The boys, looking pale and thin in their uniforms, had been taken straight from their homes and into the war. They were to replenish the ranks. Thousands of young men like them had already been killed by the snipers on Grozny's rooftops, in mountain ambushes or by their own troops during the first chaotic weeks. The boy beside me had blond, almost white, hair and ruddy cheeks; he craned his long thin neck across the soldier next to him in order to see out of the window. We sat without speaking. It was as if we were each already on our own journey. I could still turn back. He couldn't.

As soon as we were airborne, an officer emerged from behind the front curtain. He invited me, or, more precisely, commanded me, to come to the forward cabin. The front of the plane didn't have rows of seats as in the back; instead, it was a small compartment with little tables and soft chairs. I was offered a brimming glass of vodka, black bread and pickled gherkins. It wasn't quite seven o'clock in the morning.

The officers on this side of the curtain had been in the war before and were going to crush the enemy, squeeze the scoundrels, wipe out the bandits, make mincemeat of the wild men; yes, the Chechens are wild, explained the officers. They cut off people's heads, ears, noses, fingers. You can't trust them, they shoot you in the back, they trick you; they're devious to the core, and always have been, these mountain people. *A wicked Chechen crawls on to the bank, and sharpens his kinzhal.*

White rows of snow-covered cliffs shone beneath us. Delicate wisps of clouds danced around their heights. From the edge of the carpet of snow, rivers and streams rushed downward to disappear into lush forests. At the bottom of one valley lay villages trapped between mountainsides almost too steep to climb and cut by deep ravines that gaped towards the mountain's dark interior.

During the landing I was allowed to sit on a folding seat between the two pilots. Hundreds of planes would come in this direction. They would fly this route to drop bombs on forest groves, on villages, roads and on people. By now, most of the fighting was taking place on the ground; but a heavy stream of planes still took off from their bases. The war was still young.

Thud, we landed on a makeshift landing strip. *Bump*, we sped along rough concrete. *Click*, the doors were opened and we disembarked. Out on the landing strip the pilots pulled a helmet and a bulletproof vest from the baggage compartment. A farewell gift. They wished me luck.

The Russian army was going its way. I had to find mine.

The sun baked down from high overhead as I lugged the heavy gifts away from the plane. Military vehicles were already picking up the soldiers; they were crammed together in the back of a lorry and quickly left the runway.

I looked around.

First towards the airport building, where the windows had been broken long ago. Some twisted metal frames were all that remained. The walls were riddled with holes, the counters smashed. Through the building I could see a road leading from the main entrance towards the city, that is to say, most probably towards the city. Where else would it lead? There was nobody to ask. I stood there with my backpack, the heavy helmet and a bulletproof vest the size of a Russian bear. Dragging the war kit with me, I headed towards the front of the building. From there I could probably work out how to get further.

Two men, one tall and thin, the other shorter and heavier, came towards me. They walked mechanically, arms hanging loosely at their sides, making their way up the steps of what had once been the entrance to the airport. Their faces bore a stony expression. When they began to speak I realised what it was. Terror. Something I'd never seen before. Fear of death. It created a mask that made facial expressions disappear, features harden and bodies go limp. Only words were left, and they too were lifeless.

I was crazy to think of coming to Grozny, they told me dully.

'There are snipers everywhere. They lie on the rooftops, shoot down whoever they please,' said one of the men in a rasping voice. 'The Russians have control during the day, but towards evening it turns deadly.'

'The machine guns sing all night,' the other added.

They were Germans, working for *Stern*. Or was it *Der Spiegel*? No matter, they were going home, would try to get on a transport plane to Moscow, and I ought to do the same.

The men sat down with their backs to the cement wall, and each lit a cigarette. They seemed out of breath; was it their walk along the bombed street, or because their hearts were beating twice as fast? Perhaps it was that their fear was beginning to lose its hold now that they were going home. Clouds of cigarette smoke mixed with cement dust in the air.

My head was swimming under the midday sun; there wasn't a shady spot anywhere, everything tall had been bombed flat. Come back on the plane with us. *Snipers everywhere.* Back to the anemones by the cool building. *They shoot down whoever they please.* Back to Luda and Sasha and the TV set. *They lie on the rooftops.* Back to my desk. *A symphony of machine guns at night.* You're crazy if you stay.

For the first time, I felt I was weighing my life in my hands.

Did I walk? Did I find some transport? Did I meet someone? Was I offered a ride? I no longer remember how, but somehow I ended up in the centre of Grozny with my forbidding equipment. I'd passed row after row of devastated buildings, demolished homes, gaping holes – the city lay in ruins. Already now, four or five months into the war, the destruction was worse than that suffered by Sarajevo in two or three years. People tramped over stone blocks and pieces of concrete, walked around deep holes, bent under wires and cables, balanced on planks laid across the bomb craters. After the catastrophic New Year invasion, the minister of defence had got rid of some generals; he remained, himself, but changed tactics and began high-altitude bombing.

Hospitals, orphanages, waterworks and homes were demolished – despite the fact that Russia's prime minister maintained that 'the aerial attacks strike only military installations from which the enemy is shooting', and the Security Council in the Kremlin declared 'the Chechens simulated explosions in residential areas'.

Some people had set up small tables where they sold cigarettes, sweets, a pair of stockings. Spare car parts were displayed on one wooden crate, batteries on another. Hotel? Motel? A guesthouse? People shook their heads. I looked up at the rooftops. That's where they were supposed to be lying, the snipers. The massive air attacks had forced the separatists to withdraw from the capital and continue the fight in the mountains. But they stole back in smaller groups and carried out nightly surprise attacks on the Russians.

The sun would soon disappear, and here in the south at the foot of the mountains night fell very quickly. But it was still light now, and during the daylight hours Russian soldiers patrolled the city, which lay there like a pile of sleepy ruins. Where should I go? What should I do? People gave me curious looks, but when I met their gaze they turned away. I had to get rid of the wretched gifts the pilots had given me.

The sun sank lower. A young girl came carrying a large bucket. I imagine I must have stopped her somehow.

'Follow me,' she said.

I followed. A pair of worn-out sandals, a skirt that dragged on the ground, and, when I raised my eyes, a floral-patterned scarf. We left the main street and started up a steep path that crossed a hillside above the city. Low houses whose doors were pockmarked with bullet holes clung to one side of the footpath; opposite them was a stinking garbage heap. We didn't say a word on our way up the hill. The low afternoon sun burned the back of my neck. Perspiration dripped into my eyes. My face was coated with sticky dust. There was a metallic taste in my mouth. My heart beat wildly.

The girl knocked at a door. It was opened from inside. 'Welcome,' said the girl I had followed. Women of all ages came towards me. The oldest, a stout woman with wavy grey hair visible under a black kerchief, took my hand and led me into a room that was divided up by white sheets hanging from the ceiling. A young girl set out a wash basin and a piece of soap; the stream of water was like music as she filled the basin from a pitcher. In the cracked mirror above the wash basin, I met a pair of gimlet eyes. Steady, staring, wide open. A look I'd never seen before. It was my own. *I don't belong here.*

When I came out into the yard a pale reflection of the setting sun danced in a corner by the fence. A table had been set with slices of bread, a soft white cheese, sweet peppers and golden tea. The women let me eat in silence. They weren't going to have any food themselves. I saw that they had put away the helmet and bulletproof vest, which I'd set down outside, and they were evasive when I asked any questions. After all, who did they think I was — a young girl, part soldier, part adventurer, with equipment from the Russian army?

'I'm going to write,' I said.

They nodded.

The air was mild, soft as velvet, and around us the grasshoppers

were singing. A chilly breath of air brought some coolness; gradually the heat was drawn out of the hill, the benches we sat on and
the wall behind us that had been sizzling-hot before. *You're going
to the high mountains*, Ludmila had said. I went inside and got one
of the scarves she had stuffed into my backpack, and returned to
the yard as the first gunshots ripped the evening's stillness. Replies
crackled against the sky. Another attack. More replies. Round
after round of a frightening song. The women didn't light a lamp.
We sat there in the dark. It was pitch-black when we went to bed.
The girl who had come with the water pitcher went inside with
me holding a candle, and left it flickering on the floor beside me.
Shadows spiralled up the whitewashed wall. I was alert to every
sound. Bullets carried on an exchange of deadly messages, back
and forth, back and forth, far away, then closer. I lay with my eyes
wide open.

The cool breath of air had been an illusion; now the darkness
was hot and heavy. The sheets were clammy. It was hard to
breathe. The salvoes came closer, they were fighting right outside
the wall. Soldiers broke down the entrance and stormed the
house; they kicked in the door, yanked the sheet off me, pulled
me out of bed, threw me to the floor. I screamed. And woke up.
Then I dozed off again into a restless sleep accompanied by shots
that came and went, until slowly they grew silent.

At dawn I was awakened by a cock crowing. The door to my
room was ajar and opened out towards the backyard, where hens
were clucking and scratching. Soon I heard cheerful voices from
the yard, something rattled in a dish that was being filled – peas,
perhaps, or dried beans; someone sifted something, shook something; a gas flame was lit, tableware clinked. They were homey
sounds, safe sounds, and I allowed myself to be lulled by the
murmur of subdued everyday noises in a futile attempt to become
part of it all.

I realised how ill-prepared I was. I didn't know where the
battle lines were, had no idea how I was going to get around, and
no notion of what surrounded the city. The women looked at me

in amazement when I meekly asked at breakfast if I could stay for a while. But they nodded. I went with the girl who had found me – or whom I had found – to the market, to the well; we cleaned beans, we hoed vegetables, we stirred pots, we sat in the backyard. Little by little the women told me their stories.

Luiza Magomadova had five daughters. Her husband had been killed during a bombing raid that winter. I saw no sign of her sons, or of her daughters' husbands. The women didn't say where the men were, they avoided the subject, talked about something else. Because, after all, who was I?

The men were most probably in the mountains, continuing the battle there. Otherwise the women wouldn't have been so reticent. I knew I ought to go somewhere and report about the war, but I had no idea where or how. So I played with the children, talked with the mothers and waited for courage I didn't have. The youngest daughter in the house, seventeen-year-old Bereta, was also waiting. She was well into her tenth month of pregnancy, waiting for a child that didn't want to come. She waddled around the yard with much difficulty and sighing, or she sat dozing in the shade in a mended armchair. She was dark-complexioned, taciturn like her mother, and seemed weighed down by sorrow that sapped all her energy. One afternoon as we sat drinking tea, each lost in her own thoughts, she said slowly in her laborious Russian:

'I know why . . . I know why.'

She stared off into space, and then turned towards me.

'During this whole war I've held back my feelings. Now my body is holding back the child.'

She told about sitting in a cold cellar during the worst attacks, about lying sleepless, night after night, listening to the bombs and machine-gun fire and wondering how life would be when the baby came.

'If it comes, that is. It's almost ten full months now,' she sighed, and grew silent again.

The third night I was awakened by loud moaning while it was

still dark, while the gunshots were still crackling, long before the cock crowed. Bereta's waters had broken, the baby was on its way, but it was too dangerous to go to the clinic now during curfew. They sent for a neighbour. Bereta sweated and moaned, sweated and screamed. They would go to the clinic as soon as it got light. There was an extra space in the car.

'Can I come along?'

When we got to hospital I was directed to a bench in a corridor. It was a hospital like all the others in Russia, the same pale yellow walls, the same linoleum-covered floors, the same numbers and letters on badges and posters, the same smell, the same shirts, the same sheets. The only way you could tell this wasn't just any hospital in Russia was by the windows: they were covered with thick tape to prevent them from being blown out by bomb blasts.

As I sat there in the corridor under the taped-up windows, the senior doctor came and asked me to follow her. She led me into a room a few doors away, where another woman was also waiting to give birth. The woman lay motionless with her face turned to the wall. Some days ago she had been on her way down from the mountains in Shatoi and had got caught in an exchange of gunfire. Her husband and six-year-old son had been killed. She herself had shrapnel wounds in her breast. The woman looked at us without seeing us. Alone, waiting for her child, with her face to the wall and metal fragments in her breast.

'I just wanted you to see how terrible the war is,' the doctor said quietly.

She led me back to the bench and disappeared. I sat there listening to the murmur of hospital sounds.

Then I heard a loud, clear cry.

A nurse came to get me, and I was allowed to see Bereta. A tiny head with masses of dark hair lay at her breast with one ear turned towards his mother's heart. The baby's chest rose and fell with healthy, steady breathing. His skin had a deep pink glow.

A mother who didn't know where the father was, or if he was

even alive. A father who didn't know his first son had just been born. A mother who had lost a child and awaited another. A father who had waited, but who now no longer waited for anything.

This was my first war reportage.

3

The First War

One week later I'm lying in a ditch.

Bullets rip twigs from the trees overhead and graze the top of the incline, triggering a cascade of stones and weeds. In the field next to us the shots land within a few metres of each other. When they hit the ground earth spurts up – just like in the movies, I say to myself. Yes, that is in fact what I'm thinking as I lie with my face in the dry turf and prickly thistles. Fortunately, it's difficult for the soldier in the tank to fire into a ditch. My mouth is dry, so terribly dry that if only I had something to drink, I say to myself, if I had something to drink I'd open the bottle, put it to my mouth and swallow. But I don't have anything to drink, and it wouldn't have helped, because the thirst isn't thirst. It's terror.

Someone is actually trying to kill me.

To be shot at: an absolute certainty that if you're hit, the bullets are more powerful than you. In a second you can be gone. Everything you are, everything you know, everything you've read or thought or heard. You're at the mercy of the person with the weapon, who he is and, not least, how afraid he is. The time it takes when someone is trying to kill you does something to you, if you survive.

What the hell am I doing here? This isn't my war.

Next to my face lay the feet of Martin Adler, a Swedish

freelance journalist I'd met at 'Konservny', the mass grave outside Grozny where people came to look for their lost loved ones. The bodies lay in deep ditches. A sweet and nauseating odour hung in the air. The corpses were black with flies. Fat white worms crawled around among the dead. Some bodies were naked, others partially clothed; some had shirts tied around their heads, others had their hands bound; some were missing arms or fingers, their skulls crushed, their bodies pierced with bullet holes. Others had been burned and could only be identified by their teeth. They were photographed, given a registration number and reburied. If their relations managed to identify them from the lists displayed at Dynamo Stadium, they would be dug up again so that what was left of them could be buried, according to Chechen tradition, in their own villages among their forefathers. These were the people who had disappeared at the roadblocks, who had been dragged from their homes, who had disappeared in the Russians' *zachistki* – clean-up operations. Men who had been tortured to make them give information about rebel positions and inform against their comrades, or who had been subjected to pure sadism, which poisons all wars, and then tossed into this mass grave to hide the evidence. There were mostly men in the ditches, and mostly women searching.

Martin turned to me. 'What should we do?' he asked.

What should we do? I lay with one side of my face on the ground, my eyes turned towards the field where the earth was still spurting up each time a bullet landed.

'We've got to get out of here,' Martin said hoarsely. 'They might come out of the tank and shoot into the ditch. They don't ask who we are before they shoot.'

I nodded. I couldn't speak. I had no voice.

Behind me lay Martin's interpreter, a young boy from Moscow who kept saying, even before we ended up in this ditch, how much he regretted accompanying the blond Swede. Beside him lay Jennifer, a one-woman television crew from ABC, and, behind her, the Chechen driver.

It was too dangerous to stay.

We crept forward. We wriggled flat on our stomachs along the bottom of the ditch, and the whole time I thought about water – thought that soon I couldn't crawl any further if I didn't get something to drink. My knees smarted, my hands were scratched, my mouth was full of earth. More bullets showered over us. I noticed that Martin lost his map as he slid, reptile-like, over the stones. It lay some way from me, and I wondered if I shouldn't try to pick it up; it was a very good map, and such a thing was hard to find. I looked at my grass-stained fingers smarting from the thistles; with one hand I clung to the ground, with the other I pulled my bulletproof vest over me. If I reached for the map, what would I do with it, which hand would I hold it in, how would I hold on to the vest then? It would be harder to crawl. So I wriggled past the map, left it lying there like a red marker.

I had been living in Luiza Magomadova's house for a week when I met Martin at Konservny. He'd rented a car, he said, and wanted to look around, go to the front lines. He asked if I would come along.

We left Grozny the next morning and drove some distance south of Shali, a town controlled by Russian forces. Six months into the war no clear front lines existed: they were everywhere and nowhere. Martin wanted to go to the other side, to the *boyeviks* – the resistance fighters – in the mountains. If we followed the highway and crossed the invisible line where Russian control ended, we would find them.

'Outside the city, heading south, there's a huge stone at the side of the road,' we'd been told. 'You can drive that far. But no further, then you'll be fair game for both sides.'

We spotted the stone and stopped. Stood there a while. It seemed so peaceful. The heavy branches of a walnut tree arched over the road, the fruit on the wild plum trees had begun to ripen. Ahead of us, a flat plain stretched towards a distant hill. We decided to drive on. I'd taken off my bulletproof vest; it was too heavy to sit in. Instead I padded my side of the car with it. My helmet rolled around in the boot. If I'd worn it, it would look as if the driver was carrying a soldier in the back seat, and he'd have none of that. He put his foot down, raising a cloud of dust; we left the stone, the highway was deserted. I leaned my head on the vest.

The khaki colour of the tank blended almost perfectly into the road. Gunshots crackled in the air. The brakes squealed and our car swerved to the side.

'Out!' Martin shouted as he threw open the right-hand door and dived into the ditch. I tumbled after Jennifer, who had been sitting in the middle, and managed to grab my vest, which now lay on top of me like a rug. Shells boomed on the road.

As we crept forward, the tank slowly changed direction and targeted its attack on a spot some twenty metres from us. Evidently the drivers of the tank thought the attack had come from our red Lada. Had we gone a few metres on, the car would have been riddled with bullet holes.

Lying in the ditch ahead of us was another man. Martin stopped, as did the trail of people snaking behind him. The man indicated with his eyes towards a car hanging over the edge of the ditch. He had neither seen nor heard the shooting before his front tyres were punctured.

Up on the road, another car braked sharply. We leaped up, threw ourselves into the back seat, and shouted: 'Turn round! Turn round!' The driver sped back towards Shali, as armoured vehicles thundered past us in the opposite direction.

At the first Russian checkpoint we were stopped by a drunken young soldier who ordered us out of the car. Waving his Kalashnikov at us aggressively, he shouted that we were under arrest.

'Backs to the wall!' he whined, pointing towards some sandbags next to the barracks a few metres away.

The soldier was of medium height, skinny, with hollow cheeks and a defiant look in his eyes. Eager to fight. He staggered around

with his rifle and began to interrogate us in a sniffling voice. Who
were we? Where were we going? Who did we work for? Who had
we met? What had we seen?

An older Chechen was sitting on the sandbags with us. 'It was
a young boy who attacked,' he whispered when the soldier turned
away. 'He got away through some pipes. The Russians don't dare
get out of their tanks during an ambush. They don't know how
many snipers might be nearby. The soldier on the roof of the tank
was killed.'

The Chechens had lost their foothold in more and more areas,
and had been forced to withdraw towards the Caucasus
Mountains in the south. But they infiltrated the Russian zones and
launched surprise attacks on roadblocks, military camps and
vehicles on the highways.

The soldiers reeked of vodka and stale sweat. We sat silently by
the sun-baked cement wall. Suddenly the bellicose soldier aimed
his gun at me and bellowed:

'Get up! You're coming with me!'

'Me?!'

'I'm taking you to headquarters to question you properly.
Come this way,' he commanded, and pointed. The highway was at
the top of a slope that led down to a field; beyond the field was
a dark grove of trees. The Kalashnikov was aimed at my
stomach.

'But your headquarters are in Shali. There isn't any reason to
go through the woods . . .'

'It's a short cut,' he replied coldly, without moving the
Kalashnikov.

'Shali is straight ahead!'

'Shut up! Nobody asked you, you're under arrest!'

He grabbed my arm to lead me down the hill. The other soldiers didn't say a word. Martin was calmly trying to negotiate via
his stammering Russian interpreter when a thundering drowned
out his voice. A tank. Now I had to act fast. I tore myself from the

soldier's grip and began shrieking and howling and waving my arms at the side of the road.

'I don't want to go into the woods! I don't want to go into the woods!' I shouted, and thought: tears, tears, make tears, scream for mama, scream that you want to go home, scream anything at all.

The tank stopped. What incredible good luck – the vehicle was manned by a group of soldiers who had taken Martin and me on their rounds in Grozny some days earlier. My face grimy with mud and sand, I sobbed:

'I don't want to go into the woods!'

'Why do you want to take her into the woods?' the soldiers asked the commander of the post.

He mumbled something.

'Let them go, all of them,' said the tank officer. One soldier was sent to get our car, which amazingly enough still had its tyres intact. We sped away without looking back, and reached Shali just before curfew. Darkness fell and gunshots cut through the night.

We stayed overnight with a local family, and I lay there thinking about the fear they must have felt – all those who were detained at roadblocks and then taken away, into the woods, where they had to dig their own trench before being executed. Many people had disappeared at such checkpoints. Who can imagine what they went through? The terror before the shot was fired, before the bullet pierced their flesh, before they rotted away at Konservny.

The next morning Martin rummaged through his backpack.

'Damn it, I've lost the map!'

I felt a stab of guilt. But said nothing. Martin wanted to go on. I was uncertain.

In the end, I went with him. We travelled south. The goal was the same: to reach rebel territory. The Russians advanced further, leaving behind demolished buildings, more people killed and wounded. Soon only the snow-covered mountains were controlled by Chechen forces. We passed the villages they had abandoned, and when it was close to six in the evening we sped towards Duba-Yurt, one of the last towns the Russians controlled in the south, a few kilometres from the front. Our driver went fast, taking the bends at breakneck speed on the narrow hillside roads; after six o'clock you were fair game, and the usually thorough soldiers rushed us through:

'You'd better move fast, if you value your lives!'

Duba-Yurt lay surrounded by lush green hills at the foot of the mighty Caucasus Mountains, which for centuries the Russians had tried to conquer. Alexander I annexed the kingdom of Georgia in 1801, but in the area where we were the tribes fought the Tsar's forces until the middle of the nineteenth century. During that time the Russian army set up a line of military posts – *stanitsi* – along the Terek River. They were held by Cossacks, who set out on raids of the *auls* – villages. They destroyed grazing lands, seized livestock and took as many prisoners as they could. Chechen reprisals came swiftly. Often the Russians were attacked even before they got back to their own lines. Or, as night came and the army camp settled down, bullets whizzed out of nowhere, guards' throats were slashed, tents were set ablaze, prisoners released. The most resolute fighters were the Dagestanis and the Chechens. Their leader, Imam Shamil, had rallied his men to wage holy war against the Christians.

The Caucasus represented adventure for young noblemen who couldn't adapt to the salons of St Petersburg or Moscow. They dreamed of romance, daring feats, riding in the mountains, brotherhood under canvas and fearless battles against *the wild ones*. War offered the means of becoming a man. Russia's two greatest poets, Alexander Pushkin and Mikhail Lermontov, who were both killed in duels, reinforced the myth about the freedom-loving, bloodthirsty Chechens.

Under the tsars, political opponents were generally sent to forced labour in the Caucasus, because they would probably never return home alive.

Twenty-three-year-old Leo Tolstoy travelled to the Caucasus from his estate, Yasnaya Polyana, in the spring of 1851. The journey took nearly two months. His dog Bulka rode with him in the carriage.

Cadet Tolstoy's first battle experience came when the Russians were attacked in a deep ravine; his comrades fell around him. The general ordered a massive counterattack. Cannons began firing and 'the horsemen disappeared into the forest in clouds of dust'. Tolstoy described how the Tsar's soldiers later plundered the enemy's *aul* – for flour, blankets, chickens – and then set the houses on fire. In his autobiographical tale 'The Raid' he ridiculed the commander-in-chief, Prince Baryatinsky, who exclaimed after the attack: '*Quel charmant coup d'oeil!*' His aide-de-camp replied in French, as was right and proper: '*C'est vraiment un plaisir de faire la guerre dans un pays tellement joli!*' – It is truly a pleasure to fight in such a beautiful country!

In a skirmish by the Michik River, one of the enemy's cannonballs tore the wheel off the cannon Tolstoy was manning; another killed a horse right next to him. 'I've never been so frightened in my life,' he wrote in his diary.

After six months in the Caucasus the cadet wrote to his brother: 'Hunting is magnificent. In this open landscape the moors swarm with grey rabbits and low bushes where foxes hide. I've been out nine times and have ridden about eight or ten versts from the Cossack village with two dogs, one excellent and the other useless. I've shot two foxes and sixty rabbits. When I return I will go deer hunting on horseback. If you want to impress people with the latest news from the Caucasus you can tell them that the most important person here – after Shamil – a man named Haji Murat, has just surrendered to the Russians. The boldest and bravest man in all Chechnya has committed an act of cowardice.'

Haji Murat would be Tolstoy's last great work, written fifty years after his experiences in the Caucasus.

As time went on, the young nobleman lost his fascination for the life of a soldier; during the summer of the second year he

complained in his diary: 'Drill, cannon practice, idiotic repri-
mands from Alexeyev, stupid drinking bouts, hunting (shot five
sandpipers, three pheasants and two partridges), toothache, reading, women, boredom.' A few days later: 'I'm twenty-four years
old and still haven't done anything, accomplished anything. I'm
sure it wasn't for naught that I've struggled with all my doubts
and all my passions the past eight years. What will be my fate?
Only time will tell. Shot three sandpipers.'

Tolstoy was transferred to Groznaya, a fort on which the present city of Grozny was founded. 'Everyone drinks, especially my
brother. How I hate it! Tonight Knoring came in drunk. Brought
port wine. I drank a little too. Some officers brought prostitutes.
Arguments, insults, we just barely avoided a duel . . .'

After almost two years in the Russian army he was dis-
heartened.

'War?' he wrote in his diary on 6 January 1853. 'What an
incomprehensible phenomenon. When common sense asks: Is it
right, is it necessary? the inner voice replies: No.'

At the entrance to Duba-Yurt sat village guards. The Council of
Elders had reached an agreement with federal forces: if the villagers made sure no rebels were given refuge there, the Russians
wouldn't go into the houses. Both sides kept the agreement more
or less. We met rebels in the village, and heard about houses that
had been searched by Russians looking for vodka in the evenings.
As everywhere, we were met with great hospitality. The Council
of Elders contacted Isa Adayev, who was in charge of culture in
President Jokhar Dudayev's administration. He invited us to stay
in his home at the upper edge of the village. It was a large house;
Isa was a rich man.

We sat at a table in the garden as darkness fell softly around us.
A fierce struggle for control was being waged in the hills. Highest
up were the Russians, whose searchlights swept the hillsides.
Below them were the Council of Elders' appointed guards. In
between them crept the rebels.

Duba-Yurt was remarkably fortunate compared to neighbouring villages; only the outlying homes had been destroyed. To prevent the place from being razed by Russian artillery, the rebels had withdrawn two days before our arrival. You could walk around the village relatively safely until eight o'clock; after that, tanks thundered through the streets.

Crackling gunfire and the dull, distant rumble of heavy artillery drowned out the twittering birds. Isa identified precisely where the shots came from.

'That was one of our boys with a machine gun,' he said now and then. 'There are two of them, now three.'

Most of the rockets landed a few kilometres away. Isa named villages nearby.

'We're fighting against machines. If we'd fought face to face, we would have defeated them. They've got planes, helicopters, tanks, heavy artillery; all we have is guns and grenades.'

At times the whole sky blazed with rockets, turning the night into day. They hung there briefly before slowly descending to earth.

'Finally – the Russian government is providing lighting for us,' Isa said sarcastically.

He wasn't happy with President Dudayev's war strategy. With thirty years of experience in the Soviet army, the president should have realised this strategy would not work.

'Chechnya is too small to defeat the Russian bear, but at the same time we're too proud and freedom-loving not to try,' he sighed.

Isa had lost what he most valued: Chechnya's cultural treasures.

'The national museum in Grozny was bombed after Russian forces looted what they thought worth preserving: European paintings, anything made of gold and silver, precious stones and metals. Chechen and Caucasian art was blown to pieces.'

Isa grieved also about the architectural treasures that had been lost, both in Grozny and in the mountains.

'Small, unique clusters of buildings, dating as far back as the twelfth century, have been levelled to the ground,' he sighed. 'The Russians have almost destroyed us materially, but not spiritually. For three hundred years they've tried to subdue us. But we have something they don't have – we know what we're fighting for: freedom and independence,' he said, but added sadly: 'Now we're fighting mainly to survive.'

The next morning we saw the result of the night's rockets. They had been aimed at the town of Chishky, three kilometres from Isa's house. We drove down into the valley first, then up the mountain on the opposite side. Out of three hundred houses, only a few remained unscathed. The inhabitants were in shock.

'We had an agreement with the Russians that they wouldn't bomb the town if we didn't shelter the fighters. We handed over all our weapons and posted guards to make sure no fighters came here,' one man told us. 'Every week the Council of Elders and the Russian troops held talks. We thought it was safe to stay here; because of the Russian promises, few people fled. When the bombardment started, all we could do was rush down into our cellars.

'After twelve hours, the bombing stopped and we could go outside,' the man continued. He had lived twenty years in Siberia in order to earn enough money to build a house for his family. Now everything was gone. 'Until the very last day, they said we didn't need to worry.'

'They call it war,' said another. Some of the walls were still standing in the once stately house where he lived with his wife and five sons.

'They said on TV that they had killed so many Chechen fighters. That's a lie. There weren't any fighters here, just peaceful villagers. They shoot as if they have a real enemy, but only civilians die. For us, it makes no difference whether Dudayev or Yeltsin is the leader; let the Pope rule, for all I care, if only we can live in peace.'

The night's rocket attack had killed five people and wounded several dozen. Later, we found one of the wounded at the hospital in Grozny: nine-year-old Elisa, a pale, thin girl who had serious shrapnel wounds to her leg and talked in a barely audible voice. Her mother and sister had been hit by a rocket and were killed. They hadn't made it down into the cellar.

'I never want to go back to Chishky,' the child whispered from her sickbed.

We went down into the valley again. On the flat stretch of land between Chishky and Duba-Yurt, beside the peacefully flowing Argun, the 104th Paratroop Division had its base. From here they fired heavy artillery towards targets in the mountains and the Argun valley. The projectiles could reach up to fifty kilometres.

'Every third day we move a few kilometres further south,' said Sergei, an officer born in St Petersburg. 'In a few weeks we'll have taken the whole area as far as the mountain range. We took these two towns in just a couple of days,' he said proudly, pointing towards Duba-Yurt and Chishky.

As he was holding forth about their successful battle strategy, a voice suddenly shouted: *Snaipery!* Snipers!

'Get down, get down!' yelled Sergei as he rushed away. I lay down, but where are you supposed to lie in a flat field? What's behind, what's ahead, and where were the snipers? The camp bustled with activity. Martin took pictures. He wasn't one to hide. The ABC one-woman crew filmed. Soldiers shot towards the place where the crawling marksman supposedly was; four times they threw grenades. Then someone shouted:

'We got him!'

A proud soldier came towards us.

'He stood up, and I got him with a machine gun. One less Chechen to fight.'

The camp quietened down again and the soldiers rescued the scorched samovar that everyone had forgotten about when the lone fighter decided to test himself against the Russian army. Some soldiers went out to find him, but returned empty-handed.

Later, people in Duba-Yurt said the whole episode was a

performance put on for us, to demonstrate that the Russians faced a dangerous enemy and didn't only bomb peaceful farmers.

'But they did manage to kill a goat,' the villagers said.

Once again I was at a loss, wondering what to believe. Everything in Chechnya had two explanations, one Russian and one Chechen. Was it that the Russians were bored and wanted to show off for us, or was it that the villagers wanted to hide the fact that they harboured rebels?

The officer invited us to eat *shashlik* with him – grilled meat on skewers. He pointed to a slaughtered goat lying in the hot sunshine.

'Come back this evening,' he said, even promising a military escort back to Duba-Yurt after the meal. He tried to tempt us with the prospect of vodka and meat, songs and jokes, and the whole war became absurd and unreal in Sergei's smiling face.

Back at Isa's house, we told him what we'd seen. His expression hardened when we mentioned the officer's dinner invitation, but he didn't say anything. Later his son approached me.

'Father doesn't think you should go to that dinner. For one thing, it's dangerous; the Russians are often attacked after dark, you know, and down there you're an easy target. Besides . . .'

He looked at me silently. He didn't need to say more. *Besides* meant: you are our guests, you can't live here and then eat roast goat with those who kill us.

My three fellow travellers decided to go anyway for the sake of the story. I stayed with Isa, whose face bore a stormy look all evening.

It grew late. Shouldn't they be back soon? It was almost midnight. Had something happened? It was frighteningly quiet. Wasn't it?

Despite the danger, Isa sent his son to investigate. As he opened the door to leave, a tank thundered past. We heard it stop a short distance away and back up. Three figures hopped down from the vehicle. Isa gave them a tight-lipped nod and we all went to bed.

The next day we left Isa, and I never saw him again.

We made a quick visit down to the base to tell the Russians

which direction we were going, so they wouldn't shoot at us. Sergei said he had a gift for me; he went into his tent and emerged carrying a red silk banner with gold fringes. A pale Lenin in suit and tie adorned the banner. The hammer and sickle were embroidered in gold thread. 'Beneath Lenin's banner – forward to Communist victory,' the banner said, and in the lower right-hand corner the soldiers had autographed it: 'In memory of the 104th Paratroop Division. Ulyanovsk – Grozny – Chishky.'

I carried the banner with me well hidden, stuffed far down in my backpack. I felt I was carrying blood. Still, I couldn't bring myself to throw it away. I also carried with me my reflections on the spontaneous generosity they showed us outsiders – and the hate, anger and vengefulness they felt towards each other.

We finally achieved Martin's goal for the trip – a meeting with the *boyeviks*. Not where they were fighting, but in the village of Goity, where they came to recuperate. After several weeks in the mountains they came down to get rest, food, hot water and a bed before taking up arms again.

'I was on my way to the karate World Championship in Malaysia when the Russians invaded Chechnya,' said one of the commanders, a strong young fellow named Rizvan. 'There was no question but that I'd stay and fight for my people. I've never been interested in politics, but I've always wanted autonomy. Russia is not a free country, and it's disgusting to be governed from Moscow. There's no third way for us. We have enough people to take over after us if we're killed. *Svoboda ili Smert*. Freedom or death. Above all, we fight for our families and villages.'

Just before my meeting with the Chechen fighters, a soldier from Nizhny Novgorod, a Russian city by the Volga, had said as he stood guard outside Goity: 'The most important thing for me is that my wife and daughter have a good life.'

Tonight perhaps one of them would kill the other.

Rizvan would not discuss whether the struggle was worth the countless innocent victims. '*Svoboda ili Smert*,' he replied again.

'We'll fight to the last man and the last drop of blood. But don't look on us as fanatics; we want a secular state, like Norway, for example.'

The oldest man at the table, a shepherd in peacetime, disagreed about the secular state. 'I fight in Allah's name,' he said.

As we left the *boyeviks*, I thought about the pity of it all: the children in Goity had lost a karate trainer, the sheep a shepherd, and perhaps tonight a little girl in Nizhny Novgorod would lose her father.

At this point in the war, May 1995, 80 per cent of Chechnya was controlled by the Russians. Boris Yeltsin had hoped to win the war by 9 May, when the world's leaders would gather in Moscow's Red Square to celebrate the fiftieth anniversary of the end of the Second World War. Yeltsin declared a ceasefire during the week of celebration, but the generals in the field completely ignored it. Presidents and prime ministers from around the world sat passively in the VIP stand as the Russian army marched past.

After the celebration Yeltsin wanted to crush the separatists once and for all. By the end of May, only a few villages were still fighting, among them the legendary Vedeno where Imam Shamil had taken a stand against the Russians in the nineteenth century. When Vedeno fell in early June, the Chechen leadership changed its strategy – they would no longer have bases, but had to fight in small mountain units.

One of the leaders adopted a whole new tactic.

The sun was at its height and the morning freshness long gone when a police car followed by two military trucks drove into the centre of Budyonnovsk, a sleepy provincial town in southern Russia. They calmly parked outside the police station. Bearded men got out of the cars and trucks, and opened fire. They were the feared Shamil Basayev – *The Wolf* – and his men, around a hundred and fifty in all. Like his famous nineteenth-century namesake, this Shamil also came from Vedeno. Ten days earlier he had lost eleven members of his family when the village was stormed. Attacking a Russian town should wake up the Russian people and make them protest against the injustice in Chechnya.

From the police station the men moved to the city hall and the central square. They raided two apartment buildings, battered down doors, took residents and people on the street as hostages. They forced them towards the city's most vulnerable target – the hospital, which had the area's only maternity ward.

By evening twelve hundred people had been taken hostage. The Wolf set forth his demands on the hospital telephone: Russia must stop the war in Chechnya, pull out the troops and begin peace negotiations.

On the morning of the fourth day, the city's inhabitants were woken by the sound of heavy artillery firing on the hospital; the building, which had been a convent before the revolution, had thick concrete walls. The attack was answered by furious gunfire from the hospital's windows and skylights. Six armoured vehicles were hit by grenades and set on fire. When a doctor forced his way through the sea of flames with a written plea to end the shooting, it stopped. A hundred and twenty hostages lay dead; more than a thousand remained. The women who hung out of the windows of the maternity ward waving white sheets had made the Russians appear to be the aggressors. For the first and only time, the authorities decided to negotiate with a terrorist leader. Prime Minister Viktor Chernomyrdin was in charge of the negotiations, since Boris Yeltsin had left to attend a G7 summit in Halifax the day after the drama began. Four telephone conversations later, Basayev released two hundred hostages. Chernomyrdin promised a ceasefire and guaranteed the Chechens safe conduct.

In an interview some weeks later with Carlotta Gall, Basayev said that at first he hadn't supported the idea of fighting in Russia. 'Because I knew what it would cost. But when we were thrown out of Vedeno, when they drove us into a corner with wild, terrible destruction – wiping out villages, women, children, the elderly, indeed an entire people – then we decided to go. "Let's go to Russia," we said, and felt better. "We will fight there, we will stop the war, or we will all die."'

Months of half-hearted negotiations, and fierce battles, followed. When the war was one year old, a cold January day in 1996, the next raid on Russia occurred. The action was the same as in Budyonnovsk, except with a new leader; this time it wasn't The Wolf but *The Lone Wolf* – Salman Raduyev. Now it was the border town of Kizlar in Dagestan that suffered. Yeltsin was furious. He called a meeting of the Russian Security Council and roared at the generals, the security ministers and the border troops.

'What's the meaning of this, generals? Are you playing with dolls? The border guards fell asleep! Eh? We have several thousand troops guarding the roads, and these men just went right by!' he bellowed, while everything was filmed and broadcast on Russian television. Yeltsin ordered a decisive response that would 'neutralise the bandits, painfully and completely'.

'Our cities are devastated,' replied the Chechen president. 'We need houses, our fighters have to live somewhere, and we also need a new hospital. That's why we decided to take action in Kizlar. Three hundred years ago the first battles between Russian and Chechen forces occurred here. It was here the war between us began. And it will also end here,' said Jokhar Dudayev.

Again the Chechens were promised safe conduct, but they brought several hundred hostages as protection. When they crossed the Chechen border they were attacked from helicopters and had to barricade themselves in the nearest village, Pervomaiskoye – 'First of May Town', where they forced the hostages to dig battle trenches. After suffering great losses from the well-armed resistance fighters, the Russians for a while halted their attacks.

Some days later I sneaked across the border from Dagestan, the same route by which the fighters had made their retreat. With me were American photographer Heidi Bradner, Anders Sæther from *Dagbladet* and a local driver. The driver said he knew how to evade the Russians, and which areas weren't mined. Hunched down in the moonlight, we crossed a broad, frozen marsh; when not frozen, the area was impassable. In the cold, starry night the flat marshland seemed endless. But we crossed unnoticed into Chechen territory.

We drove to Novogrozny, where The Lone Wolf had gone with the hostages after the rebels' retreat. They had stood their ground there for five days. Only when Salman Raduyev heard on the military radio that the Russians planned to bomb the village because 'the hostages have already been killed' did he pull out with the hostages as cover.

The driver stopped the car by a group of houses and we were ushered in to see Raduyev. He sat in a bare, frigid room. Gas and electricity were long gone. A small, thin man with deep wrinkles etched into a ravaged face, he looked older than his twenty-eight years. He gave us a dark, gloomy look through blurred, yet shining, eyes under heavy eyelids.

Through a broken window we could see black branches reaching nakedly towards the sky. Raduyev's words were barren and desperate, too.

'There will be more raids if the Russians don't pull out. We've discovered that military actions outside Chechnya serve us better. When our towns are bombed, nobody raises an eyebrow any more. But if we go beyond our borders, the world press stands on tiptoe looking for sensational news. We are all on Allah's path of our own free will. We are suicide warriors ready to die. The best way to die is through jihad. For the Dagestan campaign I took only those who were ready for Allah's paradise.'

Two gold teeth glistened between thin lips.

The rebel leader deemed their hostage action a success. 'We were attacked with all kinds of weapons. We broke through three lines of Russian soldiers. No military analyst can explain how we managed to do that. I have just one answer: Allah.'

Raduyev was restless. His eyes flitted here and there, from the door to me to Anders and back again.

'Do you want to come up to the base and watch us plan our next attack? It can happen at any time, and at any place. Two or three more strikes at Russia, and they have to give in. If we attack strategic targets, the war will become so expensive that Russia will have to pull out her troops. When the workers strike and the students scream for their monthly cheques, the authorities will have to give in. We'll destroy them economically, the way they destroy our women and children.

'The war has made our lives a nightmare,' Raduyev continued in a thin, sharp voice. 'What kind of person do you become when you've seen children blown to pieces?' Raduyev had no military background when the war started, but had studied business in Moscow and Budapest and had worked for the local Komsomol – Communist Youth Union – in Gudermes, Chechnya's second-largest city.

'I thought I was going to help build my country when Dudayev came to power. Now I have to plan sabotage instead.'

At any mention of Boris Yeltsin or Pavel Grachev, The Lone Wolf bared his teeth. But he believed that with different political leadership in Moscow the war could be ended.

'With men like Gaidar or Yavlinsky in power, Russia could become a civilised democratic state. But financial aid from the West encourages leaders in the Kremlin to continue the war: six billion here, nine billion there. The money goes directly to financing the war. The West, with its so-called humanitarianism, could have helped us, but you don't say a word!'

Raduyev was silent for a moment, then he repeated his invitation to take us to the secret base. We looked at each other, shivering in our jackets. And shook our heads. He pointed at our Polaroid camera.

The camera that had helped us in so many situations. A photograph of themselves could be among the things needed to get Russian soldiers to let us through roadblocks. Preferably posing with a Kalashnikov. For many soldiers this was their only photograph from the war; very few could afford a camera in the nineties. Salman Raduyev also wanted a photograph, so Anders took pictures of The Lone Wolf in a sheepskin coat with me in my dark pink jacket. The young man put the picture into his breast pocket, and later I would hear from people who met him that he showed them the picture and said: 'This is my sweetheart.'

'Come with us and see,' he urged one last time.

Again we declined. The Lone Wolf was at the top of the Russians' hit list, and we weren't all under Allah's protection.

The wolf – *borz* – was a symbol of freedom that had become established through centuries of battling against the empire. The free, wild wolf was the Chechen; the tame, cowardly dog was the Russian.

The separatists chose this beast as the emblem of their republic. They saw the wolf as the only animal that dared to take on something stronger than itself. What it lacked in strength and size it made up for with limitless audacity and courage. Moreover, the wolf was loyal to the pack and ready to sacrifice its life for the others. It loved freedom, could not be tamed, and would rather die fighting than surrender.

The Chechens focused on the characteristics they liked best, and forgot that the wolf is a beast of prey that mercilessly pursues every weak, defenceless animal. The wars of the 1990s destroyed the Chechen social fabric and drove brutality to the extreme; slave trade with hostages, killing of innocent people, torture and abuse – on both sides – became widespread. But tales about the wolf have been kept alive and told from generation to generation. This poem is from the Soviet era:

> *We are wolves,*
> *Compared to dogs, we are few.*
> *To the sound of double-barrelled guns*
> *We have declined over time.*
> *As in an execution*
> *We soundlessly fell to the ground,*
> *But we have survived,*

Even though we are banned.
We are wolves.
We are few.
There are hardly any of us.

We, wolves and dogs, share one mother,
But we refused to surrender.
Your lot is bowls of food,
Ours is hunger on frozen ground.
Animals' tracks,
Snowfall under silent stars.
In the January frosts
You are allowed inside,
While we are surrounded by
A tightening ring of red lights.
You peep out through a crack in the door,
We roam in the woods.

You are really wolves
But you had not the guts for it.
You were grey,
Once you were brave,
But you were handed scraps and became slaves.
You are glad to serve and flatter
For a crust of bread,
But the leash and chain
Are your prize — and well deserved!
Tremble in your cages
When we are out hunting!
Because, more than any bear,
We wolves hate
Dogs.[1]

1 Translation by Moshe Gammer in *Three Centuries of Chechen Defiance of Russian Rule*.

4

Wolf Hunt

'Take as much sovereignty as you can swallow,' boomed a husky voice.

In 1990 Boris Yeltsin toured Russia, encouraging its regions and small nations to claim more power from the Kremlin. As leader of Russia, one of the fifteen Soviet republics, Yeltsin was seeking to undermine President Mikhail Gorbachev, as he tried to save the USSR from collapse.

A year later, while Gorbachev was on holiday in the Crimea, the old communists staged a coup in Moscow. All telephone lines to the luxurious dacha were severed, and the leader of the Soviet Union was cut off.

Boris Yeltsin threw himself into the battle against the coup plotters. Standing on a tank in shirt sleeves, he roared to the masses gathered to protest the takeover.

In Grozny, then a Soviet provincial capital, Jokhar Dudayev nodded in approval.

As chairman of the executive committee in the Chechen national congress, he called for a mass mobilisation against the coup, while others sat on the fence. He demanded that the Soviet administration resign and the parliament be disbanded.

Jokhar Dudayev, the only Chechen with the rank of general in the Soviet army, had commanded a division of long-range strategic bombers carrying nuclear weapons at the military base in Tartu, Estonia. The general had shown sympathy for the Baltic nation's fight for independence early on. He left the air force in March 1991 after refusing to participate in the military intervention and killing of civilians in the Lithuanian capital Vilnius. He went home.

Take as much sovereignty as you can swallow! That was exactly what Jokhar Dudayev intended to do.

After the coup a series of demonstrations – and eventually a general strike – took place in Chechnya in protest against the local Soviet government. Dudayev's men occupied official buildings and the radio and television tower. The revolt was a real revolution, not a quiet one as in other Soviet republics. Dudayev also liberated a prison with six hundred inmates, some of whom became his guardsmen. Criminals, from con men to convicted murderers, were released.

During the autumn of 1991 Dudayev consolidated his power, took control of the police and their weapons arsenal, bought, stole and coerced equipment from local Soviet troops who operated without leaders while the power struggle went on in Moscow.

In October, Dudayev won the presidential election with 90 per cent of the vote, and nationalistic groups won all the seats in parliament.

The first week in November, parliament declared complete independence from Russia. The second week in November, Yeltsin proclaimed a state of emergency in Chechnya and sent in six hundred Interior Ministry troops. They were immediately surrounded by Chechen snipers at the airport, and locked in the terminal. No Soviet troops, who were under Gorbachev's command, were called in. Russia's Supreme Soviet denounced the state of emergency, and the conflict was solved within a day. The soldiers were disarmed and bussed out. They left the republic. For the time being.

Dudayev was absolutely determined to see Chechnya break away – not just from the Soviet Union, but also from Russia. In December 1991 the Soviet Union was dissolved, and the fifteen republics received their independence. Chechnya had status only as an 'autonomous republic' within Russia, and did not have the right to break away. Boris Yeltsin, the driving force behind the fall of the Soviet Union, wanted to keep Russia's borders intact at any cost and refused to accept secession.

As a result, these two men who once had fought the same fight – against the Soviet Union – now became bitter enemies. And it is these two men who must bear the main responsibility for the Chechen tragedy.

Dudayev began a war of words with Yeltsin. 'Russianism is worse than Nazism', 'Boris Yeltsin heads a gang of murderers' and his regime is the 'diabolic heir to a totalitarian monster'. For its part, the Russian government introduced an amazingly ineffective trade embargo and cut important subsidies; the only thing the Russian state paid was pensions to help local Russians remain in Chechnya. The huge reduction in financial aid from Russia added to the chaos and corruption, and soon Dudayev's regime was even less able to pay salaries than governments elsewhere in Russia. A Moscow bank robbery by Chechen criminals netted almost a billion dollars; most of the money was brought back to Chechnya. Grozny became a centre for smuggling, fraud and money laundering, while the government's role in the republic was collapsing.

Meanwhile, the hawks in Yeltsin's administration wanted a 'small victorious war', something that would increase their popularity among nationalistic Russians after an ultra-nationalist candidate, Vladimir Zhirinovsky, had won about every fourth vote in the parliamentary election. However, the main reason for invading Chechnya was the political ambitions of Yeltsin and his inner circle. If Chechnya seceded, the spirit of rebellion could spread to the rest of the North Caucasus, and all of Russia could fall apart.

During the winter of 1996 the war became even more intense. The bear, with all its strike power, was on a wolf hunt. But the chief wolf – Jokhar Dudayev – always got away.

Anders and I were on a hunt, too.

We were transported from place to place, to new houses and streets, with new instructions to wait. We were given food, a bed, a seat in a new car; often we didn't know where we were, but were driven to a house in darkness, taken into a room. To wait.

He never slept in the same place more than one night. 'He was here yesterday. He's in the area. He's on the other side of the border. He's everywhere, so if you want to meet him, you'll just have to wait. Sooner or later he'll turn up,' Dudayev's soldiers told us.

One evening the Chechen middlemen drove us to a house at the edge of Urus Martan. 'Stay here,' they said, and disappeared. The evening passed. And the night. Late the next evening they took us to another house. 'Wait here.'

Almost the entire Chechen leadership was in the house. We were told to sit on a sofa. The rebels had communal worship – *zikr* – tramping after each other in a circle with heavy steps and shouting out prayers. When they sat down to eat, they looked worried, worn out.

The Russians had begun a new offensive, and wintertime was difficult. When the earth is frozen and the rivers dry, heavy Russian vehicles can move around easily. When the foliage is gone, when the ground is white, it's harder for the Chechens to hide their bases.

We were led from the living room into another room. At about two o'clock that morning, Dudayev's press secretary appeared and fastened a flag to the wall. He set down a chair and left the room again. Then the head of security arrived, along with a man who introduced himself as Chechnya's public prosecutor. We sat on soft cushions on the floor with a small gas light burning. The press secretary returned, and we understood that it was time to take out our notebooks, tape recorders and camera equipment.

The door opened. The distinguished general, genial and smiling in a freshly pressed field uniform, shook everyone's hand and then seated himself in front of the flag bearing the Chechen wolf. He was small and lithe, with a thin face, an eagle-beak nose and a well-kept moustache. His eyes were dark and intense. When he began speaking, his manner and speech were as meticulous as his dress. He seemed self-satisfied. At this point in the war he was the separatists' undisputed leader, even if some people thought he'd lost his judgement after a year in cellars and bunkers while others led the resistance. In rebel-held territory children stood along the roads with clenched fists and shouted, 'Jokhar, Jokhar, Jokhar!' when we drove by.

Tonight he had decided to direct his shots at us: the West. During the first year of the war the Chechen attitude towards the West changed. Oh yes, the West criticised. Oh yes, the West protested. Oh yes, the West mentioned the war in conversations with Yeltsin. But what happened? The war continued.

'You didn't strike a blow to make Russia respect human rights. While they bomb our towns, you shrug your shoulders and are content as long as you're left in peace,' thundered the former Soviet general. 'The UN's inability to act is shameful! We had hoped to get help in establishing a democratic state governed by law, but you betrayed us. Since the OSCE and the Council of Europe began mediating, the conflict has become ten times worse. The UN should have instituted harsh economic sanctions against Russia. Instead, you admit Russia as a member of the Council of Europe and "assign a little homework"!'

These quotations come from my interview for *Arbeiderbladet* with the rebel leader. Since 1996 the global picture has changed radically, and today it's interesting to read of Dudayev's vision again:

'Within a few years, the conflict will spread. It will be a battle of the Muslim world against the West. And it will be the end of the Western world, because you're not ready for combat.'

He added that lack of Western help in building a democratic Russian state after the Soviet Union's collapse was what made the Chechens look towards *Sharia* – Muslim laws and regulations.

'You've forced us to become a Muslim society,' said the man who had never seemed a particularly strong believer, and who is said to have shouted at a public meeting that Muslims had to pray three times a day. When someone corrected him, he cried: 'Yes, five. Let it be five. That's even better!'

There was something desperate about his criticism. He was more interested in talking – in his calm, hypnotic way – about the West's future destruction than about the course of his own war.

'You can no longer create anything, and you betray humanistic ideals when you close your eyes to what's happening here. Western Europeans are fascist and egotistic. You can't produce anything new, except make money and package Snickers. You're a group of imperialistic nations that want to conquer the others. Every week refugee reception centres in Europe are set on fire, with live human beings inside them. Isn't that fascism?'

The remaining hours of the night were spent mocking the great battle bear himself – Boris Yeltsin.

'One day he wants to pull out the troops, the next he wants to kill me. At first the war was going to be over in two hours, then in three days, then by the fiftieth anniversary of the Second World War, then by Yeltsin's birthday, then by Grachev's birthday, and now by Election Day.'

The performance ended with a menacing comment to those of us with notepads. 'You ride around gathering information that you give to the Russian intelligence service!'

Then he walked out, upright, erect.

One spring evening a few months later, when new foliage once again hid the rebel bases, the Chechen president left his headquarters to make a telephone call. He was driven into the forest above the town of Gekhi-Chu, along with his bodyguards and two advisers. They parked the jeep in a narrow gully and the advisers hooked up a satellite phone, which only worked under the open sky. There Jokhar Dudayev dialled the Moscow number of Russian parliament member Konstantin Borovoi to discuss possible peace talks.

It was a long conversation, a little too long, or just long enough for a Russian warplane to pick up the signal, take off from the base and fire an air-to-ground missile that found its target with a direct hit. According to the bodyguards, all of whom survived, the president's last words were: *Continue the fight till the end* . . .

The trips to Chechnya changed me. When I went back to Moscow to recuperate, I became depressed, had lost my drive. I just wanted to go back again. Real life was in the mountains, where people were waging a life-and-death struggle. Little by little I became almost anti-Russian. From being captivated by the poetry, the music, in search of 'the Russian soul', I became aware of the racism, the nationalism, the corruption of senior government officials, the ignorance, the bleak history; as Anton Chekhov put it: *Russian life is like a thousand-pound stone, it grinds a Russian down till there's not even a wet patch left.*

The basement apartment was still a basement apartment. The Moscow smog, the jostling in the metro, the clerks' dour faces. Capitalism was spreading, and things began to get on my nerves: the watch factory I passed every day that was now a casino, the luxury shops only the mafia could afford and, not least, the lies on television.

One evening I telephoned my foreign editor to say that I was planning to leave for Chechnya the next morning. He said I couldn't go.

'I can't go?' I said in amazement.

'No, it's too dangerous,' Øyvind Johnsen replied.

'Has it *suddenly* become too dangerous?'

It came out that he had received numerous telephone calls from Lillehammer. I called home.

'Mama, have you telephoned *Arbeiderbladet*?'

Silence on the other end.

'Mama?!'

'Me? Yes, once in a while I call to have a chat. Øyvind Johnsen is such a nice man. Besides, he agrees with me; he doesn't think you should go to Chechnya any more.'

I sat sulking in an armchair in my room looking out of a window grey with exhaust fumes towards the mist above Leningrad Prospect. Everything was packed, the tickets purchased, my travelling companions were going to pick me up the next morning: Didier from *Libération*, Isabelle from *Le Figaro* and Tom from *The Times*. I called the French. The tough journalists were speechless when they heard about my mother.

'Have a good trip,' I said meekly, and straightened the shabby cushions. As a freelance journalist, to a certain extent I did as I pleased. But now, with this travel ban, I suddenly had no money for the trip. Covering a war is expensive; you have to rent cars, the drivers demand sky-high prices because of the risk and on top of it all come the bribes. Didier had a bright idea:

'You can come along as the interpreter, and the rest of us will split the cost of your ticket!'

We slept on the floor. We ate soft cheese and dry bread. We read maps. This summer of 1996 we were looking for Chechnya's military leader, Aslan Maskhadov. Once again we were taken from house to house, from car to car, until we were set down at a crossroads and told to walk up a wooded path. I was startled by a pair of dark eyes staring at me through the foliage. Then another pair. And yet another. Several dozen men with dark beards, green headbands and black uniforms stood concealed among the trees with weapons loaded, like stone statues, all the way up the hillside; and there, suddenly, just ahead of us, sat Aslan Maskhadov on a tree stump. He'd been watching us for some time when we finally raised our eyes, and he smiled at us as we made our difficult ascent.

Aslan Maskhadov stood out among the Chechen leaders; he was quietly spoken and had calm, gentle eyes. He was the strategist behind the Chechens' amazing military capability, a few thousand soldiers against one of the world's largest armed forces. Today he looked at us with a sly grin.

The beech forest sparkled in the mild May sunshine, everything was shades of green – the leaves, the grass, the moss, the Chechen leader's uniform; I, too, was wearing green combat trousers as I sat by the tree stump. If helicopters happened to circle overhead, they would see little but green forest.

We asked him how the war was progressing. We asked about the Chechen will to fight, the mood, tactics and strategy. Then he said:

'I'm going to meet Yeltsin.'

'When? Where?'

'In Moscow. In the Kremlin. May the twenty-seventh.'

We looked at each other, the same thought in our minds: we've got a scoop. It would be the first time those two leaders had met, which in itself was a major victory for the Chechens, who had been asking for a meeting with Yeltsin all along. In two months a presidential election would be held in Russia, and Yeltsin was not doing well in the polls. Peace in Chechnya would have a positive effect. Maskhadov admitted that the meeting was a calculated risk; he knew it could give increased support to Yeltsin in the presidential election, but even if he didn't trust Yeltsin, he believed this was the only way to end the war. Yeltsin's toughest opponent was the Communist Party's candidate, Gennady Zyuganov.

'I don't trust Yeltsin, but the communists have deceived us more than anyone. Our grandfathers believed in them,' the Chechen strategist concluded.

Peace talks! Negotiations! Maskhadov to Moscow! This was major news, and on our way back we pondered how to get that news out. None of us had a satellite phone, and the only functioning telegraph offices were far away, in Grozny or Shali.

At a crossroads we happened to meet a correspondent for Agence France-Presse. She graciously let us use her telephone, provided she could report the news at the same time.

We each wrote our own story. I dictated mine with satisfaction to a secretary at *Arbeiderbladet*. Then Øyvind Johnsen came on the line:

'I've read your story. Great, exciting. But I can't use it.'

'What?'

'I told you not to go to Chechnya. I can't forbid you one day, and then print your story the next. I'm sorry, Åsne.'

So much for *that* scoop. Thanks, Mum.

The other three couldn't believe what they'd heard. He wouldn't take the story?!

They told me to try once more. Back in Grozny, I went to the devastated telegraph office, where cement dust blew in through the shattered door, and got Øyvind Johnsen on a sputtering line. He chuckled.

'You win,' he laughed. 'One-nil to you!'

Had he gone crazy?

'We got a wire report translated from Agence France-Presse saying that Maskhadov was going to meet Yeltsin in Moscow "according to correspondents for *Le Figaro*, *Libération*, *The Times* and *Arbeiderbladet*". When *Arbeiderbladet* is cited as a news source by Agence France-Presse – the first time ever in my years as an editor – well, I've got to use the story! It's out already!'

I hung up, slightly dazed. So the woman with the satellite phone had saved me.

Peace negotiations were held in Moscow. After a two-hour meeting on 27 May an agreement regarding a ceasefire and an exchange of prisoners was signed. Yeltsin got his peace before the election and the Chechens got their meeting with the president. Further discussions between the two parties were scheduled for the following day in a government dacha outside Moscow. But that morning Yeltsin went to Chechnya for his most brilliant performance of the entire election campaign; he proclaimed that the war was won and 'the bandit groups destroyed'. Meanwhile, the Chechen delegation was isolated in the dacha, with neither meetings nor access to the media. They had been part of an election stunt.

In the first weekend in July, Boris Yeltsin won the presidential election.In the second weekend in July, Russian planes bombed the high mountain town of Makhkety, where Chechen military leaders were gathered. Several buildings, including the city hall, were devastated and dozens killed. The rebel leaders fled in different directions. Maskhadov crept along the riverbank. Former President Yandarbiev walked up towards the tree line, where he waited until nightfall, and then rode further on horseback. Basayev fled westward. For three days they kept moving around, ate leaves and drank water from streams. They made their way through deep forests, gorges and ravines, and when Maskhadov and Basayev met up again they would almost be swept away in the strong current of a tributary of the Argun River. The entire leadership and all the *boyeviks* escaped from Makhkety; the only casualties, as so often before, were civilians.

In any case, the peace was over.

And when the presidential election was over, my time in Russia was over, too. For the next ten years I watched events from the sidelines.

Chechnya got independence of a sort by agreeing to put off the question of constitutional affiliation. Aslan Maskhadov was elected president by a large majority in 1997. He never managed to control the republic, or to prevent the spread of *wahhabism*, a radical form of Islamic fundamentalism to which Osama bin Laden, among others, adheres.

Chechnya lay in ruins. Most of what Russia sent for reconstruction disappeared along the way, while money from the Middle East was used to build mosques and *madrasas*, as well as for weapons. Islamists destroyed the relationship with the outside world by executing Western health workers, engineers and journalists. An open power struggle emerged between the moderate Aslan Maskhadov and the more extreme Shamil Basayev, The Wolf — between Chechnya's traditional form of Islamism and the new current imported from the Arab world.

The neighbouring republic of Dagestan had begun a campaign against Islamic extremists, who then fled into Chechnya, where they were welcomed by Maskhadov's enemies and radical groups. Their aim was to strengthen the pro-Russian regime in Dagestan and then, together with Chechnya, create an Islamic federation in the North Caucasus.

During the summer of 1999, Russian troops massed along Chechnya's borders once again; bombs were dropped on what military spokesmen called 'bandit bases'. People began hoarding food again and made plans to flee.

On 7 August 1999 a few thousand armed men, led by Shamil Basayev, moved across the Chechen border into Dagestan. They took control of several towns and declared Dagestan independent from Russia.

Two days later, Boris Yeltsin announced the name of his new prime minister, one unknown to most Russians – a former intelligence officer who had dedicated his life and career to the KGB. His name was Vladimir Putin.

The new prime minister would distinguish himself by following a harder line against Chechnya than even Boris Yeltsin.

On 9 September 1999, a bomb exploded in the basement of an apartment building in Moscow. About a hundred people were killed. Four days later, another building was blown up, leaving another hundred dead. The mayor of Moscow talked about 'Chechen traces', Russia's new prime minister did the same. Despite the fact that neither The Wolf nor other Chechens claimed responsibility for the explosions, the Russian media were positive: Chechens did it. But then on 22 September something happened that threw a new light on the case. In Ryazan, a city east of Moscow, a man noticed sacks being unloaded from a vehicle with concealed licence plates and then taken into the basement of the apartment building where he lived. He called the police, who found the sacks, along with a detonator. The sacks were filled with a highly explosive material called hexogen, the same material that had been used in Moscow two weeks earlier, local investigators reported. They also revealed that the sacks had been unloaded by employees of the Federal Security Service, the FSB. Two days later the FSB said that the whole thing had just been a means of testing 'public awareness' and that the powder in the sacks was actually sugar. The inconsistencies in the statements could make one believe the FSB had been caught in the act – preparing the excuse for a new war.

By the end of September, Russian bombers had drawn Shamil Basayev back from Dagestan. The Second Chechen War had begun.

The new war would be even more brutal than the previous one. Additional tens of thousands would be killed. Individuals would again disappear. People fled in great numbers. On the clogged Baku–Moscow highway, cars waited for days. People streamed across the border to refugee camps that were quickly set up in the neighbouring republic of Ingushetia. Each family got one corner of a tent, and once a day they lined up by a tanker, where their saucepans were filled with soup and they were handed a loaf of bread.

Aided by extensive media coverage in Russia, the image of Vladimir Putin was transformed from one of a grey bureaucrat to that of a tough, decisive and dynamic leader. On New Year's Eve 1999, Boris Yeltsin announced that he would step down, and that he had found his successor.

The prime minister was to become president.

Boris Yeltsin became the first Russian leader to leave office voluntarily, but he had insured himself well. His family was plagued by corruption scandals, and Putin would not disappoint him. The new president's first act, on New Year's Day 2000, was to sign a decree granting Yeltsin full immunity.

Then the Chechen leaders were to be liquidated, one by one.

The Lone Wolf, Salman Raduyev, was captured by Russian Special Forces in 2000 and sentenced to life imprisonment for terrorism, banditry and kidnapping. He died from internal bleeding in the 'White Swan' penal colony in Perm in 2002. The circumstances surrounding his death are unclear. That same year, our former host Khunkar-Pasha Israpilov was killed. Another man who had housed us, Commander Ruslan Gelayev, was shot in February 2004, when he tried to enter Georgia. Zelimkhan Yandarbiev's car was blown up in Doha, the capital of Qatar, in 2004; two agents from the Russian security service were later convicted of the murder. President Aslan Maskhadov was killed in a Russian attack on 8 March 2005 in the Chechen village of Tolstoy-Yurt. Pictures of the dead president lying on the ground with his shirt open and arms outstretched were displayed like a trophy on Russian television. The body has still not been delivered to his family for burial.

Martin Adler, who helped me on my very first trip, is also gone. The Swedish journalist was killed in June 2006 by a shot fired at close range during a demonstration in Mogadishu, Somalia. He was one of the few journalists who managed to meet Shamil Basayev, Russia's most wanted man at the time. The Wolf was killed three weeks after the Swede, when the truck he was standing next to was blown up. The backbone of Chechnya's resistance movement was broken.

Almost ten years would pass after I left Chechnya before I thought: it's time to go back.

5

Return

She wants to exchange the sky-blue silk scarf for a brown one that's smaller and thicker. It has a design of yellow flowers with dark centres. A long skirt, a coat belted at the waist, and pointed high-heeled boots complete the outfit.

'You need make-up,' she orders, taking out pencils and brushes and scrutinising the colours. 'Our women want to be beautiful.'

My eyebrows and eyelashes have already been dyed black; now eyeshadow and glistening lipstick are applied.

She takes out gold jewellery, earrings with a tiny tear-shaped pearl, a necklace, and something that looks like a wedding ring. 'It's better this way,' she says, content with her work.

The dark brown scarf is knotted firmly at my neck.

'Now you look like one of us!'

Two women from the North Caucasus, one a native, the other disguised as one, are going to board an aeroplane. Scarves on their heads, full skirts, clicking heels.

'But most important of all: don't smile all the time, and stop looking around as you usually do. Your open expression gives you away immediately. Keep your head down, frown and look unfriendly.'

*

The birch trees at Vnukovo airport in Moscow have grown ten new rings since I was here last. It is 2006. We lower our voices. I've promised not to say anything more than is absolutely necessary. When we land, my mouth should stay firmly shut.

Zaira is from Grozny; a tall, beautiful young woman studying law in Moscow, she's going to try to take me back to Chechnya. She decided we should fly to Vladikavkaz in North Ossetia, where she knows a woman working at the airport who will try to get us in without having to go through passport control and travel registration.

The plane is completely full. I note with satisfaction that I'm dressed properly and smile at Zaira, who gives me a severe look in return. People press forward from all sides with an impressive amount of baggage. When we reach our row, my travelling companion briskly commands me to sit by the window. Sweat glistens on her forehead. Her scarf is about to slide off her long dark hair. Mine hasn't moved an inch, fixed as it virtually is to the roots of my hair.

In the grey morning light the plane's worn interior appears even more ancient with its stains, tears, cracks, loose seat backs and tables that no longer fold up. The luggage racks above our heads creak depressingly under the weight of the bags stuffed into them.

The engines roar as we bump along the runway. The heavily loaded plane takes off, and we are airborne. I see a man two seats away from me still talking on his cell phone. 'Tell him to hang up,' I whisper to Zaira, but she just shrugs. Then I hear several other passengers talking on their cell phones. 'Yes, we're in the air now,' says a woman behind me. 'I'll see you in a few hours,' adds a young man in front of me. 'Turn off your damned phones,' my look says. It has absolutely no effect.

The fog hangs like dirty cotton wool outside the window, and a sleepy silence settles over the cabin.

After flying due south for a few hours, the clouds dissipate and there below us, rising proud and gleaming, are the legendary mountains. We are nearing Vladikavkaz, which means 'Ruler of the Caucasus'. It was once a popular spa. During the nineteenth century the aristocracy came to take the waters here in order to be healed of their various ailments; they rode on horseback under parasols held by servants and promenaded in luxuriant gardens to breathe the healthy air. During the Soviet years, the working classes took over the sanatoriums; entire factory shifts were moved from noisy industrial cities to the gentry's former playgrounds. Today the Ruler of the Caucasus is one of Russia's backwaters, on the fringe of a war that has had such tragic consequences for the Ossetians as well.

It is twelve years since I first flew this route, seated between two pilots in army uniforms; back then, nobody asked who, what or where. Now I have to hide from the authorities. Putin has understood something that never concerned Yeltsin: the power of the free word. Whereas you could travel freely to Chechnya at the beginning of the war, it is now illegal and almost impossible for a foreigner. First you have to get authorisation from the Foreign Ministry in Moscow and, after that, special permission from the Interior Ministry. Moreover, you are required to travel with a government representative. 'For your own safety,' we are told. When we criticise the Russian authorities for restricting journalists' work, they bristle. Several times a year the Russian Foreign Ministry arranges brief trips for selected journalists to specially chosen areas of the Caucasus; they are trailed from morning to night, and all interviews are monitored. I wanted to find my own way into the region.

When the pilot announces that we will soon be landing, passengers begin telephoning to report that we will shortly be on the ground. Conversations buzz around us; several passengers stand up and begin pulling their baggage out of the overhead racks. An elderly woman makes her way forward to the front curtain in order to be the first out. The stewardesses, who are seated with their belts fastened, scold the passengers like schoolteachers and try with firm hand gestures to make them sit down. But the passengers have made up their minds: they are going to disembark as quickly as possible, get home as fast as possible; it's their own business after all. Ignoring the Russian stewardesses' tongue-lashing, they continue taking down their baggage undaunted, then *bump*, we hit the tarmac. The unruly passengers hang on to the seat backs, lean forward a little, get jolted backwards; but they stay on their feet, so what was the problem?

Most of the passengers are out of their seats as the plane rushes along the runway. They take their remaining bags out of the racks and from the seats and begin pushing towards the exit.

'Stay in your seats!' comes the voice of the stewardess. But people just crowd more tightly towards the door, and surge down the steps with all their paraphernalia when it opens.

We're swept along in the stream. Zaira's contact is waiting for us. She leads us through the staff entrance and tells us to hurry past the police with our heads held high. Soon after we find ourselves in a waiting car. The woman from the airport leaves with a bottle of perfume in her pocket and a box of sweets in her hand. Zaira has thought of everything.

But now she is unsure. Should we wait until evening? It's more dangerous to travel after dark; bullets fly with greater abandon at night. On the other hand, one can hope that the soldiers at the checkpoints are tired, worn out, by then. Besides, they're afraid themselves as they stand there in the dark; they too prefer to avoid noise or trouble. But if we wait here, or drive around aimlessly until nightfall, we might attract attention. The first border crossing is only half an hour away.

'Let's go,' Zaira says firmly.

On the way from the airport we pass a cemetery. The white gravestones are all exactly the same and stand in neat rows, like a military cemetery honouring war dead. On each grave is a simple plaque; elaborate funeral wreaths hang at the gate. But this is no ordinary graveyard. Attached to the gravestones are teddy bears and dolls, angels and children's pictures. There are 330 graves here, one for each victim from School No. 1 in Beslan. One for every child killed after being forced into the school building on a day that was a celebration all over Russia. Ever since the Soviet period, festivities have taken place on 1 September to mark the start of the school year; in Beslan that day turned into hell on earth when terrorists seized the school. They wanted the world to turn its eyes towards the injustice and human rights violations in Chechnya. One of the terrorists said to a mother who begged them to release the youngest children: 'My children have been shot too. Are your children better than mine?'

Several children died from lack of water, others were shot, others blown to pieces by explosions inside the gymnasium when Russian forces attacked.

Three women are entering the cemetery gate. They walk with bowed heads and heavy steps. Perhaps they are stricken by the feeling of guilt that Timothy Phillips describes in his book *Beslan* — guilt for having survived. Zaira whispers a blessing and asks the driver to turn on to a smaller road. The main highway, where my passport would certainly be checked, is out of the question; I don't have permission to be in North Ossetia, where we are now, or in any of the other Caucasian republics. For that I would need a KTO card, that is to say, permission to be in an area of *kontra-terroristicheskaya operatsia* — counter-terrorist operations — and in order to get a KTO card you have to be on a government-organised visit.

The first crossing, into Ingushetia, goes smoothly; it is swarming with soldiers, but only the driver is asked to show his documents. Once we're in Ingush territory we take a smaller road, driving alongside fields and forests. On the far horizon we can vaguely make out the mountains, almost hidden in grey mist. It starts to snow. The driver is going at a breakneck speed. I remember that about Caucasians: they're not made for safety routines, and even less for safety belts. In fact, the belts have been removed from the car; they just get in the way. I beg the driver to slow down. He turns and laughs. 'Anyone who's afraid shouldn't go to Chechnya.'

Zaira does not smile. Her eyes scan the landscape. The trees along the road are bare – their leaves fell long ago – but the earth is not yet covered with snow. The tiny white flakes melt when they touch the ground. It's more than a year since she has seen her family. She is taking a great risk by entering with me. 'But somebody has to tell the world what's happening to us,' she says. 'That's more important than my studies.'

We approach the Chechen border. Just ahead we see two barracks behind heavy sandbags and a stone wall. The road is barricaded in such a way that people can't speed past but have to zigzag between concrete blocks. There is also a barrier across the road. Two lorries and some passenger cars are lined up ahead of us. I sit with the newly acquired look of cold aloofness on my face. Zaira stares out of the window with contrived disinterest. We are just two tired women on our way home. Between us lies a dirty bag of scruffy apples. The car stops, a blond Russian peers in, looks us in the face, glances at the contents of the car, asks the driver to get out and open the boot. If he opens my bag he will find only baby sleepers, soft playsuits and teddy bears.

The driver gets behind the wheel again, steps on the gas, turns round and smiles. He didn't even have to bribe. The two gloomy peasant wives weren't deemed worthy of a document check, and are now whizzing across the border into Chechnya.

'You see,' Zaira says contentedly and turns to me, 'Allah is with us!'

At first it only appears as something red in the distance. A red speck where the cracked brown earth blends into a misty sky. It's as if colour has been drained from the landscape; life is in hibernation, everything is faded, dust-covered, buried – except for the red speck ahead. It grows larger, takes form as we speed towards it, and becomes a tall arch curving over the road, a triumphal arch of red stone, a victory portal that rises up to the sky in the midst of desolation. What victory? Who is the victor? And who are the vanquished?

The arch is anchored solidly on each side of the road and, for some unknown reason, there is an opening on either side of the main portal. The structure has an almost naive quality about it, with square teeth at the top – it looks like a larger version of the entrance to a Lego fort.

'Welcome to Grozny' appears in ornate letters at the top, and on each side of the arch is an inlaid portrait. 'We are proud of you!' it says above the picture of an older man. 'We are with you!' reads the lettering above the picture of a younger one.

We drive on the rough road beneath these two Caucasian Napoleons – Kadyrov I and Kadyrov II – who gaze at us sternly through the gravel we throw up as we pass.

'They built it last summer.'

Zaira rolls her eyes and shakes her head.

On our way into the devastated city we see the two men more and more frequently. As portraits on exterior walls, on monuments, plaques, lamp-posts, billboards, in shop windows and as statues. Banners announce that the younger man's fan club is to arrange a concert in support of him. The ruined remains of the presidential palace, where rebel leaders once barricaded themselves, have been levelled and the area has become a memorial park to the older man. The park is complete with fountains, lights, evergreens and flowers. In the centre is a huge statue of the older man – greatly slimmed down, but with broadened shoulders – who, until his sudden death, ruled Chechnya with an iron fist. After a farcical election in 2003, Akhmed Kadyrov was inaugurated as president and became Moscow's puppet. As mufti of the republic he had supported the rebels during the first war, but later reached an agreement with the Kremlin. The statue has a perennial sheen. A worker, with brush and cloth in hand, is polishing the granite as we drive past.

This grey winter's day it's as if the entire history began with these two men; there was nothing before them, and a glowing future will come after them. No leaders from other eras have warranted even the tiniest picture; just these two pairs of eyes following us, along with the inscriptions: 'We will always remember you!' 'We will always follow you!' and 'United for you'.

The portraits look best, of course, on buildings that are still intact. They are fine on entrances to city buildings, and in places where a TV cameraman can pan across the surroundings and not see a single ruin through the lens. They do not appear among the rows of devastated buildings and heaps of gravel, the vestiges of factories and apartment blocks, twisted metal doorways, the naked frameworks of houses standing on narrow plots, or the foundations of expensive homes once surrounded by apricot orchards. But people still live in those buildings, without any exterior walls on which to hang the portraits. Their homes are like doll's houses: you can look straight into them from the street. To block the view, clothes lines strung with trousers, blankets and undershirts are hung like curtains. Here people aren't bothered by the penetrating stares of the two men. The only things that hang here are signs warning against landmines.

Along the parade route – Victory Prospect – the government ministries, the city hall, the police station and the courthouse have solid whitewashed walls. On the government buildings yet another portrait has found a place, a thin, pallid, almost anaemic-looking man between the two more vigorous-looking ones. He stares down at us with pale eyes beneath a smooth brow. His expression says that he really didn't have time to be photographed, and that it annoys him when someone looks at him.

The victor. The true Ruler of the Caucasus, and the one who appropriates money for grand gateways and monuments, as victors have always done.

Vladimir Putin is only the latest in the line of conquerors. The latest to try to tame the wolves.

Myself, I am more interested in the wolf cubs. Zaira knew where I could find them, and had promised to take me to a woman they called the *Angel of Grozny*.

6

The Angel of Grozny

The car stops. It's dark. Zaira gets out and knocks on a green door. Whispering and low voices can be heard from inside. A young boy opens the door a crack and peers out. Zaira says something in Chechen, and we quickly enter a yard where a single lamp glows dimly. A woman comes towards us. She embraces Zaira in the Chechen way – shoulder to shoulder, arms around each other's waists – and extends a soft hand to me. Speaking softly, they exchange quick messages. Zaira must go home to her family. I will stay here.

'You're safe here,' she says, and slips quietly out of the door. The engine starts and the car drives away.

The woman leads me up a staircase to a small living room. Light from a glowing stove dances on the walls.

Her name is Hadijat. She's a large, stout woman with deep beautiful eyes and long, slightly greying hair covered with a loose headscarf. Her pale skin is dry, and she looks ten years older than she really is.

It's late. Everyone else in the house is asleep. In front of the stove are two deep armchairs. A pot of tea and two cups have been set out on a small table.

When we are seated comfortably on the soft cushions, Hadijat begins to tell her story.

She grew up in a Soviet orphanage in Grozny during the 1960s. When she was four years old, her father died and her mother fell ill. The family's five children were sent to different orphanages. Hadijat never knew what was wrong with her mother, who was hospitalised for most of her daughter's childhood and until she died. On rare occasions, when she was strong enough, she came to see Hadijat, but the people in charge of the orphanage feared she might infect someone, so she was only allowed to stand outside the gate and wave.

'Once Mama sent me a bag of sunflower seeds and two roubles – that was a lot in those days, two roubles. I hid everything in my mattress, and at night I took it out and smelled it. It was Mama's smell. One night I woke up very hungry, so I dug out the bag and thought I'd crack open two or three sunflower seeds; but I couldn't do it, and put the bag away again. I breathed in the fragrance instead. Then one night everything was gone. Someone had robbed me. Eaten the sunflower seeds and taken the roubles. I cried and cried. What I wanted more than anything in the world – do you know what that was? Someone to call Mama.'

The matron rapped the children's temples with her knuckles if she was displeased with them. If Hadijat didn't finish her food, if she got dirty, if she did anything wrong, the matron whacked her fingertips with a stick.

'I still remember her. Vera Vasilyevna was her name. Vera Vasilyevna. The name still makes me shudder. We got a thrashing if we spoke Chechen. As you can hear, I speak Russian without a Caucasian accent, because we lived in a Soviet Russian environment. We even kept pigs; there was no talk of excusing the children from eating pork, although we were Muslims. We were brought up to be atheists, like all children in the Soviet Union. The pigsty was, in fact, the only place I felt safe. I often sat there and talked to the pigs. In Chechen. But the loneliness, the loneliness of an orphanage, that was the worst,' she sighs. 'My deepest desire was to have my own family.'

*

She met Malik on the bus from Mineralnye Vody during the last year of peace. When she boarded the bus at the last moment there was only one empty seat. Beside him. They hardly exchanged a word during the entire six-hour journey. But halfway through it, she offered him some pears. He gave her a bottle of mineral water. It was the middle of winter and bitterly cold. Under the seat Malik had a large box of fur hats he had received from a company instead of wages. Because of the cash crisis in Russia, people were paid in kind. He put his feet into the hats to keep warm, and invited Hadijat to do the same.

It was dark when they got off the bus. He asked if she wanted a lift in his taxi; he could drop her off on the way. Two weeks later he stood at her neighbour's door making enquiries. Yes, she is unmarried. He also found out that she had a birthday the following week, so he bought imported sweets, shaped like shells, she recalls, and knocked on her door. He was actually on his way to Siberia to sell the Caucasian fur hats, but he wanted to see her before he left. It turned out that she too was going to Siberia. So, with an aunt as chaperone, they skimmed over the Russian steppes and into the taiga. When two hundred fur hats were sold, they returned to Grozny and got married.

It was 1993 and chaos reigned. Wages were not paid, rubbish was not collected, telephones were dead. There were strikes and protests; people spent entire days at public meetings. Nationalism spread. Malik and Hadijat decided to return to Siberia. There they opened a shop where they sold coats, fur hats, school uniforms – anything that could be cut or sewn. In the evenings they drew warmth from their plans. Their dream was to save enough money to build a house with a garden in Grozny. Hadijat's stomach swelled. Malik did the figures and counted and put money aside. One evening as they drove home from a buying trip to a factory, the car slid on the icy road, swerved into the opposite lane and crashed into an articulated lorry. They were left lying unconscious at the side of the road. When Hadijat woke up in hospital, she knew something terrible had happened. She felt her stomach. The child was no longer alive.

The doctor spoke to Malik first. 'You will be fine, but your wife will be crippled.' Later Hadijat was told: 'Unfortunately, as a result of the accident you will never be able to have children.'

She was devastated. And inconsolable. Malik pushed the sorrow deep inside him. They lay with broken hips and legs in splints, grieving in their separate ways. Over the child they had lost, over the children they would never have. Although it was against the rules, they were allowed to share a room; there, amid tears and the fog of painkillers, they watched through the cracked windows as the world outside turned white and the minus-forty-degree cold penetrated the building. After a while the windows were so thickly covered with frost that they could no longer see out. They acquired a television set for the room. Bed-bound, thousands of kilometres from home, they followed the news as the unrest in Chechnya turned into a war. Columns of tanks rolled into their city, rockets whistled into the walls of buildings and gunshots rang out in the streets. They saw the dead children, the old people wandering around out of their minds. They looked at each other. And wept.

Six months after the accident they were able to leave their beds and hobble around on crutches. They wanted to go home. So, in February 1995, they made the difficult train journey back to Grozny. Total war raged. But the young couple chose to stay, and established a café near the market.

During the war their broken bones healed. After the peace talks with Russia in 1996 they both got work – Hadijat as a nurse, Malik as a driver for a medical team – at the interim government's military headquarters, the pulsing heart of the city. Everything went through this office. Here people looked for relatives, posted notices, begged for help. Amid the chaos people asked: What shall we do with all the homeless children?

Some weeks into the new administration the commandant told Hadijat to take two children home with her. They needed a place to sleep. When Malik came home later that evening, Hadijat pointed at him and said to the little boys, 'This is your Papa.'

Malik had forced a smile. He never talked about his deep sorrow that he would never have an heir, someone to bear his name and carry on the family line. 'I think people are physically attuned to having children in a family. It's almost a necessity,' he said to me later.

The first children who came home with Hadijat were two twelve-year-olds, Adam and Abdul. They were complete opposites. Adam's eyes flashed like black lightning beneath a bushy head of dark hair crawling with lice. He was short and stocky, brusque and impudent. Abdul was a thin boy whose pale face was sprinkled with freckles the same colour as his hair. He was quiet and shy, and followed Adam everywhere. They had both been homeless for a long time. Adam had adjusted to life in the street and had managed to get what he needed. Abdul was too afraid to steal, preferring to go hungry instead. Whereas Adam was fearless, Abdul was always scared. But both had shown courage during the war. When only ten and eleven years old, they had been messengers for the rebels and had sneaked past Russian blockades with bread and information.

The next evening two more boys came, then another pair, and then still more. Many had lived on the streets for part of the war and had behaved according to their own rules. Malik often had to return things they stole. A television set. A cassette player. Bread. Once Adam stole a car he was washing. The key was in the ignition and he jumped inside. In order to reach the pedals, the little fellow had to lie on the seat while another boy steered. It looked as though the car was rolling down the street without a driver. They didn't get far. Grozny's streets, with all their cracks and potholes, required experienced drivers.

One evening before New Year, Adam had taken Abdul to the bombed-out theatre in Grozny where the minister of culture, Akhmed Zakayev, had once played Hamlet. The minister had arranged for a large fir tree to be set up there for the New Year celebrations this first winter of peace. When the boys got to the tree, Adam climbed up, sawed off the top and calmly climbed down again. Then they stole home in the winter darkness; whenever a car drove by they stopped and hid behind the tree, so that all people saw was a Christmas tree on the pavement. They crept quietly through the gate at home, and the next morning everyone woke up to a New Year tree in Hadijat's and Malik's backyard. The boys said someone had given it to the children's home. The tree was allowed to stay. But one morning when Malik went out to the yard you could hear the roar: 'Adam! Aslan! Aslambek! Murat! Abdul! Who hung this up?'

The tree was decorated with the skeleton of a dead Russian. A *sniper* – sharpshooter – who had been shot on a rooftop, had rotted there in the blazing sun and was later washed clean by rain and snow, now hung in pieces, complete with skull, in Malik's and Hadijat's yard. Adam finally confessed.

But not until Malik heard people talking about the vandalising of the New Year tree in front of the theatre did he make the connection. The treetop was immediately chopped into small pieces and burned.

The boys had to be brought up all over again. Be weaned off glue sniffing and drugs, trained for a life in peacetime. Adam was incorrigible. He didn't want to listen, didn't want to learn, couldn't sit still. However, he did believe that dogs could be trained by example; when he saw a dog hungrily devouring a corpse, he caught the animal, hung it on a wall and slowly chopped off one paw after another as he lambasted the creature for eating human flesh. The mongrel howled. Adam chopped. Finally, he slit its throat and left it hanging with slashed throat and no paws as a terrifying warning to other dogs.

Children streamed into Hadijat's and Malik's flat. Dirty. Sobbing. Hungry. Some were later found by relatives and went home with them; others stayed. After a while people began to bring children they had found, all sorts of children, from a few months old to gangling teenagers. Hadijat rescued children from the ruins herself, and she never turned away anyone who needed a home. That's how she came to be called the Angel of Grozny.

These were the hopeful years. Command headquarters thought this was the most important job Hadijat and Malik could do for an independent Chechnya. They were given two apartments close to the devastated Dynamo Stadium, and money to feed the children. They started a laundry in the basement; the older children helped with the work in order to earn a few roubles. Soon they had fifty children. *Maskhadov's children*, they were called, because he had provided the apartments. That name is something Hadijat and Malik have to struggle with today now that the former president has been labelled a terrorist in Russia. Others called them *Basayev's children*. The rebel leader Shamil Basayev, who would later mastermind the Beslan hostage action, often came with toys or pockets filled with rolls of dollar bills. Once he came bearing a large television set. The children ran to him, tugged at his trousers: Uncle Shamil! Dear Uncle Shamil!

It was that same Uncle Shamil who gave Putin the pretext for a new war when he invaded Dagestan. Once again, bombs exploded over Grozny. The children's home fled to Ukraine, but the war stayed with the youngsters. They had nightmares, woke up at night, cried; they were afraid of everything: aeroplanes in the sky, men in uniform, the tram conductor, loud noises, cars that slowed down, a knock at the door.

'The fear stays with them for years. I have dreams about the war myself, wake up sweating, ready for disaster,' Hadijat says pensively in the semi-darkness. 'Boys think they shouldn't cry, and keep everything inside. They scream, run to us sobbing, and tell us what they've dreamed. They fall out of bed, they wet themselves,' sighs Hadijat.

'When children hear gunshots when they are doing their homework, how can they learn anything?'

7

The Abused

'Liza . . .'

A whisper steals into my dream.

'Liza . . . Liza!'

Sunlight filters through my eyelids. I open them and see a laughing young woman standing over me.

'Time to wake up, Liza. Tea?'

Suddenly I remember. My name is Liza. Hadijat gave me that name last night. 'So the children won't make a slip of the tongue and use your strange name among other people,' she said.

I look at the clock on the wall. Almost midday.

'Your breakfast is ready in the kitchen,' says the woman, whose name is almost the same as mine: Luiza.

I look out of the window through a leaf-patterned grille. The yard is paved with attractive flagstones that end at a tall gate with sharp spikes at the top. Behind it are the dark silhouettes of trees. Yesterday's snowfall has already melted. It trickles down the neighbour's corrugated tin roof and leaves wet patches; only in the grooves do a few white strips remain. Without going outside, without even opening the window, I can sense the mildness in the air.

I'm going to stay here a while, and spend the rest of the day getting to know the house and small yard. 'Don't go out without me. Stay indoors. If anyone knocks, hide!' were Hadijat's clear orders to me last night.

She left the house early this morning. So on my first day here, I am waiting, like the children, for her to come home.

The door opens wide. They crowd around her, hug her.

'Mama! Mama's home!'

The taller children throw their arms around her neck; the smaller ones tug at her skirt. Hadijat was certain of one thing when she suddenly became responsible for a flock of street children: she would not create an orphanage like the one in which she had grown up. She wanted to have a family. Mama, Papa and children. Malik became Papa, Hadijat became Mama, the children became brothers and sisters. During the last ten years she has been exactly that – Mama – for hundreds of children, both Chechen and Russian. Some have later gone to live with relatives or have grown up and established their own families. But to everyone she is Mama – the person who was there for them when no one else was.

'Where's Papa?' a little boy asks suddenly.

'He's coming this summer,' Hadijat replies. 'He has so much to do where he is.'

Hadijat hasn't told the children that Malik can't come back for a while. 'They need to believe Papa can come home at any time. They've lost so much. We can't let them think they've lost their father. Again.'

Malik lives in Lithuania with twenty or so of their children. They went there for a summer holiday, and the Lithuanian government allowed them to stay. They're mainly children who need medical treatment and some older boys who could be drafted into the army, or, even worse, accused of participating in the resistance. Often, just having relatives among the rebels puts you in danger.

After the kisses and hugs, it's time for the evening meal. Following the war, the family bought this solid, red-brick house and Malik fixed it up. They got support from the German relief

organisation Cap Anamur. The largest room is the kitchen. Its
tiles create rows of flowers across the entire floor. Children's
drawings hang on the wall, and the windows are misty with con-
densation from food simmering on the stove. Malika, who is
married to Hadijat's brother, stands by the cooking pots wearing
a big apron and a chef's hat. She is beautiful and as round as a porridge bowl. Her face is flushed from the steam. When Hadijat is
away, she leaves the house in the charge of Malik's younger sister,
Madina, a small, pretty woman with quick movements and an
intense gaze.

Several girls on the kitchen crew are energetically slicing bread,
setting the tables, ladling soup into bowls.

One girl stands out from the rest because she seems so distant,
as if in her own world. She doesn't talk to anyone and keeps to herself while setting the tables. She almost floats when she walks, her
steps are barely noticeable. She's thin as a rail, with no hips, no
waist, and long arms and legs. Her face glows with a strange light,
as if a Renaissance painter had chosen the colours. Her skin is
almost translucent, her cheeks soft pink. When she meets my gaze
the colour deepens and she looks down quickly, but after a while
she checks to see if I'm still there, if I'm still watching.

She is on the regular kitchen crew along with four other older
girls. As if in an effortless, well-rehearsed dance, they set the tables
with bowls, spoons, forks and cups, gliding lithely between tables
of different heights that correspond to the children's ages. There
are girls' tables and boys' tables. Everyone has a set place.

When the kitchen crew has finished, the children enter in single
file. Hadijat is already seated at the head of the adults' table. The
youngest children want to give Mama yet another kiss, which they
are allowed to do before being sent kindly to their places.

'Without discipline,' says Hadijat, 'this would never have
worked.'

The children sit down and reach for thick slices of bread.

'This isn't an orphanage, it's a family,' Hadijat explains. 'We
don't practise the kind of discipline they had where I grew up.'

Hadijat remembers those meals with horror. They had to line up, march in step to their assigned places, and stand there until Vera Vasilyevna said, 'Please start.' Then they all had to shout in chorus: *S-P-A-S-I-B-O!* before they were allowed to sit down. T-H-A-N-K Y-O-U!

Spoons clatter. First soup. A hum of small talk. Then macaroni. Laughter. A cup of weak tea completes the meal. The kitchen crew clears the tables.

Something about the elfin girl piques my curiosity. She seems to be smiling to herself, but at the same time to be hiding; her head is sunk between her shoulders.

I ask Hadijat about the girl.

'Oh, her – we were about to send her away.'

Hadijat glances at her.

'She was so awful. Stole like a magpie. Everything she could find. Money. Food. She even took bread, sugar lumps, anything at all. Or she stole things she could sell in the market. It took a while before we realised what was happening. We just noticed that things were disappearing. Suddenly we all had less money in our wallets, even if she was careful to steal so that we wouldn't notice things were missing; the wallet was never entirely empty. We thought the culprit was one of the boys; we asked, we threatened, trying to get the guilty one to confess. We couldn't tolerate such things here. Nothing like this had ever happened to us before. In the end, the other girls told me. They said she always had sweets. Always had money to buy things.'

Hadijat speaks softly as the girls clear away the last soup bowls before saying goodnight. The elfin girl gives me a final glance.

'I took her aside,' Hadijat continues, 'and gave her a good scolding. I thought she'd never dare to steal even a kopek after that. But she kept on, more slyly than before; she stole things from the storeroom and sold them. She took only coins and small banknotes from us, but then she got caught again, and this time I was harsher. Nonetheless, things continued to disappear. I cried, I raged. She kept on stealing. I screamed at her, I put my arms around her, I comforted her. She cried too. "I can't help it," she sobbed. "It's not me; my hand just does it by itself . . .'"

Hadijat shakes her head. The kitchen is quiet and a long fluorescent light casts a greenish glow.

'What is her name?'

'Liana.'

The light is uncomfortably sharp. Now that the kitchen is empty, it seems bleak and cold.

'Let's take our tea up to my room,' Hadijat suggests. We go up to the second floor, to the room we share. It has two beds, each against a wall, and the small alcove where we sat by the gas stove the previous night.

'I held her tightly while she hit and kicked,' Hadijat recalls. 'She fought out of my grip like a cat. This couldn't continue. I had to think of the other children; having her here affected them. She was so difficult, unmanageable, just like her brother. When he came to us, he went around smashing things. Hit other children when he thought we weren't watching. Swore. Smoked secretly. Broke all the rules. As with Liana, I just held my arms around him when he grew wild. Told him about God's love for all people, for all living things. Timur adapted more quickly than his sister. One evening when we'd caught her in the act again, I shouted that we'd had enough now; I had to send her back to her uncle. A howl split the air. I never thought a child could shriek like that, like an animal in pain. It was Timur, her brother. He threw himself on me, pummelled me, and screamed: "You can't do that! You can't do that!" He ran in circles. "Send me instead! Send me instead!" Then he grabbed Liana's hair, held her fast, and shouted, "Don't you understand? You've got to stop stealing!" Sobbing, he begged me: "Give her one more chance." Liana stiffened in her brother's grasp and then broke down. For the rest of the evening I just sat and held my arms around them both.'

Hadijat looks into the flickering gas flame.

'Ai, ai, ai, how she has suffered . . .'

*

The brother and sister had been at the children's home for six months when I arrived. After living on the streets for a while, Timur had no longer been able to bear the thought of the sister he had abandoned. Sniffing glue didn't help any more, strangling dogs didn't help; he couldn't erase from his mind what he knew was happening. One day he met Liana on the street. They devised a plan. The uncle always locked the door when Liana had to stay at home. Today she would make sure the door was unlocked so that Timur could expose what was going on. That afternoon Timur ran home. He opened the door and found the uncle and his sister on the sofa. His sister was crying. He slammed the door and ran. Ran and ran. To the local police station, and shouted: 'Come, come quickly! Save her!'

Two officers went with Timur to the uncle's home; they took the two children into custody and left the uncle at home. A woman at the police station who knew about Hadijat telephoned her to ask if she'd take the children.

'That's how they ended up here,' says Hadijat. 'It's so sad. There's so much of this sort of thing here. Adults who abuse children. I know it happens everywhere, all over the world. But most societies have ways of limiting it – norms, rules. We have them too, of course. Very strict rules, in fact. But when a society comes unravelled, the rules unravel as well; nobody pays attention, people have their own concerns, so sadists can find ways to sneak off and do their wicked deeds. I've seen so much of it, so many abused children, some of them in nappies. Maybe you'd like to talk about it with Liana?'

'It's probably not wise to reopen all that?'

'Maybe not.'

I don't go outside the front gate.

Little by little I find my place in the daily routines of the children's home. I'm most in demand for help with lessons. The children attend school in two groups, some in the morning, others in the afternoon, so there are always children at home. Schoolwork is based on memorising, not on understanding.

Poems need to be learned by heart. Entire dialogues in English must be committed to memory. It's not so important that the children understand what they're saying. Several times a week they are given tests, and they come home to Hadijat with grades — twos, threes, fours and fives.

The children take turns getting help with schoolwork. One day it is Liana's turn. She looks at me with that distant yet determined angelic look of hers. 'Now you are mine,' it says.

'Maths is so hard,' she says.

'Not at all,' I answer.

Liana is thirteen now and in class five. They have started equations. The problems she needs to solve contain 'a' and 'b' and 'x' and 'y' and multi-digit numbers. I have to think hard to remember the rules for dividing, setting on one side, and solving the equation section by section. I help Liana divide up the problem so that in the end 'x' stands alone. But no matter how I explain it, Liana just looks at me pleadingly: 'You answer, you answer. . .' I make it as simple as possible, but after a while I realise that Liana doesn't know the multiplication tables. So how is she supposed to divide? I try to teach her to multiply, at least the small numbers. This will take more time, I recognise. I help her solve the problems for the next day; understanding them will have to come later.

'We have to solve the problems together,' I say. She keeps on giving the wrong answer. I simplify the task again, and finally we're left with two minus one.

'Three,' Liana answers.

I demonstrate with my fingers: first I hold up two fingers, then I take away one.

'Two,' Liana answers.

I try with apples. 'You have two apples and eat one. How many apples do you have left?'

'One,' Liana answers.

Liana doesn't understand numbers, at least not arithmetic. Not at all. She's in class five because that more or less corresponds to her age. But numbers get pushed out of her mind.

I'm exhausted.

'English,' she says. 'Teach me English. It's so hard.'

We're supposed to fill in 'is' and 'isn't'. And learn the difference between 'on' and 'under'. On the table. Under the table. The pen is on the desk. The cat isn't on the desk, it is under the desk. When I ask Liana to read, everything becomes very confused and she sits there mute.

'You read,' she says. We read word for word. It turns out that Liana hasn't learned the English letters. She has transcribed the assigned texts into Cyrillic in her notebook. When the teacher read them aloud she wrote down the sounds. She can rattle off the alphabet like a poem, but she doesn't know what the letters for those sounds look like. I try to teach her the letters. It goes slowly. She guesses, rather than trying to remember.

'You won't learn anything by guessing,' I say.

She looks at me for a while. And keeps on guessing.

'Don't guess. Take a little time to think instead. You don't have to answer right away.'

We go all the way back to Lesson One. It has pictures of familiar things. Hat. Cat. Dog. Box. Desk. Pen. She should be able to do this; then we can go on from here. But after an hour she knows no more words than when we started. Sometimes she guesses correctly. 'Now I know that! Now I know that!' she exclaims, her face brightening. Then she makes mistakes again. Box. Cat. Dog. Everything becomes a jumble.

'Why is it so hard for me to remember?' Liana asks dejectedly, her eyes narrowing as she looks at me. 'If I have to go to the blackboard I never remember anything, and the teacher tells me to sit down again.'

I don't have an answer. But she persists.

'Why can't I remember things?'

'Maybe because there's so much you're trying to forget.'

Her face becomes distorted. Her eyes fill with terror, then with tears. Her lips tremble. She hides her face in her hands, her shoulders are shaking.

'Liana, what is it, Liana . . .?'

I stroke her back. She looks up at me, her face dissolving in tears.

The sentence explodes in my head. *Maybe because there's so much you're trying to forget.* They can't choose to forget one thing and remember something else, those who have experienced the very worst. Memory is not selective, as some people say. For her whole life Liana has used all her energy to push away, not notice, not feel.

The strength she uses to forget is all the strength she has.

Liana grew up with just her mother after her father went away. 'It was the only good time in my life,' she tells me after we have given up on the lessons. 'I played with dolls, Mama's stomach grew, we cooked food. Then I got a little sister. One day Mama had to go to the market to buy bread. Bombs were falling all the time and we didn't have any food at home. I was in charge of my little sister, who was only one year old. I heard the planes and saw the bombs; my little sister cried. She was soaking wet. It got dark outside. The neighbour came looking for Mama. When I said she'd gone to the market early that morning, the lady came in, looked around and put dry clothes on my little sister. "Your mama will probably come back soon," she said, and went away. My little sister crawled around on the floor. A car drove up and I ran to the window; the neighbour was already down by the car. I went out-side. She was screaming. She stood with her hands in front of her face, screaming. I ran towards her, but she shouted: "Don't go to the car, don't go to the car! You mustn't look!" They had Mama with them, you see. When I came back, my sister was lying in a big puddle. She had crawled to the stove and spilled a pot of boil-ing water all over her. She died. The same day as Mama.'

I knew the rest of the story. Liana was turned over to Uncle Omar. Sitting on the floor with the sofa as a backrest, she tells me what happened next.

'He told Timur and me: "You have to work for me." I was only seven or eight years old, so I could easily slip in and out of crowds. If we came back without money, he beat us. After a while he looked at me with an ugly smile and said, "Come here. Come to me." I hid behind Timur. My uncle was so vicious to Timur. Once when it got dark he gave Timur a beating, threw him out in the hall and locked the door. Timur shouted: "What are you doing with my sister?!" He screamed and pounded. Uncle Omar raped me. Every day. Every day for six years. Here and here and here.'

Liana points to various parts of her body. She sobs. Tears stream down her face. I put my arms around her and hold her.

'It's over now,' I tell her. 'It's over now.'

What can I say?

To say 'It's over now' seems like empty words. Because it still goes on in Liana's head.

She twitches, a shudder goes through her body, her breathing calms down, her weeping stops and we sit silently. 'Should we continue the English lessons?' she asks softly.

I have no words.

She looks at me with a swollen face. 'Don't go!' she cries, gripping my arm tightly. 'Don't go. Cat. Dog. Hat. Pen. Box,' she chants in quick succession. 'Don't go! Cat. Dog. Hat. Pen. Box. Don't go.'

8

Living in a Fog

Dinara shuffles across the linoleum-covered floor. Her hands tremble. Her head shakes from side to side, as if in a perpetual spasm. The expression in her eyes changes constantly; sometimes they're wide open, sometimes listless and half closed, sometimes firmly focused, other times flitting about. Her lower lip sags, and her sallow complexion speaks of years without sun. Her cropped hair is almost striped: black with greasy grey fringes. A threadbare, floral-patterned dressing gown is wrapped around her body.

Nearby, other women in old dressing gowns sit staring vacantly as a cleaning lady mops the brown-flowered linoleum with tepid water and soap that neither foams nor smells. The stale odour in the building doesn't disappear even if the floor is sparkling clean. It's the smell of confinement.

Hadijat wanted me to meet Dinara. A friend with a car drives up to our gate, we walk out, get in without a word, the car turns off the small street, and we are on a country road heading west.

Just outside Samashki, where one of the worst Russian massacres of Chechen civilians occurred during the first war, we cross the Valerik River, turn off to Zakan-Yurt, and drive under another gleaming portal with portraits. After turning on to yet another road, the car stops by a heavy iron gate with a sign that reads Samashki Psychiatric Clinic.

From here we go on foot, past a row of whitewashed brick buildings. Long, five-storey structures. One stinks of excrement, another of urine. The young trees outside the buildings all have bare branches now. The beds of black earth are bare, too. At the fourth building we take a small footpath where two cats are playing, rolling around and hissing happily. The path leads to a door with an outer iron grille that is secured with a heavy padlock.

The inner door is open to the mild winter day; only the grille is locked. Through it we can see Dinara shuffling around. She scarcely lifts her feet as she moves across the floor, back and forth, in circles, in half-circles, back and forth. Her eyesight is almost gone. Whether this is due to her illness or the medicines Hadijat does not know, but when Dinara hears the familiar voice through the bars she shambles towards us step by step, her hands groping ahead of her. She clutches Hadijat's arms. 'My angel, my angel,' she sobs.

The attendant lets us in. 'Don't stay long,' she tells us sternly.

Dinara's eyes and hands never leave Hadijat. She puts her arm around Hadijat's waist, pats her face. 'My angel, my angel,' she croons.

We sit down on a bench and Dinara looks straight into Hadijat's eyes.

'How are my children?'

'They're fine. They're doing well at school. They have a good life now.'

'Adlan too?'

'Adlan too.'

'Lida too?'

'Yes. Lida has become so beautiful.'

'Can they come and visit me?'

'They have so much to do at school, but we'll see if we can arrange a visit. They asked me to say hello to you.'

However, the doctors have decided that it is best if Dinara does not see her children. Or rather, it is best that the children do not see their mother, Hadijat thinks. She didn't bring greetings from them. The children don't know she's visiting their mother.

Once they were a family, mother, father and two children. That was before the wars. Dinara was a popular Islamic ethics teacher at a high school in Grozny. 'She was smart, well read; everyone looked up to her,' Hadijat told me on our way to the clinic. 'And she was so elegant, always had fashionable clothes, lovely hair and nice make-up.'

After her marriage, Dinara gave birth first to Lida, then Adlan. They were five and four when the bombing began. Her husband went off to fight, and Dinara was left alone with the children. She became ill after long weeks in the basement, not knowing where her husband was, or whether he was alive, and when he returned the young woman he'd married no longer existed. Dinara now had grey hair, sallow skin and shifty eyes. The husband left Dinara and the children in their high-rise block and went away again.

'How could I live with a madwoman?' he said to people. 'He surely deserves better than that – a strong, handsome man like him,' his family insisted.

He never returned. Dinara didn't know whether he had been killed, or whether he had just abandoned her.

The second winter of the war she broke down completely. She lay in bed most of the time, without sleeping or eating, while Lida and Adlan sat in the living room as quiet as mice so that she wouldn't get angry. On the rare occasions their mother got up, the children just hoped she'd go back to bed. She would give Lida cigarette burns while asking with a smile: 'Does it hurt? Does it hurt now? Now?'

The little girl screamed and begged for mercy, while her younger brother Adlan sat in a corner wetting himself. The children got hardly any food, they were unwashed, they were cold.

'Tolstoy wrote that madness comes from a lack of love. That

fits in Dinara's case,' Hadijat said in the car on our way to the clinic. 'Or it comes from terrible fear,' she added. 'Many of us have lost our minds during these wars.'

One morning Dinara had been awakened by Adlan playing in the kitchen. She stormed out of the bedroom, picked up the five-year-old, and took him out on to their ninth-floor balcony, where she swung him back and forth over the railing, shrieking: 'I'm throwing you down! You bad boy! I'm throwing you down!'

Lida tried to pull her mother away from the railing while Adlan screamed. People rushed up from the street and eventually managed to subdue Dinara. She calmed down. Hugged the children, said she was sorry, cried, and kissed them. The children remained with her. Where else would they go? But Adlan had stopped speaking.

One night they heard loud pounding at the door. Russian soldiers came and took Dinara away, paying no heed to her screaming children. As the wife of a resistance fighter she was a target, regardless of his whereabouts.

Long before we drove out to Samashki Psychiatric Clinic, Lida, who was now sixteen, had told me about the time her mother was taken away by the Russians.

'We sat waiting for her the whole day. Then it got dark. We didn't know how to turn on the lamp, so we went to bed in the dark. When we woke up early the next day, Mama still hadn't come back. At first we tried to play, but finally we just sat and cried. We tried to be as quiet as possible, so the Russians wouldn't find us. Why is the world so bad? I wondered. Now it was just the two of us, Adlan and me. We knew an old woman across the hall, and after a while I asked her for something to eat and she gave us food. We slept at home, and ate with her.

'Then Mama came back. She had hardly any money, only fifty roubles, and she sent me to buy bread before she went to bed. She stayed in bed for days. We ate bread, nothing else. One morning she started to clean up the flat, but when she began making the bed she just lay down in it and stayed there. She didn't see us any longer, she didn't take care of us, she got sicker and sicker. She screamed a lot. We were the poorest people in the neighbourhood and we begged for bread at a little market. We knocked on people's doors, too, and came home with small pieces of bread for Mama. I told her that people had given them to us. She said Papa was dead, but once in a while she said she didn't think Papa was dead. In a way we lost both of them.'

Lida doesn't remember much about her father. 'He was hardly ever there, he was strict, and he yelled at us a lot. In the evenings he told us folk tales, such terrible stories we could hardly sleep. Everything around us seemed frightening. We stood on the balcony with him when the war began. I remember the strange sounds, before we were sent into the basement. Then Papa disappeared. The Russians have taken so much from us.'

One day as Lida and Adlan walked barefoot, hand in hand, in their tattered, filthy clothes, they met Hadijat in the market. She recalls that the girl looked up at her and the boy stared at the ground. If he happened to raise his eyes and met someone's glance, he quickly looked away again.

'What are you two doing here?'

'We live here,' Lida had answered.

They had gone out that morning to escape their mother's screams and abuse. Adlan said nothing. It had been more than a year since he stopped speaking.

'She bought so much bread, so much delicious, fresh bread,' Lida remembers. 'I went over and asked her for some. "Who are you?" she asked. "Where are your parents?" "Papa is dead and Mama is mad," I said. She promised to come to our flat the next day. So we waited for her at home. She came and talked to Mama. "I saw them begging in the market," she said. That weekend she came and fetched us. We cried and cried, didn't want to leave Mama. But when I got to their house I thought I'd come to Paradise. So many children, so many toys, such good food.

'I don't really know what happened to Mama. She visited us once. "I see you're doing fine here," she said, and asked Hadijat to take care of us. I know she loves us, but her head isn't put together right.'

Lida's little brother has thin, stooped shoulders and walks with his head down. Adlan still looks away when he meets someone's eyes. He is told when to wash himself, when to change his clothes, when to eat.

After living with Malik and Hadijat for a while, Adlan began to speak again, first only short words, then whole sentences. But he isn't able to keep up in school and although he is fifteen now, he can barely read. He's very good at repairing bicycles, and he dreams of learning to drive a car.

At the children's home he generally kept to himself, and after a few years he went to live with Hadijat's brother in the country. There he looked after three horses. He was with his horses from dawn to dusk. When he got a sugar lump with his tea, he put it in his pocket to give to the horses; likewise if he got a toffee. If he happened to find some small change he bought sugar lumps for them.

I met Adlan during the summer. He was sitting under a tree wearing a dark blue Burberry T-shirt with buttons and a checked collar. A donation from abroad, like all the children's clothing. His shirt disappeared into the waistband of shimmering black track-suit bottoms. On his feet were pink plastic sandals.

He was chewing sunflower seeds. *Crack*, he split one between his teeth, teased it from its shell, spat out the husk and bit into the kernel, which tasted of light roasting and sunshine.

'I remember how she prepared food,' he said. 'And she kept saying, "Be a good boy, Adlan, be a good boy." I was always unhappy, because I wasn't good.'

Adlan sat with his elbows on his knees, looking around. Then he got up and walked over to a currant bush. I assumed this meant I shouldn't enquire further about his mother. He squatted down, almost under the bush, and found the most hidden branches, the heaviest, far underneath – those that no one had found yet and were still full of berries. Slowly, he plucked red, bittersweet berries and put them in his mouth. His face had a focused yet far-away expression. Gentle sunlight and the fresh smell of grass and currant leaves filled the air. Adlan looked at me and smiled.

'Horses are nicer than people,' he said between two mouthfuls. A few berries rolled around in his hand. 'They never leave you. They always wait for you. They're good and intelligent and faithful.'

He looked towards the door, where some children were coming down the steps into the morning sunshine.

'I know they dream about me at night,' said Adlan.

About twenty iron beds are lined up close together on either side of the large room. An aisle has been created in the middle. The space between the beds is just big enough for a nightstand. Women are sitting or lying on the beds with wide open, searching eyes or an empty apathetic gaze. Some are sobbing, one is making strange sounds, others are shuffling around. Dinara's bed has a deep groove down the middle. The springs have gone. The little door of the nightstand is half open; there is nothing inside. We give her the few things we have brought: underwear, a nightgown, soap, a hairbrush, some fruit and biscuits. She puts them aside without taking her eyes off Hadijat.

For a third time the attendant comes over with the padlock key in her belt. 'If you don't go now . . .'

'We have to leave,' Hadijat says to Dinara.

'We can't risk . . .' Hadijat whispers to me, whom she has introduced as her Russian friend.

Dinara's head shakes and she gives Hadijat a desperate look. 'Say hello to my children,' she says, grasping Hadijat's hand tightly. Hadijat promises to say hello to them.

Dinara starts to weep when we rise to leave, and she shuffles with us towards the door. She remains behind the grille; we stand squinting in the sharp light on the steps outside.

'Will you say hello to Adlan too?'

'Yes, Adlan too.'

'Lida too?'

'Lida too,' replies Hadijat, as a nurse tries to pull Dinara away from the door. We walk backwards down the path, waving. Dinara stands with both hands clutching the bars and refuses to be pulled away. When we leave the footpath, she's no longer in sight. We follow the gravel road. Then we hear a voice, muffled by distance but still clear enough:

'Tell them that I love them!'

9

Friday Evening

During the day it's the children's space; in the evening the women relax in the family room, down a short flight of stairs from the dining hall. It's carpeted and comfortably furnished with soft, well-worn sofas and a few easy chairs. Here, in this world free of men, they lie on their sides with their heads resting on their hands, or with their legs along the back of a chair. Their working day stretches from dawn until long after dark. When it's over, they turn on the old television set in the corner. There are two channels. One Russian, one Chechen.

The Russian news broadcasts have acquired an increasingly Soviet quality, as if edited in the Kremlin. Every evening the viewers — whether in the Caucasus or Siberia or by the Black Sea — are informed about Vladimir Putin's doings. Putin greets government leaders. Putin receives governors. Putin appoints governors. Putin removes governors. Putin attends an exhibition. Putin observes the production of aeroplanes, cars, boats; he follows the development of new tanks and rockets; he presents a medal to Mr Kalashnikov, inventor of the Kalashnikov, and a diploma to Second World War veterans. Putin holds a meeting of his ministers and puts them in their place on live television. Powerful ministers get reprimanded like naughty schoolchildren. There they sit, the headmaster and the students, at a little table. Putin says to the defence minister, for example:

'Sergei Borisovich, how is the building of new apartments for our officers progressing?'

'Vladimir Vladimirovich, in the past year we have built a hundred thousand apartments for officers. We plan another hundred thousand by 2012.'

'That's not good enough, Sergei Borisovich. You need to work faster. Every officer must have an apartment for himself and his family by the end of 2008. It's vital we make every effort to reach this goal.'

'It will be done, Vladimir Vladimirovich.'

Every evening TV viewers are shown a short film clip, a parody of a conversation. The men – for Putin chooses to associate with men – sit with serious expressions and talk about the state of the nation until the images fade out. God knows what they talk about when the cameras are turned off and the TV crews are banished. Equally absurd is the footage from meetings of the Security Council, which Putin has invested with increasing power. The meetings remind me of something I've seen before, in Baghdad in 2003, during the months before Saddam Hussein's fall. Iraqi television carried endless meetings with Saddam and his ministers. However, on Iraqi television classical music overlay the ministers' voices. On Russian television you hear the voices; the ministers are always ready with statistics, quantity and size in answer to questions from the president, who listens sceptically with a wrinkled brow. Not once during my time in Russia in 2006 and 2007 did I hear any criticism of Putin from TV journalists.

When it comes to news about Chechnya, all the channels show that it is peaceful there. If they broadcast anything from the republic it's about the reconstruction or a religious holiday or people dancing and celebrating something.

'We will be the new Switzerland! Tourists will flock here!' Chechnya's beaming minister of tourism said to the TV camera.

'We have everything tourists could want: mountains, fresh air, beautiful nature, drama and adventure!'

'Just like the Soviet days,' says Hadijat. 'They treat us like children. Do they think they're fooling us?' she asks, changing the channel to Chechen TV and the local news. There President Putin is replaced by Prime Minister Kadyrov, soon to be President Kadyrov.

'Do you notice anything?' Hadijat asks in the middle of the broadcast.

'That they praise Ramzan Kadyrov so much, you mean?'

'Where is our president? Chechnya has a president, his name is Alu Alkhanov. But suddenly, he's never in the news. That means he's on his way out.'

We are approaching New Year 2007, and everyone expects Putin to appoint Ramzan Kadyrov as president. Kadyrov Jr just had to reach his thirtieth birthday first, which he did in October amid great festivity, so his appointment can occur at any time.

As an old Kremlinologist, Hadijat judges the current power status by the TV broadcasts, in which the actual president, Alu Alkhanov, never appears. It's young Ramzan Kadyrov who controls the republic, and thereby the media. This evening he meets the inhabitants of a mountain village who shout: 'Thank you, Ramzan! Now we are safe! Thank you for peace!' Ramzan's security forces guard him closely, and after having watched a few news broadcasts I even begin to recognise the bodyguards' faces. Ramzan opens a school, he inspects a building site, he gives away a car, a minibus, the keys to an apartment. Often half the news broadcast is devoted to showing the young prime minister, who both the television crews and the people are on first-name terms with, giving gifts to the deserving and the needy, who crowd around him, applauding. Sometimes they dance for him and he throws money at them.

Like Vladimir Putin, Ramzan Kadyrov gets no criticism in the national or local media. The TV cameras cover only what is permitted.

'People are more afraid now than during the war,' Zaira had said to me after we crossed the border into Chechnya. 'It's like Moscow in the thirties. People inform on each other, they disappear in the night and never return. No one trusts anyone else any more, because Putin had a stroke of genius: he let Ramzan Kadyrov do the dirty work. Now it's Chechen against Chechen.'

It's called 'chechenising' the conflict. Whereas before, Russian forces committed the worst abuses, now the Chechen militia maintains control in a society maimed by fear.

Despite the official 'normalisation' in the republic, murders, disappearances and torture continue. What people fear most are Kadyrov's security forces, the Kadyrovtsi. They operate prisons and camps, and are notorious for their brutality; the few prisoners who have returned alive tell of gruesome torture. Films taken by the executioners themselves and now circulating on video cassettes and mobile phones show people tortured to death. In one, where a man is being given an electric shock, the executioner shouts: 'We're not going to kill you, and we won't let you live. We'll keep you like this for a few months, until you're neither man nor woman!'

Anna Politkovskaya was completing a major article documenting abuse and torture in Chechnya at the time of her murder. The unfinished work was printed in *Novaya Gazeta* on the day of her funeral, with murky pictures from a video showing two prisoners being tortured by Kadyrov's men. The video ends with a man lying on the ground as one torturer says to the other:

'Is he finished now?'

'Yes, finished.'

In June 2004 Anna Politkovskaya interviewed the newly appointed deputy prime minister, Ramzan Kadyrov.

'How do you see yourself? What are your strongest character traits?'

'How . . .? I don't understand the question.'

'What is your strong side, and what is your weak side?'
'I don't see myself as weak. I'm strong.'
'What do you like doing best?'
'Fighting. I'm a soldier.'
'And when there's no one left to fight?'
'I have bees, bulls, fighting dogs.'
'What else do you like?'
'Partying. I love women.'
'And your wife doesn't mind?'
'I do it secretly.'

The last thing Kadyrov says to Politkovskaya is: 'I'll show you. You're an enemy. I'll force you. I'm no gangster. I'll force you. I won't let you go.'

The interview was conducted one month after Ramzan's father, nowadays a robust bronze statue, was blown up by a bomb in Dynamo Stadium in Grozny on 9 May 2004. Akhmed Kadyrov was the republic's mufti – religious leader – until he became Putin's presidential candidate. He fought on the side of the separatists during the first war, but later became Moscow's man and a dictator in the true sense of the word. As time went on, the puppet tried to break free. But he was killed with all the strings attached. Ramzan was in Moscow the day his father was blown to bits.

The following day, Putin received the twenty-eight-year-old son, who attended the Kremlin meeting in jogging pants and T-shirt. He was instructed to continue his father's work. Unofficially. Interior Minister Alu Alkhanov was promoted, of course. But he was completely ignored by Putin, despite being a staunch Moscow supporter. A young Russian, Sergei Abramov, became prime minister.

Ramzan Kadyrov was appointed deputy prime minister, but he held the real power – maintained by the black-clad Kadyrovtsi. And when Sergei Abramov was badly injured in a mysterious car accident during the winter of 2006 and was 'unfit for health reasons' to continue in his position, Ramzan became prime minister. The ceremony took place in the 'Ramzan boxing club', which all day swarmed with police and various fighting units in addition to Kadyrov's bodyguards. The party began with a round of pistol shots.

The correspondent at *Kommersant*, one of the few newspapers besides *Novaya Gazeta* still critical of Kadyrov, described the party like this:

> For security reasons, only the ministers and leaders of the republic were driven right up to the building; all the other guests, including the deputy ministers, had to walk several hundred metres through slush and mud, soiling shoes that had been polished until they glistened. Some people had foreseen this situation and carried their party shoes, which they changed into at the entrance to the banquet hall. Kadyrov reiterated that Sergei Abramov was the guest of honour; every toast at the banquet was to him, and he was awarded the Akhmed Kadyrov Medal, named after Ramzan's deceased father.
>
> Abramov said he felt like a Chechen and had named his firstborn Akhmed, although the boy's passport gives his name as Nikolai. As further proof, Abramov pointed to his wife who was wearing a Chechen headscarf, as were all the other women at the banquet. During the past month Kadyrov has actively sought to have more women wear headscarves as a way of reviving national tradition. He has urged all women working in the government to wear them. Some workers who have ignored this request have already lost their jobs.
>
> At the end of the evening Mr Abramov danced *lezginka* to applause and foot-stomping, and Kadyrov honoured his 'best friend' by firing his pistol and throwing a bundle of hundred-dollar bills at the former prime minister. According to eyewitnesses, there must have been at least ten thousand

dollars in the bundle. Throwing money is an old Chechen tradition that shows you truly respect the dancer. The party lasted a long time, but no one had anything to drink; one of the objectives in reviving Chechen traditions is to keep people away from alcohol.

The women in the family room sigh when the TV announcer says that Hodj Akhmed Kadyrov will now reply to viewers' questions. The face of yet another Kadyrov fills the screen, this time Ramzan's uncle, brother of the deceased president; he has been given his own Friday night television programme. He leans back comfortably on a leather sofa, dressed in dark clothes and wearing a round cap with a gold border. Beside him sits a well-dressed young man who looks like an Armani model and has a list of questions about Islam. The programme opens with religious music before Hodj Akhmed Kadyrov speaks:

'First of all, remember that every step you take is written down by Allah. God will punish you if you do not follow the right path. God forgives, but punishes. If you are a Chechen, you must act like a Chechen. You must be proud of who you are. And you must make others feel proud of being Chechen. You must pray five times a day. You must listen to the elders. If you do not follow the right path, you will burn in Hell and will not go to Paradise. Lenin said religion was the opium of the people. Quite the contrary: religion is the foundation, and the mosques must always be open. Before, we had to pray in secret; now we can pray openly. We must give thanks for this. Five times a day you must absolutely drop everything and pray. Oh, forgive me, I used a Russian word just then: *obyazatelno* – absolutely. I got carried away and forgot myself,' Ramzan's uncle mumbles.

After several hundred years of colonisation Chechens use many Russian words and expressions. Suddenly I hear words that I understand in a conversation. Expressions like 'in no way', 'at least', 'in any case', 'at the edge', 'all together', as well as official expressions for which the Chechen language has no words.

After the opening comments, the young man reads the questions that viewers submitted during the week.

'Does Islam allow me to borrow money?'

'Yes, as long as you repay it,' replies Kadyrov, 'and as long as it is not all for yourself. Borrow only if it's for your family, to build a house, for example. Remember to repay the loan within three months if you have earned money from it.'

'Is it possible to get divorced?'

'Divorce is a sin. Those who marry must be prepared, and the family that gives away a daughter has a greater responsibility than the one that receives her. The honour of the family lies in the daughter's behaviour; namely, that she is virtuous, respectful, a good housekeeper, a good mother, and does not break traditions or do anything immoral.'

'If the husband drinks, is that grounds for divorce?'

'You must help him; but if he doesn't stop drinking, you can leave. That's the law.'

Hadijat nods.

'What if a married man has a wayward eye?'

'That means he has other women,' Hadijat translates.

'This is the greatest sin. If his wife is sick, or doesn't bear children, he can marry someone else; otherwise, a man must stick with the wife he has. However, a man can have up to four wives, so he doesn't have to divorce a sick wife even if he marries someone else.'

'What is the right age to marry?'

'Once a girl has her period, she is ready to marry. Age doesn't matter. She is a woman then, even if she is only twelve years old. The parents can arrange a marriage at the time a girl is born. That's the best.'

Hadijat shakes her head. 'Did you hear that? Twelve years old!'

'When the husband's family receives a girl with her trunks and suitcases, the contents are hers and hers alone. It's becoming more and more the custom for the women in the house to examine the trunks and demand things – this for me and this for me and this for me. They snatch things the bride and her mother have assembled. Those things belong to the bride, and it makes no difference that everyone wants a gift! She doesn't need to show her trunks at all. Only her husband needs to know what is in them. It's no one else's business what kind of underwear the girl has. And, besides, not everyone can afford expensive underwear, so it should be a secret in any case. Wedding traditions have been ruined because women have controlled them; it's time for the men to take charge and set limits. Women should take care of the cooking, and I say: Woman, stay at home. Then your husband will do everything for you! The husband is master of the house, and must provide food and security for the whole family. And women, why do you need to go outside? Regarding married life, the truth is that if a woman subjects herself to her husband's will, if she attends to his needs and doesn't quarrel or behave badly, she will go straight to Paradise. But the husband also has responsibilities: if a man looks at another woman and wishes she were his while his own wife is pregnant, his child will be regarded as a bastard!

'Woman, subject yourself to your husband. It's wrong for a wife to try to rise to the man's level. Then she degrades her husband; she is a woman, after all. She can't do everything. Look at Pompeii; that was a punishment from God because people didn't behave properly. The same is true here – two wars are enough. We don't need another one! If you keep dressing that way, and if you don't listen to your husbands, there will be another war! Allah must help us, we need Him, but then we must not live in such a way that He turns away from us.'

'How much of her shoulders and bosom can a woman's wedding gown reveal?'

'Low-cut clothing is not good. Who would want to have all the men looking down his wife's bosom during the wedding? A wedding dress should have long sleeves and a high neckline. The neckline should cover the collarbone.'

Hadijat raises her eyebrows.

'The skirt should be long, of course. Below the ankles. And for a man it is *haram* – forbidden – to wear gold jewellery. In fact, even a silver ring is not good.'

'If you are sick, are you allowed to take your medicine with a drop of brandy?'

'Never! A Muslim must never touch liquor! Never drink brandy. Anything that can throw a person off balance is a sin for Muslims.'

'Should one go to Mecca?'

'If you can, you should go. But you must never take out a loan for the trip. And you must be clean, and have no wrong thoughts. If you go, you will be as if reborn, pure as an infant. All your sins will be washed away. Your children, even your unborn children, will benefit from your trip to Mecca. And you will have peace.'

'If I find a dead man, what should I do with him?'

'Unless there is a clear sign that he is a Christian, a cross around his neck or some such thing, you must wash him in keeping with Muslim custom, bury him according to Islamic traditions, and read the prayer for the dead over him so that all his sins will be taken away.'

'I am forty years old and have paid no attention to prayer until now. Is it too late to start?'

'Pray as much as you can, and perhaps you will be saved. In the evening, the next morning, during the day, as many prayers as possible, all the time. Go to the mosque. Tell your relatives that you are living according to Islamic rules. The more prayers you read, the easier it will be. But you shouldn't boast about praying correctly, or long, or five times a day. That's taken for granted. You must do it for yourself, not for other people. You should revere only Allah, no others. These words apply to women as well, but you must never pray when you have your period, because you are impure then and shouldn't call upon Allah.'

Hadijat nods. She is a believing and practising Muslim. Five times a day she puts on her prayer dress, a long shapeless garment with a hood, rolls out her prayer mat and sits down to pray.

'I am nursing my child, and my neighbour has lost her milk. Can I nurse her child too?'

'If your husband gives you permission, it's all right. And after you've nursed someone else's child five times, they will be like brothers – milk brothers, it's called.'

When the programme is over, nature scenes and religious music replace Uncle Kadyrov. Then suddenly an image of a corpse fills the entire screen. The face is bloody, battered and beaten; the eyes are shut tight and there are deep red scars on one cheek. A voice announces that the man was found on the outskirts of Grozny.

'If you know this man, report to the police.'

Then come the ads. First, for wedding dresses. Some have short sleeves, others are sleeveless, some are even strapless. We sit watching, a little dumbfounded. You expect Uncle Kadyrov to interrupt the ad and condemn it. But he's out of the picture. Out of the broadcast. 'Come in and see our catalogue! To buy or to hire,' says a seductive voice. 'You will find us in downtown Grozny, on Victory Prospect, number . . . We also offer jewellery and hairdressing services for the big day – when you want to look your most beautiful.'

We laugh at the absurd juxtaposition, but Hadijat quickly becomes serious.

'That was an interesting programme,' she says. 'There is much to learn. We need more knowledge. During the Soviet years we were all atheists and had to pray in secret, and now, now we have to evaluate so many different viewpoints.'

Scholars debate when Islam first came to Chechnya. Tribes living near the Sunzha River are said to have adopted Sunni Islam from the Ottomans in the sixteenth century. People up in the mountains held on to heathen practices longer; they prayed to their ancestors and believed the forests and fields, waterfalls and sky were inhabited by good and evil spirits that could help or punish them. They also had various gods of nature; the most important one was the hunting god Yalta.

A hundred and fifty years after people on the plains accepted Islam, the mountain tribes did too. Many religious tenets were adjusted to fit with older ideas. For example, according to Muslim tradition the world is surrounded by mountains, but Chechens placed the mountains in the middle of the world.

Sufism, a mystical movement within Islam, gained a firm foothold in Chechnya after it was introduced in the North Caucasus in the nineteenth century. It aspires to create unity with God. Among its practices is *zikr* – a circle prayer that is still alive in Chechnya. Sufism also blended *adat* – traditional rules of living – into religion, and today many Chechens are uncertain what is *adat* and what is Islam.

The brotherhood network was almost impossible for the Russians to penetrate. In the eighteenth and nineteenth centuries Islam played a central role in mobilising the population against the Tsar's soldiers and for *gazawat* – holy war.

Most Chechens refused to have anything to do with the Russian administration, and turned to Sufi sheikhs instead. To this day, disputes and quarrels are often settled with the help of the Sufi brotherhoods or their secular counterpart, the Council of Elders, rather than through the court system.

Blood feud is widespread. A murder must be avenged, and it can be avenged through several generations. Until that is done, the guilty person cannot show himself in public and cannot cut his beard. On the other hand, the avengers can never enter his house; the home is sacred. If he goes out covered with a woman's headscarf, a great shame, no one can kill him. If a father is killed, the son must avenge him; if he has only daughters, then his brother must do it; if he has no brothers, his male cousin must do it. If the murderer hides and cannot be found, his next of kin can be killed.

One way to be reconciled is to accept blood money as determined by the Council of Elders. A date is set when men from the murdered person's family sit across from the killer and reach agreement about the amount of compensation. Afterwards the murderer must shake everyone's hand and embrace each person, from the eldest to the youngest. His head is covered with a hood and he sees only the other men's feet. Then the murderer can leave; he is a free man.

During the Soviet years blood feud was illegal, but it continued in secret. It has increased dramatically since the wars of the nineties.

After the 1917 revolution, religion was suppressed throughout the Soviet Union. Together with Orthodox churches elsewhere in Russia, mosques in the Caucasus were burned or turned into barns and stables for collective farms. Many religious leaders were killed or sent into forced labour in the Gulag. But the Chechens continued to pray in secret, and the elders gathered and read the Koran.

Gazawat played only a small part in the Chechen separatist movement of the nineties. Ethnic nationalism was at the heart of that struggle. Only when the Russian invasion was imminent did President Jokhar Dudayev begin to use Islam as a unifying concept for the Chechens; like the nineteenth-century hero Imam Shamil, he urged holy war.

The war deeply radicalised Chechen youth. The brutal conduct of Russian forces created a favourable climate for receiving ideas and money from Muslim movements that saw Chechnya as a pawn in a worldwide jihad. Some rebel leaders added radical Islamic elements to their rhetoric and accepted offers of help from fundamentalist networks in the Middle East and Asia. This explains why many people adopted wahhabism – an Islamic belief quite different from the traditional Chechen form of Sufism. It was easy to attract many young men in an area where religious fanaticism had spread very little until the wars of the nineties.

In the family room the news broadcast has shifted to a weather report that shows winter is loosening its grip. Adam comes downstairs, stands on the bottom step and says with a severe and knowing look: '*Ya v eto ne veryu.*' I don't believe it.

Hadijat and the other women lying wearily on the sofas can't help but laugh when Adam wags his finger at the weather map.

The boy who hung a soldier's skeleton on the Christmas tree and wanted to educate dogs by example has become a man of twenty-two. He doesn't believe the weather report, but he has acquired a strong belief in Allah and is responsible for the younger boys' religious training.

The first thing children learn when they come to the children's home is to pray. Mullah Kadyrov's doctrines are observed. Five times a day the boys gather for communal prayer. Adam leads the prayer. The boys follow his movements.

After his godless existence on the streets, Timur – Little Wolf – has also learned to pray. One evening he comes upstairs to show me his religion book from school. In Chechnya they have the same curriculum as the rest of Russia. He opens to a page where he has scribbled over something in ballpoint pen.

'Look, here on page ninety-two. Whoever put that picture in the book should be punished. It's a great sin to make a picture of Mohammed. I've crossed him out,' he says indignantly.

'Only what's written in the Koran is true. Teachers lie. Now everything is "Russian". The teachers think they're Russian. Instead we should have some real Chechens to teach us, people who believe in Allah. If you believe in Allah, even if you're thirty years old and have never gone to school, Allah will always help. It was only when I started to pray that I realised I shouldn't smoke any more.'

Most of what Timur knows about Allah he has learned from Adam. It's Adam's thoughts and sentences that flow from the boy's mouth.

'These fish pray to Allah too,' says Timur thoughtfully, and points at the fish swimming around in a bowl in Hadijat's room. 'They pray in their own way. In their own language. They also have hearts. I used to kill living creatures. Cats, dogs, mice, spiders, butterflies. Whatever fell into my hands. I didn't think, I didn't want to think. I hit little children. Allah condemned me and made me start smoking to ruin myself. But I've stopped that. Allah has made me do the right thing. Before, when I begged for food I sat on the street and made myself as small as possible and asked for alms. "*Bismillah . . .*" I said, but I didn't know the prayer properly, I just mumbled something without thinking,' he says, and gives me a serious look.

'Allah is in everything,' he continues. 'When you cut an apple in half, Allah is written in it; Allah is written in sheep's wool. Haven't you noticed? Allah is written in the sky. In the clouds. Allah. Do you remember the tsunami? The water wrote Allah then. He sent the waves as a punishment. The war here was also a punishment from God, because we lost Him, we let Him go. I thank God for everything that's happened to me. Stalin was fine too. He kept gypsies out of the cities. Now they're everywhere, and steal like magpies. They're the ones who taught Chechens to steal, did you know that?'

Timur sits quietly. For once he sits quietly. His eyes are fixed on the flames in the stove.

'When I came here, my first thought was that I'd blow up the house. I tried to work out how to do that. Perhaps with gas, I thought. So I found out where the gas tank was. If I lit it . . . I hit everyone, kicked, shouted and screamed. But Mama never got angry, she just hugged me, held me close. So I got the bad things out of my head. Just think, Mama could put up with me,' says Timur.

'Just think, she can put up with it. With *me*.'

Adam's childhood had much in common with that of Little Wolf, ten years younger. They have similar character traits: both are rebellious, restless, violent. Adam's first memory is one of fear. Fear of his father. He remembers how his father threw him against the wall or down the basement stairs and locked the door. There he stayed, until his mother came and rescued him. 'My best childhood memory is the day I ran away from home,' he says. 'And I remember that we got the Lenin badge at school. It said:

"Learn, learn, learn". I had a red scarf, was a Pioneer. But I wouldn't do what they told me. I wouldn't sit at a desk and get my fingers rapped with a stick. So I refused to go to school any more, and Mama said: "Do you want to be a ditch digger? Have a dirty job? Collect rubbish?"'

After the intense bombing of Grozny, Adam never saw his parents again. He lived in basements and shacks. Scarcely ten years old, he found a new 'family' and became a messenger boy for the rebels, first in Grozny's high-rise buildings, later in the mountains.

When Adam talks about *war* – the *war* that was, *wars* that have been, *wars* that will come – his eyes light up. Sometimes he inserts a few sentences about Islam. About how a person should live, but mostly about how others should live.

'I want to go to Pakistan. Read the Koran. They don't understand it here. I want to learn Arabic,' he says one day.

'I want to fight, I want to be a martyr,' he says the next.

'I want to be an artist. Paint, draw, or be a sculptor, a wood carver,' he says on the third.

'In Hollywood they're not pure, they're very sinful,' he tells me on the fourth.

On the fifth day he says he likes Hitler. 'Because he fought against the Russians and because he killed the Jews. No one talks about Stalin's death camps any more,' says Adam. 'People just talk about Hitler. That's not fair.'

On the sixth day he says: 'I hate girls who smoke. And drink. You should have seen the two girls I saw today. If I were their brother, I would have killed them. I would have dug a grave for them and sent jackals down into it.'

On the seventh day he goes into further detail. 'Women need to make themselves respected. They need to let us respect them. Not tight clothes. Not short.'

The next week, *war* is the subject again.

'Just wait, an unexpected attack will come around New Year. They will come down from the mountains. New Year's Eve maybe. I'd like to build an atom bomb; if we had one, the world would be afraid of us. Then we would be respected. I could go and fight any time if I was asked.

'War,' he says, and pauses for a second. 'We'll always have war. The first war started when the sons of Adam and Eve started fighting. The Pope said Mohammed started the war! I hate that pope. On Judgement Day, sinners will get their punishment; they will have a very hard time. I don't like Catholics because the Italians killed Joan of Arc. I like her. Genghis Khan never came to Chechnya. While Russia trembled in fear for three hundred and fifty years! Ha! I'm not afraid; it's the dog on a leash that's afraid. But even Shamil Basayev was afraid. He had to go through a mine-field; there's a video of it with people exploding, they're shot to bits, they fall, they walk on mines. Basayev shouts: "I'm losing blood, ai, ai, ai!" Like an old *baba* he shouts. But if I had to be operated on without an anaesthetic, I wouldn't cry.'

Adam and I often sit up talking after the others have gone to bed. The young man has gleaming, wavy hair and a square face with pronounced features. His hero is Che Guevara, and when he poses like Che there is some resemblance. He likes to talk big, and lives in a world of tangled tales. In Chechnya the mania for mythologising has free rein. One theory or story is just as believable as the next. The most important thing for Adam is that a story fits with his own belief system.

'People say that Che was a communist, but I know differently; I know he couldn't stand communists. He wouldn't have rescued and helped people if he was a communist or a thief or anything like that. He healed people everywhere. He loved his people with all his heart.'

To Adam, communist and thief are synonymous.

'If Che had survived he might not have been so famous. What do you think? I want to die young, too. I don't want to get to be thirty. I don't want to get old.'

In the evenings the boys from Malik's and Hadijat's 'first group' often come to visit. Abdul – the taciturn, freckled boy from those early days – has found work on a building site. He's worried because he doesn't have a contract and is afraid they won't pay him. But he doesn't dare protest, because then he will just lose his job to one of the men waiting in line outside the building site. During his first week on the job two workers fell to their deaths from the unsecured scaffolding. After years when not even a single nail was hammered in, now everything has to be built at tremendous speed; it has to be ready for Ramzan Kadyrov's inauguration in April 2007. So Abdul continues to go to his uncertain work each day. He has no choice, now that he's living on his own with his wife and will soon be a father.

Abdul met his wife in a mountain village six months ago. He was on a pilgrimage to Avturi, where the daughter of the prophet Heda is said to be buried. The pilgrims travelled on foot from Grozny, and when they asked for shelter with a family in the village they were invited to stay overnight. Abdul was captivated by Diana, the daughter of the house, the moment he saw her. She was sixteen and served him *galushki*, a national dish rather like gnocchi, with a sauce of garlic and lamb. The girl went along on the rest of the pilgrimage, and they walked back together. Four days later Abdul sent a representative to ask for her hand.

'We got married here in the backyard,' Abdul tells me. We are sitting in the kitchen with our evening tea.

'She is the most beautiful woman I know.'

'Women should cover their bodies,' Adam says suddenly. 'Wear the hijab. Then we wouldn't have all these rapes. Rapists should be publicly shot. Women must at least wear a headscarf. You talk differently to women without a scarf. If we had Sharia laws here, women wouldn't have to work outside the home,' adds Adam, who has neither a wife nor a girlfriend.

'It's a pure and beautiful relationship,' Abdul protests. 'She's an honourable woman.'

'What do you want in a wife?' I ask Abdul.

'I want her to put up with everything. To never let me go. And I want to never let her go.'

Abdul is silent for a moment, and then concludes:

'You know, I just want us to have an ordinary life, like ordinary people.'

He sits there quietly, staring into the air.

'Women,' Adam interjects, 'shouldn't walk around alone. They ought to be with someone. At least they shouldn't walk around in the markets – much less sell goods there.'

Adam's 'brother' from the children's home, Aslan, has also got married, but he complains that his sixteen-year-old wife is ill-tempered and lazy. So he often has supper or stays overnight at the children's home. He wonders whether he should get a divorce.

'If a woman doesn't listen to her husband, he can send her back to her parents,' Adam asserts.

Zaur is the fourth of the older wartime boys. He is married to Luiza and has a two-year-old daughter, but is unemployed and depressed; mostly he sits at home in his Grozny flat and reads about war on the Internet.

What Hadijat fears most is that her 'sons' will be drafted into the army.

'They won't survive a single day,' she often laments over evening tea.

The only way to avoid the army is to have two children under five, so she urges Zaur to have another baby very soon. Or she considers buying papers that will attest he is in poor health; but that is expensive.

Not long ago a woman came to the children's home with a list. She said she came to see if any young men lived there. 'No,' Hadijat had replied, 'there are only little children living here.' The woman left then, but Hadijat is afraid she will return.

'I'll go up into the mountains instead,' says Zaur. 'That's better than going into the army.'

'In any event, there will be war again,' Adam says. 'If the Russians withdraw, there will be war between the wahhabis and the murids.'

Murids are Muslims who follow Chechnya's earliest Islamic practices – Sufism blended with local traditions. Wahhabism is the form of Islam that Saudi Arabia and others follow; the Arabs took it to Chechnya during the wars of the nineties.

'People should live according to the Koran,' says Zaur. 'Mohammed never said you should dance and hop around the way the murids do. The *zikr* way of praying is a sin according to pure Islam.'

'But it's based on your own traditions,' I protest. 'Why has that suddenly become wrong?'

'Tradition? Yes, but in this case a very bad tradition. A heathen tradition,' Zaur sniffs.

'I want to cleanse Chechnya,' says Adam. 'This is no life here.'

After a while Abdul, Aslan and Zaur tire of the conversation and go to bed. Adam continues talking.

'What do you think of Robert De Niro? Have you seen *Once Upon a Time in America*? There Al Capone says: "Death or your wallet!" When did he live, by the way, Al Capone? Was it after the Red Revolution?'

Adam feeds himself on bits of history, fragments he's heard, rumours and legends. He's never been outside Chechnya, has barely gone to school, and has swapped the laws of the street for strict religious education.

'Las Vegas. I hate that place. Casinos. Gambling. It's all sin,' he says. 'There's gambling here, too. Slot machines. They should be blown up. Shut down. Did you know that ten people in Grozny hanged themselves because of gambling debts? All casinos should be wiped off the face of the earth. People play the whole day, computer games, too; it costs twenty roubles an hour. People sit there from the time they leave home until the place closes. They neglect home and family. That's a sin.

'Here in Grozny you see the Pepsi generation now. Young people who want to be part of Russia. Russian youth want to be like Americans, and Chechen youth want to be like Russians. They sit together on benches and chew sunflower seeds and drink

Pepsi. They should stand up for older folks, but they don't. And on TV, half-naked women sing about love. That's a sin. And rap and hip-hop are even worse. I don't like it. You shouldn't sing like that: "I wait for you, I'm longing for you." Rock should be forbidden. If you had a daughter would you let her listen to Madonna?'

'Yes . . .'

Adam is silent; he prefers it when we agree. Then he continues:

'Why don't the Orthodox patriarchs like Madonna? They want to forbid her to sing in Moscow. That's strange, because I don't like her either. But I also don't like the Christian church leaders. By the way, I'd really like to have Madonna's songs translated. It would be interesting. What does she really sing about?'

Adam thinks for a moment.

'If she took out everything that was sinful and wrong in her songs, and if she dressed properly, then she should be allowed to come and sing in Grozny. The same with Britney Spears and Christina Aguilera. Things were much simpler in the seventies. Bryan Adams dressed like a normal person. The Scorpions, too. And Michael Jackson. Allah gave him the power to make a black man white. White Americans hate blacks, don't they? And Michael Jackson was able to become white, so they loved him.

'Well, I couldn't have stood a single night in America. There people walk around like robots. There's no sun, no nature. They go around eating on the street. You should always eat sitting down. Do you believe in God? Just think of the unbelievers. It will be terrible for them on Judgement Day. After death the true believers will have eternal life in Paradise. They will have pineapples, bananas, and gardens there; well, actually I can't imagine it. Gooseberries and blackcurrants, too, I'm sure. And there in Paradise you don't think about a woman's figure, but . . . You can find a hundred million proofs that Paradise exists. And then there are people who believe the world was created through some sort of ridiculous explosion. If so, the Most Holy One would not be here, and we wouldn't have either sunset or sunrise. Just think if all believers could gather in one spot! Then something would certainly happen, and the world would be better.

'I'd like to build a mosque. I had a terrible dream last night. The earth was burning. It was boiling hot. A mosque rose out of the earth. It seemed like Judgement Day was imminent. Do you believe that? You have to teach children to believe in God from the time they are small. The communists blew up mosques. The Russians drank vodka inside the mosques. Budanov chose the most beautiful girls to rape. And then he said it was snipers he'd caught. I would have shot him. Allah knows I would have shot him.

'In Paradise I'll bathe in misk. Or was it musk? You know, that perfume. Or was it milk? In Paradise you get everything you desire. Then I'll eat as many apples as I want. Here in Chechnya we need to have Sharia, like in the old days when they cut off hands.

'The Chechens have been put through the mincer. Beria wanted to lay a railway down to the Caspian Sea and send trains filled with Chechens straight into the sea. But Stalin didn't want that; he knew a few Chechens.

'I really wish I could watch the sunset from a mountain forest, but there are mines up the entire mountainside. I'd like to go and fight for NATO, to get their training. Learn to use weapons. Learn to fight, so I can fight the Russians. Bush dreams of taking the Caucasus; everyone dreams of taking the Caucasus. Because we've got oil. When we returned the Russian prisoners of war, they were killed by their countrymen. They were burned alive. Put in buses with locked doors and set on fire. Allah knows it's true. Did you know that Tolstoy became a Muslim on his deathbed? I have a book about many well-known people who have converted to Islam.'

Adam rushes out and comes back with the book. I ask if he can find the part about Tolstoy.

'I don't have time now,' says Adam. He jumps up quickly and leaves.

I pick up the book as Hadijat enters. When I look out of the window I see Adam sitting on the steps with his head in his hands; then he gets up and tussles playfully with one of the smaller boys. He doesn't seem to be in any hurry. I tell Hadijat about the incident and ask if I said something wrong.

'Oh, my dear,' she laughs. 'Did you ask Adam to read?'

Hadijat chuckles.

'That's something we've never been able to teach him.'

10

Sleep in a Cold Room –
Wake Up in a Cold Room

Lavrentiy Beria was Josef Stalin's most feared henchman. After a bloody career in the Caucasus, in 1938 he was promoted to become chief executioner in Moscow. His orders resulted in millions dying or rotting away in the growing network of Soviet prison camps where people were 'crushed to clay dust'. In February 1944 he presented a new proposal to Stalin: the deportation of the entire Chechen population.

His justification for such an action was that instances of treason had allegedly been found among the mountain people, and it was suspected they might fight on the Germans' side in the war.

On 20 February 1944 Beria came to Grozny. By then, more than a hundred thousand soldiers from the NKVD, the forerunner of the KGB, were already in place. The action began three days later under Beria's personal supervision.

The deportation is the greatest trauma the Chechen people have suffered. Almost a third of the population died on the way to Kazakhstan and Kyrgyzstan during the first months in exile. Not until 1957, with the easing of restrictions under Nikita Khrushchev, were the Chechens allowed to return home. The deportation was a taboo subject during the Soviet era; nothing appeared in the history books, it was not discussed. Even today many Russians hardly know about it.

In Chechen families the stories lived on as yet another example of the empire's oppression. But not until after the collapse of the Soviet Union could Chechens mark the day of sorrow – 23 February.

One dark December day I sat with Malika in the kitchen drinking an early morning cup of tea with lemon. She began to tell me about her father and her concern for him. He was exactly the same age as my own father, born in the summer of 1936, but he'd had a life whose beginning was marked by Stalin, its end by Putin.

'Today he's a broken man,' says Malika. 'He cries a lot. Mama was killed by a rocket some years ago; later one of my brothers disappeared, then the other. He says that his heart skips a beat every time he hears a car stop outside. He never locks the door, in case my brother should return. About thirty masked men came to get him. Papa is still searching.'

Malika sighs. 'And his childhood – like all Chechens of his age, it was filled with loss: fatherland, family, language, so many people he loved. If you wish, we can take the bus after the children have had dinner and go to visit him.'

Abdullah meets us on the doorstep of his house in Belgotoi, a village outside Grozny. He is thin and feeble, and more than a head shorter than me.

The entry leads directly into the kitchen, where a huge pile of walnuts covers half the floor. Abdullah has picked the nuts in the nearby woods. They have to last him the whole winter. In the kitchen, a fire is crackling in the cast-iron stove and logs are drying along the wall ready to be thrown into the flames. The house has two rooms. In the other room are a sofa, a bed covered with a patterned blanket, and a small wood-burning stove.

Malika's father offers me a chair at the kitchen table. He sits down on a stool with his back to the stove and looks out of the window.

'I was born right here,' he says. 'Well, perhaps twenty metres from here; when I was a child our house stood a little further away. It no longer exists. But I've lived in this house since I came home from deportation and military service in 1960. My roots are here.'

The frail man recalls the winter when he was seven and a half and in class one.

'Russian soldiers had moved into our village early that winter. But we couldn't talk to them; hardly anyone here spoke Russian at that time. The soldiers dug trenches. We were told that they were going to protect us from the Germans. There were trenches all along this street.'

Abdullah draws the pale lace curtains aside. 'These houses weren't here then; ours was the only one.'

His eyes scan the road outside.

'One night we heard gunshots. Then soldiers burst in with their rifles pointed at us. They were the same soldiers who had lived among us for several months. "*Davai, davai!*" they shouted. Come! Come! They gave us a few minutes to get dressed and pack. There were soldiers in every backyard; it was impossible to escape. Those who tried to were shot.'

Abdullah's voice trembles. 'They came while it was still dark, about four or five in the morning. We'd had dry, mild February weather for a long time. But that night a quarter of a metre of snow had fallen. A soldier told Mama to pack a little food. She found five chickens and some maize meal. Then he told her to bring our valuables. When she went and got her jewellery and some money she had hidden in the outbuilding, he took it all away from her. Our neighbours weren't able to take anything along. They walked through the snow in slippers. The soldiers hadn't even given them time to get dressed properly.

'We didn't understand a thing. Only when we reached the next village was the order from the Soviet authorities read to us: deportation. We were counted, crowded into Studebakers, and driven towards Grozny. I remember the huge trucks; they were borrowed from the American government, delivered to Stalin via Iran to be used in the war against the Germans.'

Malika comes in carrying a tray with tea and a jam roll cut into thick slices. She sets the thin porcelain cups in front of us with a smile and leaves. Her father continues his story where he left off.

'We were packed together in coal wagons. It was cold. We had no idea where we were going. Some said that we would be driven straight into the sea. That we were going to be drowned. Others spoke of hard labour or prison camp. We sat there in the dark and felt the train begin to move. Papa had managed to hide a knife, and with it he cut a small hole in the wall. Everything outside was white. Raw winter everywhere. Once in a while there were small houses, but they became increasingly rare as we travelled further and further east across the steppe. Our family created a space in one corner; we used the maize sacks as a mattress and lay on top of them. There was a stove in the truck on which the women made maize cakes fried in mutton fat. But because we didn't have any water, we often ate only dry maize meal. We spat on it and swallowed. Spat and swallowed.

'From the very first day, people began to die. They were thrown out by the soldiers along the way. Right out into the snow. People tried to hide the corpses in order to bury them when the train stopped. The men then rushed outside and had to scratch graves in the snow and ice with their hands. If they had time, they said a brief prayer.

'Whenever the train stopped, people went looking for others; many had been separated on the way. As time passed, people heard more and more frequently that this person had died, that person had died,' says Abdullah softly.

Mass deportations of entire nations were an escalation of Stalin's terror, which until the Second World War had been used against 'enemies of the people' based on class or political affiliation. Beginning in 1943 'enemies of the people' were also identified by ethnic origin. First to be deported to Siberia and Central Asia were a million Volga Germans who were accused of collaborating with the Nazis. Next were the Karachai, a nomadic people living at the foot of Elbrus, the highest mountain in the Caucasus. Then the Kalmyks, a Buddhist people living near the Caspian Sea, were sent east. And in February 1944 it was the turn of the Chechens and Ingush; it was the most comprehensive action since the deportation of the Volga Germans.

One week after the cleansing operation began, Stalin received a telegram from his trusty executioner: '478,479 people, namely 91,250 Ingush and 387,229 Chechens, have been deported and loaded on to trains. 180 trains are fully loaded, of which 159 have been sent to new areas. Today trains were sent with the government forces and religious authorities in Chechen–Ingushetia we utilised to carry out the operation.' Russians, Avars and Ossetians moved into the empty houses.

After the Chechens were deported, Beria sent another telegram to Stalin in which he described the Balkar people of the Caucasus as bandits and accused them of attacking the Red Army. 'If you agree, before I return to Moscow I can take the necessary steps to give the Balkars a new place to live. I ask for your orders.' He got them. Later, the Tatars of the Crimea got their turn, too. According to the NKVD, a quarter of those deported died on the way and during the first months in exile.

'I remember two children who had wandered away from the others a little. The doors closed when they were just a few steps from the train and it began to move. They ran alongside the wagons. People shouted, but the train didn't stop. The children were younger than me, maybe five years old. In the middle of a frozen wilderness. Miles away from anyone. Snow-covered taiga as far as the eye could see. I wonder how long they survived. If they froze to death, or if they were eaten by wolves. Think of their mother and father trapped in the train while the children were left alone on the barren steppe. The children's faces, their faces as they run. Those images are etched for ever, here.'

Abdullah points to his forehead. The tea in front of him has grown cold. Neither of us has touched the jam roll Malika set out.

'It was almost April. After travelling for three weeks, the train was still moving. Even more people died – from hunger, from the cold, from sickness that spread in the tightly packed wagons. At the point of departure the NKVD commanders had proudly reported to Moscow that they needed fewer wagons than anticipated because so many were children.

'After a long time we saw roads,' Abdullah recalls. 'Then buildings. And finally the train stopped. It was quite warm. We hadn't been driven into the sea. We were in Kazakhstan. We all got out with what was left in our bags, and our names were called out by family. Then we were lined up for the bath house. It wasn't just hot, it was red hot. We got our hair cut and were deloused. We'd been on the train for forty days. That evening we were given a corner in the basement of the local collective farm in Shile. Oh, how hungry we were! We got a cup of soup. That was all. Papa got work as a tractor driver. We were all poor, cold and hungry, but people helped each other. Not like now. Now nobody looks after other people.'

Abdullah stares into space. 'But that's another story,' he sighs.

'During that spring, all my brothers and sisters died. Mizan and Maruz and Belkiz. One after another. Typhus.'

The old man has turned his stool away from the table and is facing the stove. He looks down at the floor.

'The last thing my little brother whispered, so softly you could barely hear him, was: "I'm dying, I'm dying. Mama, don't let me die!"'

Malika's father weeps silently. He purses his lips before taking a breath.

'Then he died.'

He looks at me again, and continues:

'I got typhus too. I lay in a bed of straw on the floor. Mama fed me soup made from kernels of maize she had found. She sat and wept over me. I remember what she cried: "If only your mother could die instead of you!" One morning I got up. I was just skin and bone, Mama told me afterwards. I looked like a swamp rush. There was nothing to eat. Nothing. Mama made flour out of dry straw that she pounded, broke up and mixed with water. Then she made pancakes, or straw cakes. I remember that they were awfully good. I always got a terrible stomach ache from them, but it was better than going hungry. And then there was some sort of swamp rush called *tatish*; our stomachs swelled up like balloons and you could almost see through our skin. Sometimes Mama used the husks from rice; she pounded them and fried them. Then one day Papa became sick and died. In the autumn we once got watermelon. It is the best thing I've ever tasted.'

Abdullah stops.

'What sort of life? What sort of life did they let us live? Papa died. My sisters died. My little brother died. I didn't have any shoes. Had some rags tied around my feet. Was almost never allowed to go outside, because Mama was so afraid I could get sick and die. But once in a while Mama and I went to look for potatoes in the fields, after the potatoes had been harvested. There might be a few left, if we were lucky and got there before all the others who were searching for food. The potatoes were frozen and we fried them on the stove. They were so good. Once I fell on to the stove because I was so tired and weak. My clothes caught fire, my hair caught fire. We didn't have anything to put on the burns, but then I got a small piece of bread and forgot the pain. We children congregated at the rubbish dumps. Maybe we would find something. We ran. The dogs ran. If we found something, it went straight into our mouths. That was true both for us and for the dogs. We picked grains out of horse manure. Took them home, where Mama washed them and made soup. We dug up roots. Cooked them. Made cakes from them. They tasted good, but we got swollen stomachs from them, too; it hurt so much, as if our bellies were full of water and if they got punctured only bones would be left. We were sick all the time.

'There were already Kazakhs living where we had been sent, and they made soft white cheese. They set it in the cellars to ripen. We stole it. It was so good. The Kazakhs didn't scold us, they never chased us; they probably felt sorry for us.

'During our first years there I was always barefoot; my entire childhood in Kazakhstan I went barefoot. We children often sat down by the railway and waited in case something fell out of the wagons. When the train stopped, we crept under it. One day we found a lot of beetroots. First we ate as many as we could by the tracks; the rest we took home. Mama never asked where we found them.'

Abdullah rises laboriously from the stool and returns with some yellowed notebooks. They are diaries kept by his cousin, Bashlam, who was nine years old when he and his family were deported. Bashlam died several years ago, but Abdullah has saved the diaries the boy wrote about his life in Kazakhstan. During the first years it was impossible to get hold of paper and pencil; only several years later could he begin to write down his memories. The notebooks are not dated, but the handwriting and the tone indicate that these are the writings of a teenage boy. Bashlam ended up in a different part of Kazakhstan, but the suffering was the same.

Bashlam's family had lived higher in the mountains, above Shatoi, and the journey down to Grozny took several days.

> *Sleep in a cold room. Wake up in a cold room. In a strange house.*
> *We had not slept enough. We were hungry. We were dirty. Nothing*
> *to be had. We just sat up straight. We didn't know what people*
> *would do with us. What did they want?*

This is how the first notebook begins. The family had stayed overnight in an abandoned house on the way down from the mountains. The people who lived there had already been deported. At first the villagers had been ordered to walk, later they rode in horse-drawn carts.

> *In Shatoi we heard a terrible noise, some strange wagons came*
> *towards us. It was a miracle of God — wagons that moved without*
> *horses! They operated all by themselves. I fell in love for ever with*

these wagons. The soldiers opened the back door and ordered us inside. Whatever people had in their hands was taken from them and thrown away. We sat along the sides and two soldiers with rifles sat in the middle. The wagons went very fast, you would think the driver was born in the mountains. We rushed down towards the ravine by the Argun.

Abdullah passes his hands over the notebooks. Later I'll sit in the children's home and copy them, together with Luiza, Zaur's wife. The handwriting is often hard to decipher, so in the evenings after the children have gone to bed we light the stove and Luiza reads aloud from the notebooks:

All the men had to hand over their kinzhals. Our men always carry a kinzhal, it is a national dagger that is part of our clothing. It was a humiliating insult to take away their kinzhals. They felt undressed by the soldiers, like little boys. The soldiers stamped their boots on the daggers and swords. The men watched, clenching their teeth until their heads hurt, but they could do nothing. It's better to kill us than to destroy our weapons before our eyes, a neighbour said afterwards.

People were herded in small groups, like a sheep market. The air was filled with noise and clamour, soldiers, wagons, screams, shouts, howling dogs, crying children, chanting and prayers. The older men prayed to Allah for mercy for his Muslim people, the women sang old songs about their forefathers, about the graves we left behind, about the mountains and the fatherland. Commands were roared at us amid all this noise.

When they were packed into the trains Bashlam and his mother and the other younger children became separated from his father and oldest brother.

When the train stopped for a while people went to the other wagons and asked is this person here, or that person? People looked for each other, were reunited, or cried over a lost child. Some sat, some lay down. There were sick people, but we could not show that people were sick because then they would be thrown out.

Women and men crowded together. It was insulting. Men and women should not be squeezed together. I can't understand how the grown-ups stood it. How Mama stood it, how Papa stood it. They knew if they ate something, they would have to relieve themselves, and that wasn't possible. You had to sit down where you stood, where you lay. Some girls died from burst bladders because they held it in. When the trains stopped, you could go out, but anyone who went further than five metres away from the tracks was shot, and many women were too ashamed to sit side by side with the men. I wanted to eat and drink and pee, but had to wait and wait. After five days, we each got a cup of soup at a station. I remember there was an eye floating in my soup. The eye had a lot of fat and I ate it greedily.

There was a soldier by the door. He sat on a box holding a rifle between his legs and watched what was going on. One evening he cried; we must have been an awful sight. What was that soldier thinking about? Hard to guess. Maybe he remembered his sister or brother, or mother and father, who lived somewhere else. Who knows what went on in his head? We couldn't talk to him because he was the guard and because we didn't speak his language. We were enemies, he was a soldier in the Soviet army and we were enemies of the people. But we understood that he didn't choose to be there, that he was ordered there, that this was just as bad for him. The only difference between us and him was that he had a vintovka — a rifle. There was no air to breathe, either for him or for us. We sat in the dark, didn't see or hear anything. When they came with our rations they opened the door, then shut it again. A man who had fought in the war and could speak Russian asked them to keep the door open while the train was moving. But they wouldn't do that.

Mama and the other women managed to make some pancakes. Where they got water from I don't know. The pancakes were thin and small and not fried very much, because there wasn't much heat from the stove and Mama had to give her place up to other women so they could fry for their own children. Mama looked at the soldier who was sitting there feeling sorry for us, and she took a piece of a pancake and gave it to him. He smiled, put his vintovka in his left hand and stretched out his right hand to take the little piece. 'Spasibo, Mamashka,' he said, and put the pancake in his mouth and chewed it quietly.

One day there was no more wood left. The men ran along the tracks to find twigs before they had to rush back. They competed to see who ran the fastest. I watched from the wagon and hoped my brother Dilo would win. Once he only just managed to get back to the wagon before the door was slammed shut. A guard hit my brother, but he held on to the wood.

There was very little water. Every mouthful was more precious than gold. So the bigger boys had to run for water, they had to risk it, and, thanks to my brother perhaps, no one in our family got sick. We had no idea where Papa and my other brother were, but I was sure my father would not have gone for water. Break the law, survive — don't break it, perish. Papa chose the latter. At one stop we learned that he had died. He was put in another wagon and had been thrown out somewhere along the way.

Then suddenly the train stopped. Finally, we could leave the cursed goods wagon. We could drink as much as we wanted, stretch our legs, bury the dead. Kazakhs met us with sleds. They were different from us, small eyes, broad faces. They were not friendly, but they picked us up on the sleds and took us further on. Later we learned that they had been told we were cannibals. It was a different kind of people and a different landscape. We had mountains, they had plains.

We got a space under the ground to live in. It had no windows, a small door and a turf roof with a pipe in it to let out the smoke. We were always hungry, from the day we left home I never felt full, not once. Then winter came again. Nobody had winter clothes or shoes, we were almost naked, and we sat in the hut or guarded the road outside, because on that road our big brother, Dilo, would come. We watched the road wondering: is Dilo coming? We waited because he brought bread. We recognised him from a long way off by his walk, and we were always anxious to know what he was carrying. That was our main interest. In the winter we got dressed by turns, one child went out, then the next one. Everything my brother earned went towards bread. Conversation was always about food, about something to eat. We talked about what it was like to feel full, when would Dilo return from his job, what would he bring us? When would he come with bread? This went on all winter. The whole long, frozen winter. There is nothing to compare with it. It was beastly cold, it was a hell.

Then came the hunger sickness. We started to swell up, people collapsed before our eyes. My sisters and brothers lay beside me, swollen up, all of them. The sick ones helped the sickest, we boiled water and added salt and lived with the hope that this would eventually end. Mama said that sooner or later we would go home, anything else was impossible. That people couldn't live without a country. Like a bird without wings. Because we believed this, we survived. A person needs to dream of a bright future.

We waited for spring. The spring of 1945, I've never waited like that for spring. The weather grew mild enough for us to go out in the sun and we crept out of our holes. Almost all the old people from our village were dead, no one over fifty-five was left.

One day I went with Mama to visit Aunt Alpata after our uncle died. Mama was not well, but she still walked ten kilometres, from the collective farm to where our aunt lived. We found our relatives in a cellar; they lived underground, in a hole covered with a turf roof. When we went down the steps it smelled rotten, and I felt as if we were going into a grave, a grave filled with corpses. Alpata lay on her back on the ground and looked at us with empty eyes. She asked Mama to see if her two sons were alive. They were lying a little further away. They were alive, but they were sick. They lay next to each other waiting to die. Alpata's brother-in-law was also lying there. He greeted us and said: 'To die isn't bad, but to rot alive is.' Alpata asked us to shift her on to her side. Her whole back was swarming with maggots. That's where the rotten smell came

*from. They were eating Aunt Alpata's body. It was terrible to look
at the maggots crawling around on her. Mama washed everyone, or
as many as her strength allowed. The awful smell and the memory
of the maggots stayed with me a long time. A little later Aunt
Alpata and her sons died.*

After the first year of hunger, circumstances improved, although
the forties were hard years in Kazakhstan, like everywhere else in
the Soviet Union. Bashlam and Abdullah grew up in different
parts of the region, and both learned Russian. Bashlam began
technical high school in Kazakhstan and became an engineer;
Abdullah was drafted into the army after Stalin's death in 1953.

'I was proud and happy to be accepted as a Soviet citizen. But
I was only allowed to be in the building brigade. I wasn't allowed
to carry a weapon. We were still humiliated as a people, degraded
and insulted,' he sighs bitterly.

After the Twentieth Party Congress in 1956 when Nikita
Khrushchev denounced Stalinism and the cult of personality
under Stalin, millions of people were released from the gulags
or rehabilitated posthumously. The Chechens were rehabilitated,
too. They were no longer regarded as an enemy of the people,
and a year later they received official permission to return to their
homeland.

There was little basis for the charge that they had collaborated
with the Germans. On the contrary, several thousand Chechens
fought in the Soviet army.

One of them was Varkhan Musayev. He was sixteen when Hitler
attacked the Soviet Union on 22 June 1941. A year later he was
sent to the front.

On his liver-spotted forehead he has a deep hollow covered
with yellowish skin, the result of a piece of shrapnel that cut
through his helmet during the battle for Berlin in late April 1945.
He limps because of a bullet that tore his leg muscles. During the
war he was wounded five times.

I had noticed Varkhan during the parade in Grozny on 9 May. The victory over fascism is celebrated on that day all across Russia. From Moscow, where Putin watches soldiers and tanks parade through Red Square, to the smallest village that celebrates its war veterans.

Walking stiffly but upright, supported under each arm by his daughter-in-law and grandson, Varkhan had made his way to the reception where every Chechen veteran, a hundred and five in all, would receive a car from Ramzan Kadyrov. Varkhan got the keys and immediately gave them to his daughter-in-law. 'I want you to use it,' he said.

We talked briefly then, and a few days later they invited me to their home. Now we were sitting under a vine arbour in his garden in the village of Achkhoi Martan.

I notice that Varkhan squints, but at first I don't realise he is almost blind; in fact, not until he says so himself. I'd seen the way that he felt for the teacup on the table, but his movements were so elegant, so easy and gentle, that I didn't think anything of it. Besides, he held my eyes as we talked. Although he saw me only as a shadow.

At the beginning of 1942 the Germans reached the Terek River. They had taken Vladikavkaz in the neighbouring republic of North Ossetia, and barely advanced into parts of Chechnya. But they were pushed back before they reached Grozny, which had been their main objective because of its rich oil resources.

'I enlisted voluntarily,' he tells me. 'That is to say, I signed a statement that I enlisted voluntarily. Who goes to a war voluntarily? However, it was better to go before they came and got you.'

Varkhan speaks calmly and clearly in a strong self-confident voice, like a man who is used to having people listen to him.

'There wasn't a single German here in Chechnya, yet we were called enemies of the people,' he says. 'But I didn't know that we were public enemies, because when my people were deported, I was in Warsaw. We liberated the Suvalki camp outside the Polish capital. Several thousand Soviet prisoners had been kept there since early in the war. They could hardly stand on their feet. Anyone from the Caucasus? I shouted. Two skeletons came towards me. Two Chechens. They kissed my feet and wept. Prisoners died every night, they told me. Every night they dug new graves. Soon it would have been their turn. They planted cabbages, vegetables, where they had buried the dead, to give food to the living. Can you imagine?

'When we took Warsaw it opened the second Belorussian front; now there were ten Soviet fronts. I was in the cavalry at first, on horseback; then I was transferred to a tank brigade on the Belorussian front. Rokossovski was the commander there, I remember; a tall elegant fellow, his mother was Russian, his father Polish. After we took Warsaw, Stalin ordered Rokossovski to the third Belorussian front, while Marshal Zhukov was assigned to the first front. It was politics: only a Russian could take Berlin,' Varkhan says emphatically. 'But in the field, Chechens were clearly just as good as any devout communist. In war we were all equally valuable.'

Public enemies were good enough comrades for Stalin when he needed them. The dictator had to recall ten thousand purged officers from the prison camps because he desperately needed professional military men, and he got angry when he asked for officers by name and discovered that they had already been executed. One of the officers who had been brought back from a 'long and dangerous mission' was Konstantin Rokossovski. The meeting between Rokossovski and Stalin is described in Simon Sebag Montefiore's book, *Stalin: The Court of the Red Tsar*:

> Stalin asked one of them, Konstantin Rokossovski, perhaps because he had no fingernails: 'Were you tortured in prison?'
>
> 'Yes, Comrade Stalin.'
>
> 'There are far too many yes-men in this country,' sighed Stalin.

The outstanding abilities of generals like Rokossovski and Zhukov, plus the huge number of Soviet farm boys, were what enabled the Red Army to advance towards Berlin. One of those soldiers was Varkhan on his way through East Prussia.

'I didn't know anything. I was a child. But I could do as I was commanded. And I was a good horseman. We rode through the forest, the Germans fired at us; my horse was hit in the hoof and collapsed. I ran. The horse was left lying on the field.'

Varkhan lifts his hands to his head and drops his glass, which shatters on the flagstones.

'It's so hard to remember all this,' he whispers. 'I saw soldiers fall around me, totter and collapse. Bullets whizzed past us. In the Baltic States they fired at us from buildings. And we killed everyone we encountered, because in the Baltics many had gone over to the Germans. Later when we crossed the Donau I swam behind my horse holding its tail. Horses swim so well, you know. The Germans flew low over us. We lived on dry bread, in the trenches, many days with no food at all. We ate our horses — that's how bad it was; we ate grass, didn't give up, and pushed forward. I was wounded five times. Leg. Back. Head. We surrounded the Germans. Skirmishes. If you don't kill first, they'll kill you with bullets, knives, bayonets . . . We drove Harley-Davidsons into Berlin. Oh, how thin people were! The German women were so thin, so thin. And so afraid of us. But they were beautiful, those German women . . .'

He sits deep in thought.

'How did it feel to capture Berlin?' I ask, breaking the silence.

'When we reached the Reichstag, I just thought about saving my soul. Now Hitler is crushed, I thought; now I'll go home. I was only twenty years old when Berlin fell, wanted to come home alive. But we were sent further, liberated Prague. We took a break by the Elbe, relaxed on its banks. The river wasn't very wide, forty or fifty metres perhaps. American soldiers were camped on the other side. We swam on our side, they swam on theirs. Our commander, Movladi was his name, ordered his horse to be unsaddled. Then he mounted the horse wearing just his underpants, rode into the river, and swam to the other side. Bravo! shouted the Americans. Then the war was over.'

Varkhan has a faraway look. So much, such a long time ago.

'I was young, it was all like a dream, *raz*, *raz* – done with that, and then press onward.'

'And then what?'

'Give me a moment!'

Varkhan sits motionless for a while. Then he says softly again: 'It hurts so much to remember.'

People and houses burned. Civilians impaled. Deserters, former comrades, executed on the spot.

'War never brings anything good,' he sighs. 'The fascists had already put an end to the Jews. I knew nothing about what happened to the Chechens. In the army we were all equal. We went to die. Defended the fatherland. There were no enemies of the people there. I could read and write; many of the Russians were illiterate *kolkhozniki* – collective farmers – so many letters went through my hands.

'When the war was over and the soldiers were to go home, I was almost out of my mind with happiness. I hadn't received any letters or news about my family, and all I could think of was getting to see them again. The commander summoned me to his office.

'"I want to go to Grozny," I said.

'"That's not allowed," said the commander.

'"But my parents . . ."

'"No one is there."

I didn't understand anything.

'"I helped to take Berlin, to win the war. I've been wounded five times, I've received medals, and now I'm not allowed to go home on leave!" I said.

'"There's no home for you in Grozny. All your people have been deported to Central Asia," the man replied.'

Varkhan's fists clench. His lips quiver. Anger over the injustice has not diminished.

'The war was over; my people had been turned into enemies. I was no longer needed; I had done my duty. So I was sent by train to Kazakhstan. Father was dead. Many Chechens were dead. That was it. I wept. It was hard to think I was an enemy of the people. They didn't tell me that when I fought in Warsaw or before the war was over; they were probably afraid I would defect to the Germans. I, who had fought for, and believed in, Soviet power!'

A medal with a profile of Stalin lies on the table. The daughter-in-law has placed it there. *Nashe delo pravoie* – 'Our cause is just' – it says under the leader's face.

'What do you think of Stalin?'

'Stalin was in Moscow, I was in the war.'

The daughter-in-law also brought out a certificate that all Russia's veterans received in the mail for 9 May. It is a printed greeting with an ornate signature at the bottom. 'You surrounded the enemy's positions, saved humanity from the terrible threat of Nazism. The fate of the world was decided on the front lines of the great war for the fatherland. In memory of the heroic deeds you performed so bravely with weapon in hand, sacrificing yourself for our nation. From the depths of my soul I wish you good health, good fortune and happiness. Vladimir Putin, President of Russia.'

'What do you think of today's leaders?' I ask.

Varkhan reflects a bit before the afternoon's final words are wrenched from him.

'Everything is destroyed,' he says, gazing ahead defiantly. 'I will soon be dead. I didn't need this war, and I didn't need the previous one.'

11

Between Mecca and the Kremlin

The low February fog turns the air grey and cold. Shamil is hunched behind the steering wheel. His breath forms a frosty mist. Shamil is a handsome man, with pale skin, ruddy cheeks and a thick mane of hair. He's wearing a brown leather jacket and a white wool turtleneck. His fur cap almost touches the roof of the car.

His parents were burned alive in their beds six years ago, in January 2000. The previous day soldiers had checked the passports of everyone living on their street. Shamil wasn't home at the time. That evening his mother suddenly grew fearful and asked his sister to stay overnight with a Russian neighbour. While everyone was asleep, the soldiers returned, poured petrol over six houses and set them on fire. It was his sister who found their parents' charred bodies.

Shamil works for Memorial, a human rights organisation established in 1986 by victims of oppression during the Soviet era. It is one of the few organisations to have an office in Chechnya.

It's February 2006 and I've asked Shamil to travel around Chechnya with me. Among other things I wanted to meet families of people accused of terrorism. Suspected terrorists were sent as far away as possible, to Siberia, the Far East, north of the Arctic Circle – a macabre reminder of the deportation of prisoners to the gulags. I've a list of names and addresses from a Red Cross colleague; the organisation helps close relations cover the cost of visiting their sons so far away. We chose one of the addresses.

I'm shivering in the car; there's a draught from the door and my toes are frozen. We're going to a district that's been a key area in the resistance movement. To get on to the highway we have to drive through the centre of Grozny. Some of the buildings have huge bomb craters. The walls that are still standing are full of holes, from bullets, grenades, rockets. Clothes are hanging out to dry outside shattered windows. The openings are covered with plastic, sometimes with a scarf or some sacking. The holes in the walls are filled with sandbags or boards. Some flats still have roofs, and four, five, six people could be living in each room. People walk around Grozny with water buckets. They carry in clean water from wells and stand-pipes, and throw dirty water out of the windows.

Mine detectors search the roadsides. Resistance forces still sometimes come into Grozny and blow up military vehicles. Tanks thunder over the holes in the streets; the rattling cars try to drive round them. Swathes of ice curve like frozen serpents on the hills leading to the city centre and the car skids down over the bumps with soft thuds.

We come to *Prospekt Pobedy* – Victory Prospect. Two kilometres of good straight asphalt, and a row of what look like small Christmas trees. The ancient maples that once graced the street are gone. Only dead trunks remained after the battles.

The street was to be a New Year's gift to the people of Grozny, to welcome in 2006. It was Putin who told Ramzan Kadyrov that Grozny had to be rebuilt for the celebration.

'It will be done,' said Kadyrov.

The so-called 'Kadyrov Fund' was to be used to reconstruct the parade avenue. As far as the buildings were concerned, time was too short. But that problem was solved by covering them all with scaffolding and installing windows in the façades. If you look behind the scaffolding, you will see the perforated walls in which the new windows, still covered with red and white tape, are smiling; you will also see that the buildings have no roofs. They are mere stage sets, Kadyrov's stage flats. Just as Prince Potemkin built façades of beautiful village houses where Tsarina Catherine the Great was to pass, Kadyrov has built façades for Putin and his TV team. Just as expensive, just as useless.

However, some buildings are brand-new, such as the white and grey Finance Ministry, the pink Construction Department, and a government institution that has peach-coloured window frames. A rebuilt Orthodox church stands proudly with pale blue walls and a gleaming gold onion cupola. A red-brick mosque with a minaret rises above areas flattened by bombs.

It was ingenious of the authorities to say that Grozny would be rebuilt with the help of the Kadyrov Fund, because when people are given a parade avenue, even one with half-built houses, it's still a gift. And you have to say thank you for a gift. You can't complain about a gift either. You don't say that it should have been better; or that you don't want stage flats, but proper buildings, schools, day-care centres; or that you want the library, the cinema, the theatre, the concert hall, the health clinic or the bus shelter back. You say thank you, thank you.

On a building that's been bombed out but now lies under scaffolding, hangs a banner which reads, 'Our future lies in science and culture'. So the library and the physics laboratory can wait.

At the end of the parade avenue is a granite statue of three stalwart heroes of the revolution. In the middle, a powerful man with wavy hair and glasses, the Russian; on one side, an equally powerful but slightly shorter man in a sheepskin hat, the Ingush; on the other side, a handsome Chechen. The statue represents *bratstvo narodov* – Brotherhood of the People – and what was once called the Chechen–Ingush Soviet Republic. People usually call it simply *Tri Duraka* – the 'three idiots'.

On our way out of Grozny we drive past a sign: 'Come out of the shadows – it's time to pay taxes!' Shamil snorts.

'Let them first pay back what they've taken away, then I'll pay taxes.'

Where the presidential palace once stood, a towering statue of Akhmed Kadyrov stands bathed in light. Hundreds of glass globes on beautiful pillars embrace the square, like a sea of light in the winter darkness. Shamil snorts again.

The previous day I'd sat in the reception room at Memorial listening to people's stories.

A man came in and looked around the room. He was short, thin, red-haired, and intense in everything he did. Even when sitting down, his whole body was tense. He leaned forward, looking as if at any moment he might leap up, lash out and hit someone, either to protect himself or to put up a fight. At the same time, he seemed very tired, close to exhaustion. His name was Salman and he was twenty-eight years old. He was a primary school teacher in the outskirts of Grozny, where he taught basic safety training, a course designed for war zones. He taught the children first aid, bandaging, how to watch out for mines, what they should do in case of possible attacks, gas leaks, explosions.

One frosty morning the previous week several men in camouflage uniforms had come to get him and his twenty-year-old brother Saluddin, a carpenter, as they sat having an early breakfast. Their mother had run after the men, clutched their jackets and screamed: 'Let my sons go!' She had hung on to the car and was dragged several hundred metres along the icy street before she had to let go.

Hoods were placed over the brothers' heads and they were driven out of the city. After about an hour, Salman estimates, the car stopped and they were shoved out. Still hooded, they walked across a gravelled area with their kidnappers, a door was unlocked and they were told to lower their heads. The ground was uneven, and there was a strong, sharp odour. Then the hoods were removed. They found themselves in a dark hall and were taken to separate cubicles, like cattle stalls. The walls did not reach the ceiling; Salman thought the building might be some type of barn. He was taken to the interrogation room first. It was some kind of sports room, with a billiard table, wall bars, weights, metal bars.

'You teach children to lay mines,' said the interrogator, a big fellow with bulging muscles.

'No, I teach them to *watch out for* mines,' Salman replied.

'You teach them to become little traitors,' his accuser continued.

'No, I . . .'

The first blow. And the next. And the next, the next, the next, on his head, arms, legs, stomach, back, lower abdomen. Salman was handcuffed and pushed to the floor.

'Which wahhabists do you know?' shouted the interrogator. Several other men had arrived by now. They hit Salman and kicked him about. Then they brought out an instrument and gave him electric shocks. In his ears, his groin, his rectum. Towards evening he was thrown back into the stall.

The next morning it continued.

'You teach children to be terrorists! You recruit little children for your terrorist plots!'

The accuser demanded that he sign a confession. Salman refused.

Battered and bloody, he was thrown back into his cubicle. When the lock turned the next nightmare began: his brother's screams. Screams that came from the gut, Salman said in the austere Memorial office, as a worker wrote down everything he said.

'When you're hit and kicked like that, until you lose consciousness, you can't do anything but howl and writhe,' he explained. Through the wall he heard the accusation levelled at his brother: that he planned to blow up the new statue of Akhmed Kadyrov.

After four days of abuse Salman was taken from his stall and pushed into a car. He asked about his brother.

'Sent to the military base in Khankala,' came the reply. Salman was driven back to Grozny and dropped off at Minukta Circle. A week had passed since then. He hadn't seen his brother since they had been put into separate stalls. Each morning there had been dead bodies outside in the yard.

Salman could describe the interior of the place in detail, but he had no idea where it was located.

'All the prison guards were Chechen, there were no Russians there,' said Salman. 'They were coarse fellows and had beards like Ramzan Kadyrov; they all talked the same dialect, were clearly from the same clan. I'd recognise them if I saw them. And I remember their names: Jihad, Besrad, Magomed, Ramzan and Beshan.'

Salman straightened his fur cap on the table. He was still wearing his leather jacket. His hands shook as he spoke. He ran them nervously through his hair.

'The reason I take the risk of talking to you is that I have to find my little brother.'

Then he broke down. And hid his head in his rough hands.

'Blow up the statue?' snorts Shamil when we talk about the story from the previous day. The road is icy and Shamil drives fast. His eyes follow the road disappearing beneath us. Gradually there are fewer houses and more cattle, and then we drive into the village. Shamil stops the car at a tall green gate. It corresponds to the address we got at the Red Cross, the address picked at random from a list of families with sons in a Russian prison. We didn't get any telephone numbers, and don't know if the family is at home.

'Of course they're at home,' Shamil had said. 'Where else would they be?'

A woman in her sixties opens the gate slightly. I've been told to stay in the car. The woman surveys Shamil sceptically and stands back a little from the narrow opening. I can barely see her. She and Shamil speak briefly, one on each side of the gate, before he comes back to get me.

'Go in quickly,' he'd told me earlier. 'Don't say anything, don't look around.'

The woman gives me a brief nod. She is dressed in a worn-out skirt and a threadbare wool jacket. Like many older, poverty-stricken women in the villages of the Caucasus, she is missing several teeth. Childhood in Kazakhstan has left its mark. She asks us to follow her. The woman has a hunched back and wide hips, and walks with careful steps, as if every one is painful. She is wearing rubber galoshes. We follow a path towards a house. The yard is protected by a wall several metres high, as is common in Chechen villages.

The woman takes off her muddy galoshes and leaves them on the doorstep. I do the same with my boots. She sets out slippers and points towards a kitchen. The floorboards creak. Near the kitchen windows are a table covered with yellowed oilcloth and three chairs. The long net curtains at the windows have a woven floral pattern and a few holes. Next to the stove is a well worn sofa with a green blanket over it. The woman pours water into a kettle and asks us to sit down. When we have explained who we are, she brings out a photograph album.

In one picture the woman, whose name is Tamara, is sitting on a sofa with four boys, looking gravely into the camera. The photograph was taken ten years earlier.

'I'd just been widowed,' Tamara says.

The photograph is faded and its colours have taken on a brownish tone. The five on the sofa sit close together with their shoulders squeezed forwards or backwards to keep from pushing each other out. You can barely see the mother's head as she sits there among her sons' broad shoulders. The boys are strong and well built; the youngest one is about twelve, the oldest ten years older.

'Oh, what splendid sons,' whispers Tamara.

'Handsome,' I say. 'Very handsome.'

In another picture the boys pose around a football. They have open, happy faces, glistening with sweat. The mother flicks through the photographs; in some the sons stand together, in others they pose individually: in front of a newly built house, in a karate outfit, by a gate. We come back to the picture of them on the sofa, the only one where all five are together.

A few metres away from us is the empty sofa. I recognise its legs and the wall behind it.

'They went to the mosque, they trained in karate,' Tamara tells us. 'They helped me with everything, such wonderful sons. Now all of them are gone . . .'

She looks from me to Shamil and says something in Chechen. 'It's a long time since I spoke Russian with anyone,' she apologises hesitantly. 'There aren't any Russians here now.'

Educated in a Soviet school system, she knows Russian as well as anyone. Initially a little rusty, she begins to tell us her story.

'My oldest son, Ali, a big husky fellow, became emir in the village,' she tells us. An emir was a local leader in the resistance against the Russians.

'In 1996 they decided to take him. They came with several vehicles and ordered him out of the house. He refused. He knew that he wouldn't come back alive if they took him. People like him didn't survive; they would first torture him, then kill him. "Don't give up, don't give up!" I told him.

'That morning he and I were the only ones at home. The Russians started shooting when Ali refused to follow their orders. My son fired back. He barricaded himself by the stove. I helped him, ran for ammunition, covered him with furniture. He got hit. I held him in my arms when he died. "Allah," he cried. Then he was gone.'

Tears run down Tamara's face. 'My little, little boy,' she says. 'So proud. I was with him the whole time, what else could I do? Then they set the house on fire. I dragged him out on a blanket, and even though the flames licked us, I got him out unharmed; not a hair on his head was touched, not a whisker burned. His face shone, his forehead had an angelic light; he was sanctified. Allah had taken him and given him a true jihadist death,' she says, her eyes flashing.

The second son, Movsar, wanted to avenge his brother's death and joined the resistance. In 2000 he was taken prisoner in the village of Komsomolskoye when it was besieged by the Russians. No one has seen him since.

Russian soldiers often came to search Tamara's house. Where were her sons? Was she hiding soldiers? Did she help the rebels? Six months after Movsar disappeared in Komsomolskoye, towards the end of 2000, they came for her third son. They dragged Iznaur out of his bed before dawn and drove away with him in a truck. Tamara asked about him everywhere, but never got an answer.

That left her with just one son. Fifteen-year-old Sharpuddin. A year after Iznaur was taken, Tamara saw a line of tanks at the end of the street. She shouted to Sharpuddin: 'Hide! The Russians are coming!'

The boy ran outside in panic. He wanted to go to the neighbour's house and then sneak into the field behind it. But right outside the gate, running at top speed, he was hit, fell and died instantly.

Each time the mother goes outside she has to step on the spot coloured red by the blood of her youngest son that morning.

Tamara's only daughter, Fatima, has arrived. She stands in the doorway listening to her mother's story. Fatima has lost her husband and lives with her mother and two sons, aged seven and eight.

The young woman has her headscarf pulled well up on her forehead. 'It's important to show hair,' she tells us. 'So no one will think I'm a wahhabist.'

The worst thing a person can be in Chechnya is a wahhabist. That's what this family is accused of: contact with 'wahhabists and terror elements'. You can be branded as such if you do anything against Ramzan Kadyrov and his men. 'Just think when . . .' says the grandmother, and stops. She puts her hands to her mouth and continues:

'Think when the boys are old enough to . . .'

Tamara gives me a terrified look.

'. . . avenge my sons.'

The two women are often woken at night by the screams of one of the little boys. Always the same nightmare: 'The Russians are coming! The Russians are coming!' When will they be snatched away? The 'enemy' stigma is passed from one generation to the next.

Tamara had held a time of remembrance for her four sons. Four young, strong sons. Her life seemed meaningless. Then one day in 2002 she got word that Iznaur, her third son, who had been dragged out of the house before dawn two years earlier, had been indicted and convicted of planning terrorist activities and was in *strogi rezim* – maximum security – in a prison in Arkhangelsk.

'He was alive! I'd been so sure he was dead.'

Tamara smiles tremulously through her tears. 'But now, I'm so afraid for him. What will they do to him in prison?'

An envelope with an Arkhangelsk stamp lies in a kitchen drawer. It is decorated with a pink tulip and green leaves beside the address. And there's another stamp – 'approved by censor'. Still, Tamara didn't dare save the letter, and burned it. She kept just the envelope, the envelope with her son's handwriting on it, the only letter she has received from him since he disappeared six years ago.

'He gets two pieces of bread a day, and a sugar cube every third day,' his mother tells us. 'The prison is full of tuberculosis. He's the only son I have left. I'm so afraid he will die too.'

She lays a soft, work-worn hand on my arm.

'There are more tragedies in our family,' Tamara says. 'Last week . . .'

She grasps my hand, and I understand that she wants me to come with her. We don our footwear on the doorstep and she draws me across the yard to another room in another house.

In the entry you could already tell that something was wrong. The low voices. The sobbing. The smell of fear.

A group of women, all in black, sat in a circle on stools or cushions. When I entered the room, they glanced at me fearfully. My eyes were drawn to a young girl sitting on a sofa. Her foot, sheathed in a black sock with a pink border, trembled nervously. The movements were so small, so rapid, that they were more felt than seen. Her toes didn't leave the floor, and her foot made no sound as it tensed towards the soft carpet. Only her heel quivered. The sock was pulled over thick black stockings. Above them hung a heavy skirt, also black. Then a sweater, covered with an equally pitch-black shawl. The pink border tightened a little around the unruly foot like a glaring mistake. Apart from that, the girl was dressed entirely in black.

A little boy clung to her knee. He pummelled it with his fists, but the girl just sat with her hands in her lap. Her fingers clutched each other like claws while one hand pressed the other down. The girl's eyes were dark and distant, as if gazing through several veils. Her foot continued like a rapidly firing piston, and perhaps she clasped her fingers as she did so that they would not follow the rhythm of her foot. The boy started to cry. But the girl's face remained expressionless, her eyes wide; she was miles away from everything around her.

'Mama!' the boy howled.

She picked him up. But he brought no warmth to her eyes. Terror seemed to be trapped there.

A Persian rug protected people's feet against the cold floor. The walls were covered with pale wallpaper. Above the sofa where the girl sat was a poster of Mecca at sunset. Hanging close to the ceiling was a framed photograph of two serious-looking boys in Soviet military uniforms; it had acquired a greenish tinge with age. On the opposite wall was a clock, its face picturing Red Square.

Through the cracked windows you could hear a cow mooing out in a garden among fruit trees weighed down with wet snow. In the yard, chickens strutted about under a clothes line of frozen washing.

The women had run out of words; between the sighs and the sounds from outside, the clock ticked steadily. With every second, more time had passed since his disappearance. The clock's second hand made its slow march of time across Red Square. When it pointed straight up it slashed the colourful St Basil's Cathedral, then it continued on to the Kremlin's dark red walls, past Lenin's mausoleum, and swept along the wall of urns, Stalin's grave, Kalinin's grave, Brezhnev's grave; after half a minute it was at the History Museum and then it moved upwards along the walls of the department store that covered the other long side of the cobblestoned square before again ticking its way up to the golden onion cupolas.

The women were waiting for one of the two young boys hanging on a nail between Mecca and the Kremlin.

A week had passed since Hassan had driven out of Grozny early in February 2006 to do some errands in Nazran, Ingushetia, an hour's drive away. He left Salina and the two children in the flat early in the morning, saying he'd be back that afternoon. By nightfall he had not yet returned, nor by daybreak the following day. His car was found on the roadside near the village of Achkhoi Martan a few days later; it had been burned out. There was no sign of either him or his sister-in-law who had been travelling with him.

The police know nothing. The military know nothing. The authorities know nothing. No one has seen anything, heard anything, said anything.

Hassan's mother tells the story. About Hassan who never took part in the war. Never had enemies. Had no scores to settle with anyone. Too ailing for combat. Often sick. Not strong. Who would want to do anything to him?

'He didn't get married until he was forty years old,' his mother tells me. 'We thought he'd never have a family. But then we found Salina, who was clever and good and compliant,' she continues, and points to the young girl wearing the black sock with a pink border.

In a rasping, scarcely audible voice, as if it's rarely used and has to be tested, Salina whispers that she hopes her husband will come back soon and she prays to God nothing has happened to him.

'I can't bear to think anything else,' she whispers.

Salina was four years old when the Russians dropped the first bombs on Grozny. Her family went to stay with her grandmother, who lived outside the city, to escape the battles and bullets. After a few days her parents and two older brothers made a quick trip to their apartment. While driving on the highway, their car was hit by a rocket and they were all killed instantly. Salina doesn't remember her parents. Nor her brothers. But she remembers that they never returned, she says slowly.

Salina never got proper schooling because of the war, and has barely learned to read. When she was twelve her grandmother fell ill and was no longer able to care for her. It was best that Salina establish her own family, the old woman decided. Otherwise, who would take care of her after she died?

When Salina was thirteen, her grandmother took her out of school and married her to Hassan. At the age of fourteen she gave birth to her first son; at fifteen she had the second boy. Two months before her sixteenth birthday her husband disappeared. She telephoned his family, who brought her to their house in the village. Here, she's been in a daze for a week. She can't eat, hardly drinks and the milk in her breasts has dried up.

The little boy has climbed on to the sofa and is trying to pull off the black headscarf knotted tightly at the back of her neck. She pays no attention to him; the other child lies in her arms. Her parents. Her brother. Her husband. Her milk. Salina's life has been about loss.

The women put mats on the floor and prepare to pray. It is two o'clock. The prayer rug is facing Mecca. The hour hand of the clock points to the Kremlin.

Salina sits with the wailing child in her lap while the others are on the floor making obeisance. Their arms are crossed over their breasts. Their lips move silently. Their heads nod up and down, from side to side, and back again.

Mothers, sisters, wives and children become more powerless

with every disappearance. What is it about this family that all its men should be exterminated? And the thousands of other Chechen families that are losing their men?

After prayers one of the women remains sitting on the floor shaking her head slowly, as if in a trance. Salina is still staring vacantly into the air. Tamara rises abruptly and gestures for me to follow her. We walk back down the little path that's been trampled brown in the soft snow. The sun has finally broken through the fog and glistens on a crusted expanse of white, untouched snow next to the wall. But its warmth can't quell the horrors inside us. The horrors of dried blood, burned cars, buried sons.

'Hassan is only the last in a long line,' says Tamara when we're back in her house. 'In our family all the men disappear, one after another. Gone, done away with, locked up, vanished. One after another.'

Tamara trembles.

Shamil has started to get nervous. 'It's time, people have seen the car, us,' he whispers. He assumes the house is being watched, and thinks we ought to leave.

'Can I come back another time, perhaps tomorrow, or later in the week?' I ask.

'Whenever you wish,' replies Tamara.

'Will you promise not to tell anyone I've been here?' I whisper.

'Are you mad? I'm scared to death myself.'

She holds her clenched hands to her breast. 'I still have one son to protect, after all.'

'You're mad,' Shamil says in the car. 'Why did you say that you wanted to come back? You don't know them! You're really naive. They do their cleaning at night, that's when they come, the Kadyrovtsi, to clean out, sweep away, rake in. Or the Islamists — they'd also like to have your head on a platter, filmed for all the TV channels. If you're going back, you have to come like today, accidentally, without an appointment, drop in, and stay for a short afternoon. One afternoon, that's all.'

We drive in silence. I know that Shamil is right.

His car is freezing cold. My feet are like ice. The dreary fog once again lies heavily at the bottom of the mountain chain, and a wind sweeps across the plains. I wonder if it's possible to heat some water when we get home. If we have enough water. I wonder about that because I can't bear to think about this: to give birth to four sons, nurse them, feed them, raise them, see them grow up, play, begin school, become young men, and then lose them, bury two, search in vain for a third and know that at any time the fourth might be rotting in some contaminated prison camp beyond the Arctic Circle.

'There's something about that family,' Shamil says after a long silence. 'There's something that's not settled, that's not yet avenged,' he says almost as if to himself. 'You shouldn't go back there.'

'Won't you please take me back one more time?' I ask. 'Maybe they will find Hassan. And soon Iznaur will be released from prison . . .'

'*Inshallah*,' replies Shamil.

12

The Enemy Among Us

Zaira telephones her sister in Chechen-Aul.

After talking about the children's schooling, the sister's ulcer and the autumn's pickled peppers, she asks:

'Your neighbour, the one with the daughter who used to call me Zaza – does she still live on your street?'

There's a brief silence at the other end, then the sister clears her throat a little and replies that, yes, as far as she knows, the woman still lives there.

'Do you see anything of her?'

'No.'

'I'd like to talk to her.'

The silence at the other end of the line is long and deep. The conversation ends. Zaira regrets what she did; she shouldn't have asked on the telephone.

There are certain families no one visits. They don't visit each other either. Former best friends no longer say hello. Children are ostracised. No one says goodbye to the dying. There are certain people you shouldn't show feelings for or sympathise with.

Having contact with these families can lead you into the darkness yourself. They are burdened by a catastrophe. For some, the catastrophe is explosive.

The strife in Chechnya has entered a phase where streets have eyes, everyone watches everyone else, and anyone who doesn't denounce others is hiding something.

Only in the most inaccessible, nearly uninhabitable areas does the resistance hold its ground. Down here on the plains it has been subdued. People have bowed their heads, given in, turned away. Say nothing.

The iron fist of the republic hammers in the idea that traitors are threatening us. In our very midst. They must be smoked out, punished, generation after generation. Those who associate with these people are enemies themselves. Those who weep at their funerals are dissidents too.

This is what's called 'chechenising'. The executioners and the victims are Chechens. But the Kremlin decides who will have the power. Its henchmen operate in darkness and shadow. And in broad daylight.

The village is shrouded in thick fog. The further we go from Grozny the heavier the fog becomes, and when we reach Chechen-Aul we can barely see a hand's length ahead of us. Allah is helping us, Zaira believes. Only a dog sees us sneak through the gate.

The name of this settlement means 'Chechen village'. It gave it's name to the land, not the other way round. This was where Russian forces encountered the mountain people for the first time.

Zaira's sister paces nervously. She's been to her neighbour's home and asked her to come over to meet me. She took along a jug, as if she was going to borrow some milk. Before, they were constantly going back and forth between each other's homes with buckets and pans. What the sister did not know was that her neighbour's two cows had recently been killed, mown down by a truck, so she had to go back with an empty jug. But she had been able to give the message to the stunned neighbour, who hadn't had a visit in four years.

The sister continues to pace restlessly around the room as she speaks.

The neighbour's family had been among the wealthiest in the village, generous and lively; there had always been people in for tea, a meal, a chat, to borrow something, offer something. They owned cattle and sheep, and the father had well-paid work. They had just built a lovely two-storey house when the Russians invaded Chechnya in 1994. At that time they had six children.

The eldest son was in the resistance from the very beginning, and when he returned from the first war he was celebrated as a hero. He became an important man in the village after the peace agreement with Boris Yeltsin. When Putin's soldiers invaded in the autumn of 1999, he went to war again. A year later he was killed in a battle at Bacha-Yurt. The whole village joined the funeral procession and mourned him.

The sister stops pacing round in circles and leaves the room. A few minutes later she returns with some photographs: pictures of two girls, her married daughter and the neighbour's daughter, Mariam. She looks at them uncertainly.

'I should have thrown these pictures away, but somehow I can't bring myself to do that.'

The girls, then in their mid-teens, are laughingly putting on airs for the camera. They are beautiful, with joy in their eyes.

There is a soft knock on the little side door behind the kitchen. The sister gives a start. She turns the pictures face down and goes to open the door.

It's the neighbour. The sister had begged her to be careful and not let anyone see her. Because *those who have contact with the out-casts will themselves become outcasts*. The woman has a weathered, well-scrubbed face with high, prominent cheekbones and steel-grey eyes. She is breathing heavily after her walk through the woods, the detour she took so that no one would see her. Before anyone can say a word, she bursts into tears.

The sister gives us a disconcerted look.

The neighbour sees the photographs spread out on the table,

but does not pick them up. Her tears flow silently. Another mother, another sorrow. She looks at me uncertainly. What do I want? her look says. I tell her that I'd like to hear her story.

She looks questioningly at Zaira's sister, silently asking: Does she know . . .?

Then she looks at the photograph I have turned face up, but she doesn't touch it. The girl in the picture is wearing a knee-length turquoise skirt and a pink checked blouse with short sleeves. She has clear, peach-like skin, the same rosy cheeks as her mother, only rounder, large deep eyes, and eyebrows like Elizabeth Taylor. The laughing girl is a classic beauty.

'That's my daughter, Mariam,' says the neighbour.

Zaira's sister had already told me that it was Mariam who took her brother's death the hardest. She became silent and withdrawn. The turquoise and pink clothes were put away, she no longer left the house unless she was swathed from head to toe in a long dark skirt and cloak and a thick head covering. The gold-blonde locks that before had hung loosely disappeared under a tight headscarf. Where once there had been a curly fringe, now not a single strand of hair was visible. Her headscarf crept down on her forehead. The pale peach skin and rosy cheeks disappeared further inside the scarf. In the end Cleopatra's eyebrows were hidden too.

'We never thought . . .'

The woman barely manages to get out the words.

'We'd always let her do as she wished. There was never any nonsense with her. She was so kind and respectable, so strong and wise. Of all our children, she was the most helpful. Not so good at school, but the very best when it came to cooking, sewing and helping with the animals. She was perfect housewife material. When we gave her money to buy something new for herself, she chose instead to buy something for her nephews. She always thought of others before herself,' her mother remembered.

'Then she changed. She stopped going out, started to study the

Koran, to pray five times a day. The rare occasions she left the house it was always with one of her brothers. At home she sat bent over the writings of the Koran. We hoped that she would eventually recover from the sorrow of her brother's death, and that the happy girl would return.'

Suddenly Mariam came home one day and said she wanted to get married; in fact, she had already promised to marry someone.

'They're coming to get me tomorrow,' she said.

Who was he? What did he do?

'He's alone,' Mariam replied. 'His entire family was killed. He's only got me. He needs me. And he doesn't insist on a dowry. He'll take me as I am.'

Later that night the mother had suddenly awoken and sat up in bed. 'A cold shudder went through my heart,' she says. She was terrified, and ran in to Mariam. 'Don't do it!'

'Why, Mama?'

'It's wrong. It's wrong!'

The mother had wept and pleaded with her daughter. 'Don't do anything hasty. Let us meet him. Let us get to know him.'

'He needs me.'

'My heart says no,' sobbed the mother.

The next morning some relatives of Mariam's fiancé came and got her, as is the custom in Chechnya. The wedding was held quietly and her family was not present. That, too, is according to Chechen tradition. Only the groom's family celebrates a wedding, whereas the bride's family should stay at home and mourn the loss of a daughter. The girl can have only one family member with her, and never the mother; often it is a female cousin or girlfriend. At the wedding she becomes her husband's property and can't visit her family without his permission.

'If only I had known . . .'

The mother begins to weep again, twisting her fingers in and out of her scarf.

Those were the brutal years during the Second Chechen War. Villages that had not been touched during the first campaign were destroyed now. The authorities mercilessly struck down everyone they thought might be a separatist, or, even worse, an Islamist. People disappeared, were left in ditches, were tortured to death in prison. There appeared to be no end to the spiral of violence. Violence bred revenge, which bred new violence and new revenge.

Six months after the wedding the parents found out that their daughter's new husband was in the resistance. They were frightened. Once rumours started, it wasn't long before people were arrested. The families of those fighting against the Moscow-appointed regime could also be vulnerable to persecution and cleansing. When Mariam's parents heard that the husband was also a wahhabist, they were terrified.

Finally, the next spring, a whole year after the wedding, Mariam came for a visit. Her parents were dismayed. Gone was the smile, gone were the soft pink cheeks; the girl was skin and bone. They pleaded with her to leave the marriage. But Mariam insisted that she wanted to stay with her husband, and asked her parents to turn to Allah instead, to open their hearts to God's word as she had done.

The parents went to bed with heavy hearts, more worried than ever. Mariam left the next morning before they were awake.

The mother pauses in her story. The old kitchen door creaks in the wind, and some branches smack against the window. A storm is brewing. The sky is grey.

'I remember the last thing she said before we went to bed,' says the mother. '"Now the path leads straight ahead," she said with a faraway look in her eyes. The words sent shivers down my spine; they chilled me to the bone.'

Summer passed with no sign of her. Then, one dark evening in October 2002, some blurred pictures from a theatre in Moscow were shown on television. During the second act of the Russian musical *North-East*, forty masked men and women leaped on to the stage and fired live ammunition into the air . . .

'You are hostages . . . We have come from Chechnya. This is not a joke. We are at war,' the leader, Movsar Barayev, had shouted.

Several of the hostage-takers were related; there were sisters and aunts, uncles and cousins, husbands and wives. What they had in common was that they had all lost close relatives in the war. Some were teenagers; two girls were only sixteen years old. The women were dressed in black and had what looked like explosives strapped around their waists. The Russian media called them *The Black Widows*.

For nearly three days and nights the actors and the audience were held hostage in the theatre. The terrorists' goal was to focus attention on human rights violations in Chechnya. The mastermind behind the action was The Wolf – Shamil Basayev. Altogether there were about eight hundred people in the building. At dawn on the third day Russian forces launched a gas attack to overpower the terrorists. All the hostage-takers were killed, along with almost two hundred hostages, who were either gassed or killed in the exchange of fire between the hostage-takers and Russian anti-terror units.

Russian TV showed people being carried out of the theatre and those who lay dead. A lifeless Barayev was displayed in a pool of blood.

Several of the Black Widows were pictured leaning back in the red plush seats of the Dubrovka Theatre, their mouths open and bullet holes in their foreheads. Their belts were still intact. One of them was eighteen-year-old Mariam. Her husband was also among the dead hostage-takers.

'*Now the path leads straight ahead.*'

A few hours after they had seen their daughter's death on television, the parents' house was surrounded by masked commandos, riot police, anti-terrorist units and men from the intelligence service. The entire street was closed off, the house was ransacked; all their papers confiscated, all their photographs, all their letters taken away. What did they know? Who did they know? Who had helped her? Had *they* helped her?

The second son, who was also in the resistance, was not at

home when the anti-terrorist forces came. They found him in a house in the mountains and surrounded it. He refused to surrender, choosing instead to use his last bullets against the Russian special units. He was killed in the exchange of fire. This was the brother who had introduced Mariam to the husband she died with, and who had been Mariam's witness at her wedding.

Early one morning a few months later the police visited Mariam's third brother, who had fled to the Russian city of Samara. They brought him to the police station, and since then no one has heard from him or from the friends with whom he shared a room.

Two years later the parents had only two children left: their nineteen-year-old daughter Azet and their youngest son Isa, who was handicapped from birth and partially paralysed.

The family led a miserable existence in Chechen-Aul. All the villagers had turned their backs on them. The father lost his job and began to drink. He became violent and accused his wife of encouraging the children to become rebels. He thought they got it from her because there were many famous soldiers from the first resistance in her family.

The once prosperous family had barely enough to live on after the father lost his job. So he decided that their daughter Azet, who lived at home with her parents and her three-year-old son after her husband died in battle, should go to Georgia. There she could buy cheap goods, and then sell them in the market in Grozny, where nobody knew her.

One raw December day, when the family had saved enough money, Azet left with her son and her sister-in-law, the second brother's widow. At the border crossing to Dagestan they were stopped when they showed their passports. They were accused of being part of a secret terrorist network that was planning to blow up buildings in Dagestan. After two days the sister-in-law was released, but Azet and her three-year-old were held in custody. The sister-in-law went back to Azet's parents. Every day they visited the authorities in Grozny to make enquiries. What was the charge against their daughter? Where was she being held? Where was the grandchild? They got no response, other than a warning:

'You still have a son; if you come here one more time it will be the worse for him.'

One evening just before New Year 2004 a little boy babbling in Chechen was found in the entrance to an apartment building in Dagestan. A search for his relatives was announced on TV. The child stared blankly into the camera with frightened eyes. On his forehead was a fiery burn. It was Azet's son.

The grandfather rushed to the telephone, and then set off immediately for Dagestan to get the boy. When he arrived, the child was at the TV station. The little boy stumbled towards him. As they left, the grandfather heard a journalist say: 'He's the son of a terrorist. His mother was going to blow herself up for Basayev.'

The child had changed completely. Two weeks in prison had made him timid and fearful. He shied away when people talked to him. Just gazed at them with frightened eyes.

The grandmother sits for a while in silence.

She points to her forehead, to show where the little boy had a deep red scar. What had they done to him? Could they have tortured a three-year-old? Or Azet? Had they abused the mother in front of the son? To make her talk? Where was she? Was she alive? Little Azet. Little, peaceful, quiet Azet.

Now, two years later, Azet has still not returned, and there has been no news of her. Her son no longer lives with the neighbour and her husband; the child went to live with his other grandparents. They thought he would be safer with them. Mariam's mother hasn't talked to the boy for more than six months. She can't afford a long-distance telephone call.

All they have left is Isa, their youngest, bedridden, son. And the hope that Azet will return.

'The war, the war. Once I had six wonderful children . . . now I have only one left.'

Her cheeks are damp under the gas lamp. She apologises for her tears.

'It's so long since I've talked to anyone about my children,' she confides. 'It's so long since I've talked to anyone at all.'

The grey afternoon has begun to darken, the wind howls around the house. It's time, says the hostess's look. The houses have eyes. The streets have ears. And her nerves have been stretched enough. The neighbour rises, knots her scarf more snugly around her head, pulls her wool jacket tightly around her, and then, hidden by the fog, makes her way slowly into the woods. A good distance away, shielded by dense trees, she follows a narrow path and passes well behind the row of houses along the road. When she comes out of the woods, she walks across the road towards her own home. If anyone is out walking in the afternoon fog they could not know where she has been.

The next day Zaira's sister meets one of the neighbours on the road.

'What were you doing at *their* house yesterday?' she is asked.

'We ran out of milk and my grandchild was crying,' the sister replies.

'But their cows were killed a few weeks ago. Didn't you know that?'

'No, I didn't know. How could I?'

The neighbour nods and walks on. The sister hurries home.

Those who have contact with these families will themselves become outcasts . . .

13

Welcome to Ramzania

Grozny comprises two worlds. The haves and the have nots. Those who gloat and those who groan. After having travelled in secret and met the degraded and abused, I wanted to meet those floating at the top. But in order to travel between these two worlds, even if they are separated by only a few streets, I have to take a detour via Moscow.

There I hear that the Russian Foreign Ministry has chartered a plane and is arranging a trip for foreign journalists in connection with Ramzan Kadyrov's inauguration as president. I sign up for it, and get a pass for a day trip, Moscow–Grozny–Moscow.

It is 5 April 2007 and we meet before dawn in the nearly empty departure lounge. Sitting at a plastic table drinking airport coffee are Andy from the *Economist*, Guy from the *Wall Street Journal*, Andrew from the *Independent* and Adrian from the *Daily Telegraph*, all neatly crossed off the list held by a bureaucrat from the Russian Foreign Ministry. A young man from the Information Service of the Chechen representation office in Moscow waylays me as I'm going over to get some coffee.

'Are you excited?'

'Yes, very excited.'

'Have you been to Chechnya before?'

'No, never,' I say, shaking my head.

Standing there bareheaded and in jeans, I have little in common with the stooped woman who usually flies to one of Chechnya's neighbouring republics from this same departure lounge. I sit down at the table. It feels strange to be taking a trip with a group of journalists after such a long time alone. They are so poised, so well informed and, not least, so self-confident, these top journalists. Even at five o'clock in the morning.

The sun rises somewhere on our way south. Masses of snow soften the razor-sharp peaks of the Caucasus mountains like soft cushions you can dream yourself into from the hard aeroplane seats. Then a rasping female voice announces that it is eight degrees and overcast in Grozny, with a chance of sunshine later in the day.

Even from the air we can see the portraits on either side of the terminal. The airport is gleaming. It was reopened for Ramzan's thirtieth birthday six months ago, after having been closed for ten years. At the opening, Ramzan, then prime minister of the republic, guffawed to the TV cameras: 'I don't think anyone has ever received an airport as a thirtieth birthday present before!'

Then he danced *lezginka* and threw money about.

We stream out of the aeroplane on to the smooth tarmac. The holes in the asphalt are gone, the runway is newly marked out, newly cleaned and polished, and rows of men in suits stand to attention waiting for someone. We are herded into the terminal and past the VIP lounge, where tables are decked with an abundance of Caucasian delicacies.

The arrivals hall sparkles. Glistening squares of imitation mother-of-pearl cover the floor, the slate-grey stairs and silver metal railings and counters gleam. Outside the main exit a highway leads towards the city. A gut feeling of recognition. It was here, on the steps of the main exit, that I stood that day twelve years ago, uncertain what to do. 'There are snipers everywhere.' 'Go back to Moscow.' 'This place is hell.' At that time the city truly lived up to its name, which means *The Threatening* or *The Terrible*.

Today a bus is waiting. I am crammed into it along with the British, the Germans, the French, the Russians and a woman from Swedish Radio. Young trees with yellow-green buds have been planted, and the road from the airport is almost like a boulevard. The foliage is still sparse and stunted, but if the peace holds it will become thick and beautiful.

The military is out in force, and we are waved on our way. The city is almost deserted, although it's the middle of the morning. Later I learn that people were not allowed to use their cars that day so as not to create problems for the important guests. Soldiers with loaded weapons are stationed along the entire route, some turned towards the road, others facing the surrounding hills and fields. And such amazing buildings along the highway! The high-rise flats have red and green façades designed like the Chechen flag.

We drive past Grozny towards Gudermes, where Ramzan has his dacha and Chechen representation office. A soldier is stationed every hundred metres along the route of the hour-long drive. Amid an eager crowd of people, the man from the representation office opens the bus door and guides us through several security checks. The place is swarming with men in different uniforms: the black-clad Kadyrovtsi, the green uniforms of the Foreign Ministry, the blue of OMON – the riot police – the navy blue of the highway patrol and the olive drab of the federal forces. In addition, there are civilian guards and men in suits with earphones in their ears milling about. An endless line of people on their way to the festivities has to undergo body searches; their bags are opened, their shoes put through a metal detector. The reporter from Swedish Radio and I are hustled over to the women's queue. It's short and we are finished quickly. Instead of waiting for the bus, we walk down towards Ramzan's dacha. At regular intervals we nod towards his black-clad security guards who stand along the curving road with loaded weapons. They do not return our greeting, and suddenly a man is walking behind us.

'Why are you walking here? Why didn't you wait for the bus? Why do you want to walk alone?'

The road slopes downward, it's less than a kilometre to the cluster of buildings we see on the level ground below.

'We like walking. We're restless types,' I reply.

His laugh is a bit forced. We pass a building site, and I ask what it is.

'It's going to be a racecourse,' says the man.

'I thought Ramzan had forbidden games and gambling.'

'It's just for racing,' the man replies quickly. 'No money involved.'

We walk towards a gate displaying the republic's new emblem: a traditional Chechen tower and an oil rig, with a mountain peak above and two outer rings – a circle of wheat topped by a half-moon and a star in a kind of naive Muslim–Soviet design. At the gate we go through yet another security check. The man leaves us there, vanishes into the crowd just as suddenly as he appeared.

Inside the gate are three roads. One goes past a circle of straggly, drooping pansies that look as if they have just been transplanted from dry pots and are trying to revive. Inside the ring of pansies is a star-shaped bed of orange marigolds, with a couple of roses smiling in the middle. I peek into an octagonal pavilion with large windows. It is an art gallery, a collection of paintings that portray Kadyrov I and II in broad, vivid strokes. Putin is honoured with a portrait too, and even he has some colour in his cheeks.

Had I taken the road to the right I would have come to a cage in which four large lions growl lazily behind iron bars, while a panther and a tiger pace stealthily along the sides. Ramzan likes to say that he spits in the face of an animal before he pets it, to show who's boss.

Instead, I take the middle road, which leads towards two buildings – the president's private apartments and the assembly hall. I'm directed towards the latter. It is, in fact, impossible to go the wrong way; young men pop up everywhere and politely suggest

I move on if I stay too long in one place. Inside the assembly hall, which looks like a big top, the white walls are decorated with turquoise polyester ribbons and the ceiling is a shiny transparent material. The seats are upholstered in a silky mauve fabric. People have started to take their places. Up on the stage two women are struggling with a vacuum cleaner. The machine fails to remove some sticky red spots on the blue carpet, and after a while a woman in sky-high heels trips up to the stage with a broom. Another woman, also in a party dress and stilettos, wipes away every spot or bit of dust she sees with a grey cloth.

The sunshine that was forecast has materialised. The hall is like a steam bath. The woman with the broom gives the floor one last sweep; the glassy surface reflects the sunlight. The light is so bright that people are wearing sunglasses. It's also almost impossible to see the picturesque mountain scenery being projected on to the stage backdrop.

Many of the older men are wearing traditional costumes and *papakha* – tall sheepskin hats. The younger men are in suits, and the women are dressed to the nines. This spring, as last year, leopard-print clothes are all the rage for women of all ages.

On either side of the stage is an imitation brick tower decorated with bits of broken mirror. Two flags, the Russian and the Chechen, stand in the background. Seated in the first row are the presidents of the other North Caucasus republics: Dagestan, Ingushetia, North Ossetia, Kabardino-Balkaria and Karachai-Cherkessia. The former president of Chechnya, Alu Alkhanov – the only one, since the wars began, whose presidency hasn't ended in violent death – is conspicuous by his absence.

The hall is soon jam-packed, and in the chaos I sneak away from the journalists' assigned seats in the back off to the side, and sit down in the fifth row, behind the presidents but in front of the members of parliament.

I want to look Ramzan Kadyrov in the eye. It turns out that I've seated myself among the ministers, a couple of judges and one of Ramzan's notorious friends whose tentacles reach far down into the Russian capital's underworld. Out of the corner of my eye I see a guard heading towards me, and I immediately initiate a conversation with one of the judges. A trumpet fanfare sounds, the hum of voices subsides reverently and the guard turns away. Tramping footsteps are heard approaching down the middle aisle. A man carrying a tall banner with the Ramzan emblem – the two towers – strides firmly up the steps to the stage. He has taken three paces towards the two flags when the point of the banner crashes into the overhead projector. The man stumbles and falls; the pictures jump and a crackling comes from the projector. The man hastily picks himself up, circumvents the projector and positions himself stolidly between the flags.

Another fanfare, and who's this running? – Ramzan! Flanked by rows of boys and girls in beautiful folk costumes, he jogs up the aisle like a footballer taking the field, his arms bent at the elbows, held in front of his chest like a boxer. He takes the steps two at a time and is met on stage by the broom woman, now without her broom, and handed an armful of orange roses. A man rushes up to the podium and begins to speak:

'A telegram has arrived from Russia's president, Vladimir Putin!'

As he says *Putin* the loudspeaker begins to crackle. The man, who proves to be leader of parliament, tries to turn on the microphone and start reading the telegram. The crackling continues. He turns on the microphone. The crackling increases as he reads the greeting. *Order and stability . . . Continue the work . . . Strengthen the republic . . . Achieve security . . .* the loudspeaker croaks. The young man at the sound board off to one side presses buttons feverishly, pulls levers, turns screws, and soon all you can hear is the loudspeaker's protesting shriek. But you can't stop reading in the middle of a telegram from Putin. The leader of parliament reads louder and louder. In the end he is shouting Putin's words. We high-ranking individuals in the front rows hear him perfectly well, and so does Ramzan, and that's the most important thing. *Goodwill from the people of Russia . . . New energy . . . With best wishes . . .*

As the telegram reading concludes, the loudspeaker gurgles a few times, coughs briefly and then goes dead.

Ramzan has been squirming in his chair during the reading, as if his suit is too small, or he is too big for it. He seems to be pressed into his seat against his will and, as if in protest, he cracks his knuckles, hunches his shoulders, drums his fingertips on the arm of the chair.

The new president's friend, in my row, has pushed his expensive sunglasses on to his forehead. I've seen him before, in photographs together with Ramzan. A businessman rumoured to be behind the murder of the American manager of one of Moscow's luxury hotels. He is clean-shaven, has dark eyes and a hawk nose; he's wearing a pink shirt and a white silk suit. As one telegram after another – something they call faxograms – is read, he glances at me roguishly. Via the entire row of ministers and judges, he sends me a note with his telephone number scribbled on it. The men passing it exchange meaningful looks.

Meanwhile, Ramzan has not yet found a comfortable position and sits dejectedly with his face in his hands. Will this never end? He leans his elbows on the table in front of him. Flashbulbs go off, those, that is, of the foreign photographers; this is the type of photograph they want for their archives, for illustration when problems mount. The national press prefers pictures of the president when he finally straightens up and rises to take the oath of office. Placing his hand on the Russian Constitution he promises to respect everything within it. The orchestra, festively clad in dress uniform, plays a new fanfare, and then it's over. The man in the white suit saunters over to me.

'My name is Omar,' he says. 'Would you like to meet Ramzan?'

I turn furtively towards the man from the Chechen representation office in Moscow; he's busy herding the other foreign correspondents. I nod. Omar has put on his gold-rimmed sunglasses again. He takes me by the hand and leads me over to the pavilion among the pansies. Out of the corner of my eye I see my colleagues from the plane standing around outside. I hope they don't see me walking hand in hand with the millionaire in the pink shirt, but I don't pull my hand from his grasp.

Half a step behind the president's pal, I am led into the holiest of holies, Ramzan's world. A security guard reaches out an arm towards me, but when he sees my new friend's grip he withdraws.

The entrance is dominated by an enormous fireplace. Landscape paintings and Chechen antiques soften the impression a little, but, like so many of the new buildings that are going up so quickly, this one seems shallow and artificial. Ramzan's mother, sisters, and uncle stand by the fireplace greeting people; the grip of the man in the silk suit keeps getting tighter. He leads me further into the building, down a hallway and through a door to the reception room, where all the guests seem to be heading. The furniture is white and gold, the brocade curtains keep out the bright sunlight. It's cool and airy after the sweltering assembly hall.

Sitting by a table overflowing with elegant food is a fat Russian general. I know his face from the newspapers and TV. He pours vodka into his glass. There is clearly no ban on alcohol here, and – as if this were a comedy in the Russian theatre of the absurd – the general is already growing boisterous. He bellows to all sides, while the distinguished and decorated Chechen leaders smile politely but with a trace of disgust. What is this barbarian doing here with us? the faces say. Even in the puppet regime, the connection with the Russians is more one of need than of pleasure.

A roar goes up. Ramzan's uncle is embracing the new president at the entrance. A moment later the two men enter the room. The mother and sisters have remained in the hall, and I realise that I'm the only woman at the reception. Ramzan accepts congratulations and gifts, but doesn't he look a little sad?

The newly inaugurated president seems preoccupied as he receives people's good wishes. He replies monosyllabically or with a clap on the shoulder.

That morning he had wept at his father's grave in Tsentoroi, his uncle told me later. Ramzan had telephoned him and asked him to come to the grave so that they could say a prayer together. 'It was a very emotional day for him,' the uncle said.

I feel a tug on my hand, and the man in the silk suit, who has been greeting people left and right, now goes over and introduces the guest from Norway to the new president.

'Isn't she beautiful?' he babbles.

'Very,' Ramzan replies curtly, and looks away.

I wonder what I should say, if I can offer my congratulations to an executioner. I end up with an empty greeting and look into a pair of frightened eyes. Or is that my imagination? The robust man, the former bodyguard, the soldier, the man with his own prison, own army, own boxing club and own fan club, appears to want to get away, away from the reception, away from the masters of ceremony. He wants to ride his horses, box in his club, play with his lions, shoot targets with his pistols.

'I'd like to meet you another time,' I say. He nods. 'For an interview,' I add.

'She probably wants something quite different from you!' roars the fat general from the table. I feel my cheeks flush.

'Ha, ha, ha!' the Russian shouts, his flabby cheeks quivering.

'Later,' says Ramzan. 'Later.'

He is embraced by new VIPs and stands there, a man with enormous power over his people but who still can't get rid of one gibbering general. Because the Russian's bleary look says something else: You are no more than a pawn in our Caucasus game. You will be in power as long as we need you. Just like your father.

'Let's go,' says the millionaire, and we leave the gaudy surroundings.

'Let's make some plans,' he says, and grips my arm as we walk down the hall.

'Let's . . .' he continues as we emerge into the bright sunlight, but is interrupted by the man from the Chechen representation office who comes running towards us with wide eyes and is so agitated that he doesn't see the dark man from the glittering underworld. He is about to scold me for not following his rules, but then he sees the plutocrat, stops short and greets him deferentially, before he hisses at me: 'You can't just disappear like that. We've been looking for you! The bus is leaving! The plane is leaving!'

I'm hustled on to the rickety bus, and on the way to the airport we stop at the memorial park for Ramzan's father.

'You can talk freely with anyone you wish here,' says the man from the Moscow office. 'You have ten minutes!'

Every second person in the park seems to be a guard; to conduct interviews appears pointless. Instead, I follow a Russian television crew to see what people say to them.

'Ramzan is our hero!'

'Look how he has rebuilt our city!'

'We thank Ramzan!'

'We praise Ramzan!'

'He has given Grozny back to us.'

'Everything around us is thanks to him!'

The replies roll off their tongues, and revive memories of street interviews in Baghdad under Saddam Hussein. The same stock phrases. The same expressions of nervous happiness on people's faces. Even the government TV journalists get bored.

'Isn't there something else you want Ramzan to do? Or perhaps something you want to ask him?'

'Ramzan knows best. Whatever he thinks is necessary, that's what should be done. He does everything for our good.'

The man from the representation office comes over to where I'm standing eavesdropping on the TV journalists' interviews.

'See how freely you can talk with people,' he says enthusiastically. 'Just think, it's safe to walk around here, you can go wherever you wish now.

'I'm sure you were afraid before you came here,' he adds with an understanding smile. 'But there's no danger now. Just listen: people's free, honest opinions. No one is afraid any more.'

We are herded back into the bus with stern instructions to

hurry, because the plane is leaving. Then we drive straight to the airport, where we wait until nightfall. When the sun disappears, the terminal's large glass panes enfold us in cold air. Finally, we are crammed into the narrow cabin and fly off into the night. The mountaintops of the Caucasus are hidden beneath us.

The next morning I read in Russian newspapers about a dignified inauguration of Chechnya's new president, about a celebration afterwards with caviar and champagne, carp and sturgeon, lamb and vodka – but the president, of course, did not touch a drop.

One of the sober president's first acts was to close all the public orphanages. According to Ramzan Kadyrov, they went against Chechen tradition. 'Our customs strongly forbid us to take children from their homes. That brings shame on the entire family.'

Welcome to Ramzania!

14

New Grozny and the Green Zone

One month later I am in the Green Zone. With all my papers in order. This time everything was done openly; copies of my credentials and press card were submitted, along with information about what I wanted to do: interview Ramzan Kadyrov. Early in May I was informed that the president was expecting me.

Even before I entered the terminal my name was called over the loudspeaker. Waiting for me at the information desk were Ramzan in a suit and Sultan in a red T-shirt. Not President Ramzan, but a man by the same name from the Committee for Youth Affairs who was to take care of me during my visit. Sultan was the driver. He was plump and energetic, with a broad cheerful face and a profusion of grey curls. The Committee for Youth Affairs fellow was very pale and his forehead glistened with acne. He immediately wanted to show me everything that had been rebuilt. During the past year the face of Grozny had changed completely. The streets were tarmacked, the pavements repaired. Everywhere you heard hammering and pounding, workers shouted, construction cranes shrieked. Cement was being mixed, windows installed. On the road from the airport you didn't see a single sign of the war. Many of the buildings displayed colourful façades. Purple squares. Yellow balconies. Pale green patches of land. And everywhere the same posters of Ramzan and his father.

'This is New Grozny,' my guide told me proudly. He was in his mid-twenties and during most of the trip he was busy texting on his mobile phone. We irritated each other from the start.

'And this is the Green Zone,' he said when we drove up to the heavily protected government site.

At the barrier, our documents were checked by Russian soldiers. If you got past them, you came to a gate guarded by more Russian soldiers, and then you were checked one last time before going to your destination: the government building, the presidential administration office, the guard headquarters, the military base, the election commission, or the mosque where the president prays every Friday.

The wall around the Green Zone was ten metres high and guarded by several watch towers. Tanks were lined up inside the walls so that they could quickly create a cordon should that be necessary. A few years earlier, a suicide bomber had driven straight into one of the administration buildings with a truck full of explosives and more than a hundred people had been killed. The area was formerly the site of a large industrial plant, and some of its ruins still formed the outer part of the zone. Inside the wall there were several new buildings. The largest was the government building, a whitewashed structure with broad steps. Beyond them was a plaza with inlaid grey and purple flagstones. The gardens were new and the lawn had not yet been seeded, so weeds had spread wildly. As in the rest of the city centre, all the trees were tender year-old saplings.

'Ramzan is here,' the driver in the red T-shirt whispered knowingly, while our own Ramzan was busy with my papers in the guard house.

'See those silver-grey cars in front of the building? They're Ramzan's men,' he said. The vehicles were all Soviet-made Zhigulis.

'He recently ordered three thousand Zhiguli 110s,' Sultan confided to me. 'He often drives himself. He likes to do that. Then nobody knows which car he's in. He has to be on his guard all the time, you know; he's always in danger.'

In each of the cars sat a couple of men with rippling muscles under their shirts. Kadyrovtsi. They were strong and broad-shouldered, some wore caps and black T-shirts with the words *Presidential Security Service* on the back, others were in uniform, some were in suits; but all had the same broad faces, the same well-trimmed beards. Were they chosen for their similar look, so that an assassin would think that perhaps that one, or that one, or maybe *that* one was Ramzan?

I was assigned Room 3 at the Astoria, a grey stone building with bulletproof windows next to the mosque. Here, too, Russian soldiers were stationed at the entrance; only federal forces serve in the Green Zone. Locals aren't trusted here, so I was surrounded by soldiers from Lipetsk, Arkhangelsk, Kaluga. Only among them, mostly peasant boys and a few girls, could you be sure that no one was interested in taking part in a coup against the government.

A delegation of five men accompanied me down the corridor: Adlan, the prime minister's adviser; Mamed, Chechnya's representative to the Council of Europe; the hotel manager, the technical manager and the Russian duty officer.

'Nice,' I said, when the technical manager opened the door to my room. 'Very pleasant.'

It smelled mouldy. In a corner by the bed water dripped from the ceiling, perhaps from a burst pipe on the next floor. The ceiling panels were about to fall down and there was dirty white plaster dust on the floor.

'I'm sure you want to rest,' Mamed urged.

No, I thought. 'Yes,' I replied.

'Then I'll come and get you in a few hours,' he said.

My room reminded me fascinatingly of earlier Soviet hotel experiences. When I put a sweater in the cupboard, the shelf fell backwards on to the one below. I tried to mend it, but two screws were missing, so I balanced my clothes so as to distribute the weight evenly. All the cupboard doors were crooked, and the refrigerator was as warm as a plastic bag in the sun. But the bottles of water I'd brought could certainly be drunk warm. In the bathroom, most of the tiles were missing, the shower cubicle balanced on uneven mouldings, and when I recklessly knocked the toilet bowl with my knee it moved half the length of my foot. I hurriedly pushed it back into place. When I lay down on my bed, it was wet. I moved the bed a little and hung the blanket over the bedposts to dry. How old could the building be?

It was built a couple of years ago, I was told later. I recalled the only critical voice I'd heard on that marathon day when Ramzan Kadyrov was inaugurated as president a month earlier. When I praised the rapid rebuilding of the city, a female Chechen journalist had whispered: 'They build fast and badly. They build shells. Many of the decorative façades are already falling off. Soon everything will have to be redone.'

After two hours of rest the handsome Mamed knocked on my door to show me around Grozny. Unfortunately he was going to Strasbourg the following day. I'd been surprised to find him here. The last time I'd met him was at a conference on human rights in Chechnya, held at the Olof Palme Centre in Stockholm. It had been attended by people from various human rights organisations, both Russian and Chechen, many of them personally threatened by Kadyrov. Anna Politkovskaya had been actively and energetically present; it was she who cut to the core when the talk got too fuzzy. During the final dinner we agreed to meet in Moscow, where I planned to be several weeks later.

'Home, we must meet at home. For me, Moscow is now just my own apartment, and the apartments of my parents, my children, and my friends,' she said. 'Everything else is gross, grotesque.'

Three weeks later I was on the plane to Moscow. To attend her funeral.

But what had Mamed been doing in Stockholm? Was he sent by Kadyrov?

Mamed's office was at the Astoria, next door to the apartment of the prime minister, Kadyrov's best friend. Now he wanted to show me Victory Prospect, which had been renamed Kadyrov Prospect. We turned on to a street that had just been opened.

'It was closed for years,' said Mamed.

We looked at the memorial park for Kadyrov, and the mosque that was under construction; it would be Europe's, or at least Russia's, or at least the Caucasus's, largest mosque, designed by architects from Istanbul. While he pointed to the new shops, I asked about the Stockholm conference.

'I have to keep up with what's going on,' he replied as he admired the smooth tarmac beneath us. 'I used to have to repair my car all the time; it couldn't withstand the bumps and potholes in the streets.'

'But what did you think about the conference?' I repeated.

'They exaggerate,' he answered briefly, and drove around the 'three idiots' at the end of the new Prospect. His conclusion was: Amnesty International exaggerates. Memorial exaggerates. The Helsinki Committee exaggerates. Human Rights Watch exaggerates. The European Union exaggerates. The United Nations exaggerates. And, not least, the USA exaggerates.

'That's what they make their living from,' he said.

'What do you mean?'

'They exist on exaggeration. On telling the world what important work they do. All the abuses they uncover. That's what they make money on. That's how they get sponsors and support. I don't say that kidnappings never occur, or that people don't disappear, but it's usually common criminals or family quarrels, something the government can't do anything about, unfortunately.'

Mamed took me to a pizzeria on Kadyrov Prospect, the only one in Grozny. Yellow plastic chairs and tables were placed with a view on to the centre strip, where the thin spruces had sprouted pale green buds since last winter and young Groznians were strolling.

The sun was setting and a soft light settled over the rooftops.

People sat on benches eating sunflower seeds or drinking Pepsi. The atmosphere was calm and carefree, the May evening cool and lovely. Mamed wanted to sit inside.

'It's so dusty outside.'

The pizzeria was alcohol-free, like most restaurants and cafés in Grozny. Ramzan had decreed this. He had also decreed that discotheques should be prohibited. Nightclubs were a decadent Western idea. He wanted to have a pure, Islamic society of hard-working people. We drank Fanta.

'In some restaurants they have small rooms where you can order alcoholic drinks,' Mamed told me. 'That's fine, as long as nobody sees it.'

Our conversation was apathetic. I didn't know how much of what we talked about Mamed would later report. He was well informed about me, I could tell, and I wondered why I'd been given permission to enter the republic. It had been a surprise to receive his last email the day before I left Moscow:

Don't worry – we will try to organise you visit to Chechnya and meeting with Mr Kadyrov in a best way so that you can prepare you book in a best manner and give a present to Kingdom of Norway in a form of new best seller.

The sun had gone down, and the yellow plastic chairs were swallowed up by the darkness. The music got louder. The night was still young, and I was driven home.

15

The Youth Palace

A peach-coloured building with columns and white window frames rises proudly at the end of Kadyrov Prospect. It is built in the neo-colonial style with a prominent entrance, balconies and decorative pediments, and is set back elegantly from a plaza that has a fountain and two cannons from the Crimean War. It is said that the guns were once manned by Leo Tolstoy. Above the entrance, stretching the entire width of the building, hangs a banner that says in green letters: *We are always with you, Ramzan*. A smaller plaque by the door reads: *The Committee for Youth Affairs*. In common parlance: the Youth Palace.

Well-dressed young people stream in and out of this grand entrance. The girls are beautiful and made up like dolls; they wear skirts that reach their knees, no shorter, no longer, and tight-fitting, but proper, blouses. Teetering on sky-high heels, they cross the plaza with impressive, elegant precision and a gracefulness worthy of a ballerina.

Cheery headbands replace the thick headscarves that the president has asked Chechen women to wear. On 8 March, International Women's Day, he had summoned all the female students to the largest auditorium in the university.

'A woman is our most treasured possession; therefore, she must be honoured and protected,' he said, and instructed the professors to enforce the wearing of scarves. Towards the end of the gathering, as the TV cameras rolled, he announced expansively that he had brought gifts for everyone: a headscarf for every woman. His assistants distributed them, adding that Ramzan would be upset if the women didn't wear them.

The Youth Palace girls have reached a compromise: the wide headband gives an impression of modesty, but at the same time doesn't spoil a carefully planned outfit. Most of the girls who go in and out of the peach-coloured building are about twenty. According to tradition, if they are unmarried they can choose not to wear a headscarf.

The princes of the Youth Palace stride out with backs straight, carefully observing everything around them. Something about Chechen men gives the impression that they are always prepared. Ready to attack or to defend themselves. It's as if they are filled with a perpetual, unreleased tension. Temperament simmers in the city. There is adrenalin in the air. Judging by what you see on the streets, dreamers are few and far between in Chechnya; you don't get many people strolling about aimlessly philosophising. There are far fewer Raskolnikovs than Rambos.

The young men usually wear jeans, black or faded blue, with high waists and tight belts. They also wear close-fitting T-shirts over their bulging torsos, and walk with their chests thrust forward and their bottoms stuck out. Their arms hang slightly away from their bodies when they walk, as if their back muscles are so stiff from exercising that they can't swing their arms freely. Many have adopted their leader's look: hair cut short and beard neatly trimmed. Others wear their hair a little longer, with a fringe hanging down into their eyes; but on no account can hair be too long at the back of the neck, because that would suggest fundamentalist religious attitudes.

The minder who has been assigned to me comes from these ranks. My Ramzan is medium height, medium build, medium good-looking, with a square face, brown hair and brown eyes. Since I'm on an official visa, my steps are carefully monitored.

After the first security check outside the entrance, we meet more guards inside. They are fiddling with their guns; they examine them, polish them, pat them and pet them. There's the constant sound of guns being loaded, laid on the table, reloaded, before they are returned to their holsters to rest securely against their owner's hip as he scrutinises faces, checks documents, searches bags.

We go through a large marble hall and up an elegant stairway. On each floor long corridors stretch away from both sides of the stairs. Beautiful young people hurry in and out of the offices. My Ramzan shows me around, following the signs on the doors – Information Department, Analysis Department, Organisation Department, Innovation Department, Community Relations Department, Press Department, Foreign Relations Department, Media Department, Radio Station, Patriotic Development Department.

'Impressive,' I say.

'Yes, isn't it!'

'I'd like to talk to them all.'

'All of them?'

'Yes, all the different departments.'

Our first stop is the Organisation Department. Two young girls look up and tell me that their supervisor is not in, so could I come back later?

'I'm interested in knowing what you do.'

'We're just employees.'

'But what do you do?'

They look at each other, shrug.

'You must know what the Organisation Department does?'

My minder tells them to answer.

'We organise concerts, invite singers, groups, things like that. And then we plan public activities.'

'What kind of activities?'

'Just now we're planning the 9 May celebration of our victory in the Great War for the Fatherland. On that day we'll also commemorate the murder of Akhmed Kadyrov. Next month, 12 June, is Russia's Constitution Day. We'll celebrate it with a huge concert. On 14 July we'll have festivities to mark Ramzan's first hundred days as president. There will be a lot of concerts during the summer, too. We'll mark the first day of school, 1 September; then on 5 October we'll celebrate Ramzan's thirty-first birthday, and so on. But we're rather busy just now . . .'

We knock on the next door. The sign says Information Department.

'We provide information about different activities and concerts that support the president,' a young man tells me. 'We distribute leaflets, put up posters, invite people to events. Now we're advertising the 9 May event. It will be at Dynamo Stadium, and Ramzan will be there. It's going to be fantastic! We also travel around and tell people about Ramzan and the work his administration does.'

'Do you do anything else?'

'Next month is Russia's Constitution Day, and in July it will be a hundred days since Ramzan became president . . .'

We proceed to the Media Department. There, four young men are sitting at computers. The Youth Palace has wireless connection and twenty-four-hour access to the Internet, my Ramzan boasts. As in the other rooms, posters of the president and portraits of his dead father hang on the walls. The young men are wearing T-shirts with Ramzan on the front.

'We inform the media about rallies, concerts and events that we arrange to support the president; we also provide general information about Ramzan's work for young people. And of course we're at all the rallies, events, ceremonies and concerts . . . Ramzan is a big supporter of young people, you know.'

We go to the Analysis Department.

'We gather material and analyse it,' says a young man.

'What kind of material?'

'We ask people about different things.'

'Such as?'

'Unfortunately, I'm very busy at the moment. Can you come back another day?'

In the Foreign Relations Department, where my minder normally works, a group is planning what kind of foreign connections they should have.

'At the moment we're cooperating with different areas in Russia,' Ramzan explains.

'But Russia isn't exactly a foreign country, is it?'

'No, but we start here.'

'Who do you cooperate with?'

'First and foremost, the patriotic youth movement, Nashi. We have a lot in common with them. Some of us are in Moscow now to support them in the demonstration outside the fascist Estonian embassy. It's disgraceful that the Estonians removed the statue of the Soviet soldier in Tallinn!'

In the Innovation Department I meet the gorgeous Aigul.

'What does this department do?'

'Innovation.'

'But what do you actually do?'

'We think creatively. Come up with new ideas.'

'Meaning?'

'We come up with activities we've never had before.'

'Like what, for example?'

'Well, we invite entertainers and groups that have never been to Chechnya before.'

'So you also organise concerts and other activities?'

'Yes.'

'In other words, you do exactly the same as all the other departments?'

'I don't really know, I've only just started here. Only been here three weeks. But no, we don't do the same thing as all the others. We think of new things. We organise events and concerts we've never had before. Now we're going to hand out a calendar with quotations from Akhmed Kadyrov. That hasn't been done before.'

Quotations from Akhmed Kadyrov are hanging on the wall. For example: *I go forward bravely, because I know Ramzan is watching my back.*

We go through the door that says Patriotic Development Department. Ruslan is sitting behind a desk. He's a little older than those working in the other departments.

'We're getting ready for 9 May,' he says. 'That's when the young people and the veterans will meet here to remember Akhmed Kadyrov. It's very important,' he assures me.

'What's the most important thing the Patriotic Development Department does?'

'Our main job, the overriding aim, is to get young people to report for military service and to encourage their interest in the army. At the moment, no Chechens serve outside the republic. The past is too close; many have something to avenge. And then there is *dedovshina* – brutal bullying from older soldiers – a lot of abuse, unfortunately. As things are now, the Chechens all stay here, in the guard, in the police force, in railway and construction brigades. We're trying hard to get young men drafted at sixteen. They should already be getting military training at school, theoretical as well practical. Sports training ought to be based on military exercises. We teach children to strip a weapon, yes, even an automatic weapon, because it's important to know how guns work. Then we arrange competitions to see who can take a weapon apart and put it back together again the fastest. What's more, they compete in hurdling, press-ups and other tests of strength . . . The army gets people fit and active. They get a different view of the world.'

'What sort of view?'

'They start to see the world through different eyes.'

'For the better?'

'Yes. Of course for the better.'

'How so?'

'People leave the military wiser and more mature than when they entered it. They start to think. Before the wars, young people weren't interested in anything, the Soviet system had made them passive; everyone was supposed to be equal, but the Russians controlled everything anyway. Now young people are interested in so many things – sport, art, religion. Religion is the only real way to get rid of crime, to teach people, improve them, purify them. We've got a new start because of our great leader, Ramzan Akhmatovich Kadyrov. And you know what? Ramzan was almost in tears when he saw everything we'd done here in the Youth Palace. He's satisfied with us, he supports us.'

'Isn't it rather you who support him?'

'Yes, of course. *My odna kommanda.* We are one team.'

Ruslan looks straight at me.

'And you must also write that we publish lots of journals and brochures.'

'That's wonderful. I'd like to read them.'

'Well, my information secretary isn't in at the moment. We haven't got any here, but I think she has some copies at home,' he says, and I thank him for his time.

'We must never forget who we are,' he adds, as we say good-bye. 'What's needed now is patriotism, tradition, history. So much has been lost, burned. The library lost nearly all its books. The museum nearly all its paintings.

'So much death,' Ruslan sighs. 'So much shattered innocence.'

We next go to meet one of the Youth Palace leaders. Baslan is tall and energetic with a nice haircut, like a college boy in a 1980s American film, and dresses like a young Western conservative politician would. His hair is reddish-brown, his eyes brown, his pale skin lightly freckled. Typical Chechen colouring. Behind him hangs the flag of the Russian youth movement Nashi, 'Ours', a diagonal white X that stretches to all four corners, on a red back-ground. Baslan is the leader in Nashi's Chechen branch and in Vladimir Putin's party, United Russia.

'Nashi is a democratic anti-fascist youth movement. We are a hundred per cent democratic,' Baslan begins. 'Last year there was a summer camp with five thousand commissars from all over Russia. I was one of them. Before there were pioneer camps; now Nashi has camps. There are lectures on economics, patriotism, society – very interesting, a kind of educational camp. He who has knowledge owns the world. And, just think, Ramzan came too. See that picture on the wall of Ramzan and me? It's from that camp. I'm very proud of it.'

Baslan has the same picture on his cell phone. As time passes I notice that Ramzan's ministers, his relations and even casual acquaintances have pictures of him on their cell phones. Everyone who has ever been photographed with Ramzan seems to use it as a screen saver.

'EVERYTHING is thanks to Ramzan,' Baslan assures me. 'But we do some things ourselves. We distribute calendars, we hang posters. On 8 March we gave roses to all the women in Grozny, a gift from Ramzan. We made a video of that. Would you like to see it?'

Baslan summons an office boy, who finds the right clip. It shows young United Russia supporters in blue jerkins handing out roses in the streets. 'A present from Ramzan to you,' they say. One woman cries: 'No one has ever given me roses in my whole life, and now Ramzan's doing it. You're my hero, Ramzan!'

'Very moving,' I say.

Baslan drums on his desk with a pen. 'I'd like to be at the Estonian embassy in Moscow at the moment. With others from Nashi.'

When the Estonian government wanted to move the memorial to the Second World War dead – represented by a Soviet soldier in bronze – it made the Russians seethe. They massed around the bronze soldier in Tallinn, one man was killed in the riots. Meanwhile, demonstrators barricaded the Estonian embassy in Moscow. In no time they'd stuck up printed posters proclaiming 'Estonia is a Fascist Country'; they also had jerseys, T-shirts, jackets and hats bearing anti-Estonian slogans. Tents with identical messages appeared outside the embassy, the young people played ear-splitting music night and day, assaulted anyone who visited the embassy, and tore the flag off the Swedish ambassador's car. All this while the police stood by and watched.'

'What else do you do for young people?'

'We've just finished petitioning; we collected twenty thousand signatures requesting the erection of a statue of Nikita Khrushchev.'

'Why do that?'

'He was the one who brought us back to our fatherland after Stalin and Beria had banished us. Following his speech at the Twentieth Party Congress in 1956, we were rehabilitated. Ramzan supports us in this. He has promised that a street in Grozny will be named after Khrushchev.'

'I'm struck by how much of what you do concerns the past, the Soviet past,' I remark. Is that what happens when the present is too dangerous and too confusing?

'We are patriots. That's why we're concerned about the past. We support Russia and belong here. Russia has become stronger with Putin, and I'm happy about that. We try to help the government, Russian and Chechen. That's our job.'

'Human rights violations, Baslan, many of them committed by the government's own security forces. Doesn't that worry you?'

'In war, human rights will always be violated. After war, as well. You know, if someone destroys your house and doesn't rebuild it, then your human rights are already violated. But now we're rebuilding Grozny. You've seen that, haven't you?'

'What about the people who have disappeared?'

'The police are working on that. I think they will put things straight.'

'And the lack of press freedom?'

Baslan gives me a slightly worried look.

'Sometimes the mass media are too free, as when they wrote that our president had killed Anna Politkovskaya. They shouldn't be allowed to spread such false accusations. I call that irresponsible writing. I call that gossip.'

Each sentence is spoken emphatically.

'When the gossip got printed, we wrote an open letter to the newspapers saying that Chechen youth didn't believe our president had killed her.'

A squeal of brakes outside. Through the window we see the plaza filling up with black-clad men in bulletproof vests carrying guns and automatic weapons. This can mean only one thing: Ramzan is coming. My minder hustles me away from the window.

'But I want to watch,' I protest.

'No, you can't stand there, it's not allowed. Come out this way!'

'But it's interesting watching him arrive.'

'It's not allowed!'

Because I take such tiny steps we don't get out of sight in time; we are standing on the landing when Ramzan and his entourage hurry past. Jogging as usual, they take the stairs two at a time. Into the office of the Youth Palace leader – personally appointed by Ramzan, of course. A dozen guards occupy the sofas in the leader's waiting room and my minder orders me outside.

'*Nel'zya*,' my Ramzan says harshly. *Nel'zya* is stronger than *nyet*, meaning 'no' or 'not'. *Nel'zya* means 'forbidden' or 'never'.

'*Nel'zya smotret!*' You're not allowed to watch!

I'm driven back to the Astoria.

Ramzan doesn't say a word. I had looked at his boss without permission.

The next day I'm at the Youth Palace again to meet the chairman of the Ramzan fan club. He is sitting with his feet on the desk, but lowers them when I come in and begins rotating his chair instead.

'You could actually say that the whole republic is one big presidential fan club, because we've never seen anything like him before! He's a fantastic man. So unpretentious, so much his own person, so easy to talk to. As you know, people at that level usually have their minds on other things. I'll never forget my first meeting with him; it was so warm, so special. At first we were all very nervous, but as soon as Ramzan arrived, everything was so easy. We still talk about that meeting; it's something I'll remember for the rest of my life.'

'What did the two of you talk about?'

'Plans.'

'What kind of plans?'

'He asks us to be ourselves. That's all. But plans, well, we planned an event. We gave out T-shirts to fifteen thousand people in the Chechen colours, and then we laid them out on the plaza to look like our flag! He was really pleased when he saw that!'

The chairman smiles.

'Ramzan recently gave away three thousand cars. To ordinary people. To the neediest. That's how he is, he helps people. He gave cars to the poor, well, not only to them, but to deserving people too. The fan club got three cars to travel around in, two Gazelles – minibuses – and a Zhiguli 110. Just for me . . . me. Personally. Hah! The thought never crossed my mind that I'd benefit from this, and suddenly I have a car. And an office! Now we've got computers, printers, scanners, photo equipment, a video, a DVD player. But the most important thing is this: he gave us the republic, a republic in which buildings and roads are being constructed. And he gave us hope. In a year's time there won't be any unemployment here, I promise. *May Allah give us strength and courage, and give us a head with which to use them.* That's a quote from Akhmed Kadyrov, peace be with him,' says the chairman, and continues:

'We Chechens are hotheaded. I think Pushkin said that the Chechens can either love or wage war. There is no third way. Either love or wage war. We have several hundred active members. Girls, too. We specifically included girls, because without girls we might look like a gang, and people might say we are this, that and the other. We have girls with us to show we're civilised.

'Ramzan has said that he'll make sure he doesn't lose power. Let's have an election; we'll show people that ninety-nine point nine per cent support Ramzan, and that everyone votes. We've paid dearly for other types of leader. One started a war, another couldn't stop it, a third started a new war. Ramzan should stay in office for the rest of his life. The same with Putin, he's strong and he's smart.

'War – that's just for those who profit from it or who are sick in the head. There's nothing worse than war. We've seen a lot, we've seen dogs eat corpses, seen it here in Grozny. It stays in your mind for the rest of your life. The rest of the world is flourishing, and we sit here with terrible memories. The guilty ones are no longer to be found. Russia isn't guilty. And it wasn't the Chechen people who fought against Russia, it was the separatists.'

'Akhmed Kadyrov believed that Chechnya needed a dictator. What do you think?' I ask the chairman.

'Everything he said was right; he did the only right thing. Remember that every fifth Chechen was a wahhabist at that time. They've been converted now, they build houses, have ordinary jobs, and the guilty ones have been killed. All thanks to Ramzan. He's a good friend to everyone.'

'There's a lot of criticism of his brutal methods, torture, executions . . .'

'The people who criticise – have they even been here? How could I criticise you – for example, tell anyone that you aren't beautiful – if I hadn't seen you? Of course, I can also go on the Internet and start criticising. Every single letter of the alphabet can be criticised, because it's round and not square, because it doesn't smell like French perfume. Forget the critics! Do I, for example, have the right to criticise the President of Norway even if I don't know a single thing about Norway? Just six months ago you couldn't have walked around here without an armed guard; the wahhabists could have kidnapped you. Now you're completely safe, because of Ramzan. And plans? Yes, we've got plans . . . we're planning a trip to the mountains; we'll take horses, ride into the mountains, have a picnic. You're welcome to come along. Can you ride? The mountains are pretty wild. The weather just needs to get a little warmer, and then we'll go . . .'

*

It is 8 May. My Ramzan has taken me to Dynamo Stadium which is about to be reopened three years after Akhmed Kadyrov was blown to pieces while seated in the place of honour there. The chairs on the platform for the dignitaries are green and white, the pillars are alternately metallic and blue, freshly painted, and the artificial grass newly laid. The stadium has a boxing club and a football club, halls for judo and table tennis, locker rooms, VIP areas, and a soldier stationed every metre or so.

'A month and a half,' the construction minister's press secretary, Marina, whispers in my ear. 'Forty-five days! In March there was just a big hole here, and now, a brand-new, gleaming stadium. Impressive, isn't it?'

I nod.

'Eight hundred houses, forty streets and three bridges,' Marina continues. She rolls her eyes, as if to suggest I should take out my notebook and write down eight hundred houses, forty streets and three bridges. I do so.

Marina is beautiful and well groomed, like all the women I meet in the inner circles of power.

'Do you want to interview the construction minister?' she asks. But then the deputy construction minister summons her to straighten the red brocade cloth with gold fringes that covers the table where the guests will sit. It turns out that the stadium is not opening tomorrow as had been expected, but today.

'That's always how it is,' says my Ramzan with a meaningful look. 'It's lucky we were here. Otherwise we would have missed it. You never know where the president will be. He just shows up!'

I've been seated in a chair and told to wait three hours. So I sit there watching the final preparations for the opening.

The deputy construction minister is also a woman. She and Marina trip about on stilettos that sink into the grass.

'I thought we were just coming for an inspection today,' Marina confides as she sashays past me. 'Security. Top secret,' she giggles.

Two more women in stilettos arrive with a bucket. They wash

the table legs under the brocade. The guards hang around us, all tough-looking men with rifles, pistols and walkie-talkies. Marina asks if I have a paper tissue. She dips it in mineral water, then she and the deputy construction minister polish the delicate water glasses until they gleam spotlessly in the bright sunlight.

The armed men remind me of years back, when I spent weeks with the rebels. They would come and go in the villages, clean their rifles, eat, rest, watch TV, plan new tactics, then kneel in prayer before leaving for their mountain bases or for a night attack. They are all the same men, have the same look in their eyes, the same determination. In war as in peace. In battle as at some ceremony. They're just different assignments.

The men aren't just similar, they are the same. Most of Kadyrov's guards are former rebel soldiers who accepted an offer of amnesty. The reprieve was given on one condition: that they went straight into Kadyrov's forces. Otherwise, they were branded as outlaws.

The same is true of the women. Women who were once in their village kitchens cooking, washing, watching over the rebels, now polish glasses for the president's celebration.

Finally the construction minister himself has time to talk to me. He is a solid fellow and sits down firmly on one of the chairs.

'A month and a half ago we got an order from Ramzan that the stadium reconstruction was to be completed for 9 May. It was sink or swim. We were working until three o'clock this morning. Ramzan came every week to check on our progress; at any time – during the day, in the evening, even in the middle of the night I had to be ready.'

The construction minister is interrupted by a shout: 'They're coming! They're coming!'

About thirty silver-grey cars drive up to the VIP entrance at rally speed, sending up showers of gravel. Young women in traditional dresses and young men with long swords are lined up as a guard of honour. Photographers and ministers flock to the scene. Ramzan!

The construction minister runs towards the crowd as fast as his legs will carry him. He wants to be part of it too, get his slap on the back.

The entourage comes jogging across the artificial grass, like a football team heading for the fans. Ramzan Kadyrov seems to like running, so of course everyone else has to run, too. Cheerful music is playing. The group takes its place on the white plastic chairs. The speeches begin. Ramzan wriggles about in his seat. Cracks his knuckles, stretches his legs. Laughs and talks during the speeches. Only when some little boys demonstrate their karate skills does he sit quietly. He claps and shouts happily when they sling each other to the ground. All eyes are on him. When he laughs, they laugh. When he stands up, they stand up.

The stadium is officially opened. It's time for the football match. The president's administration against parliament. The men disappear into the new locker rooms and reappear in football kit. Ramzan Kadyrov wears white shirt and shorts. He is captain of the president's team. The leader of parliament is captain of the opposing team, which wears red. The referee blows his whistle. The men lumber around on the new field.

Then Ramzan scores. Of course he does.

The next day I am invited to the village of Tsentoroi. The Kadyrov clan's home. To get in is like entering a fortress. First you go through several red and brown arches guarded by men dressed in black; at the entrance to the village heavily armed men turn the car inside out, and you need a written pass or to be on a list in order to proceed any further. Beyond the barricades the village is like any other: cattle wander around in the streets, children play, old men sit outside their houses. But one thing distinguishes it from other villages: the palaces. Not even the tall gates can hide the towers behind them. We drive past the high fence in front of Ramzan's mansion. This is where he has his firing range, his deer park, his race track, his dog-fighting arena. It is also behind this fence that, according to witnesses, he has his private prisons.

They tell about torture. Only some have come out alive, and few have told their stories. In the closely knit Chechen society, the entire family is in danger if a victim of torture breaks his silence. Those who dare are those who no longer have anything to lose.

Sultan drives me and my minder towards the home of Magomed Kadyrov, Ramzan's uncle and deputy agriculture minister, where the ceremony of remembrance for the president's father will be held. This is a day of sorrow, and my guardian angel has given me strict instructions to buy a dark headscarf. Magomed receives me at the gate. I am the only foreign, and, for that matter, the only female, guest.

In the assembled crowd, my Ramzan gives me instructions:

'Make sure you don't touch anyone with your hands. That would sully them and they'd have to wash. Don't come near anyone with your body. Don't meet anyone's eyes. Look down!'

The plan is doomed from the start; several hundred people are crammed into the uncle's backyard. In order to watch the men dancing *zikr*, I tuck my hands into the sleeves of my respectable brown jacket and wander around, with my arms held protectively out in front of me so that, if the worst comes to the worst, people will only bump into my elbows. It works fine; most people move aside when they see me, anyway.

In the middle of the courtyard hundreds of men are running around after each other in circles ten deep. This is the Sufi prayer dance – *zikr*. The dancers clap in a quick rhythmic tempo as an older man calls out in a loud plaintive voice: *La ilaha il Allah, la ilaha il Allah!* There is no God but Allah! The prayers get faster and faster, louder and louder; the men's faces become flushed and shining, sweat drips down their backs, soaks through their shirts. The oldest dance in the innermost circle, where they can take shorter steps. In the outermost circles, the young boys gallop like stallions to keep up with those in the middle. The goal of the Sufi dance is to reach ecstasy, and in that way get closer to God. The faces of those approaching that state become even redder, their eyes glisten, the stamping grows fiercer, and they break into wild howls. Then the tempo decreases and they tramp after each other, still rhythmically, but barely lifting their feet. The dance goes on for hours, without stopping, but with varying degrees of intensity.

Ramzan does not take part in the prayer ritual. He sits with his protégés in one of the uncle's living rooms. Plate after plate of steaming mutton seasoned with herbs is carried in to the president and his men. Dishes of garlic sauce, thick slices of fresh bread, salads, rice, meatballs, chicken and mineral water are set out for them.

The women dish up food in the kitchen, and the little boys serve it. After a while, I too am relegated to the busy kitchen. Here they are doing a different sort of dance: cutting and peeling, stirring and pouring. The women appear to be working equally hard, whether they are members of the president's family or not. They tell me who's who, but I get utterly confused by aunts and cousins, sisters-in-law and wives, nieces and sisters. They are all part of the Kadyrov clan in one way or another. Several have relations in Norway.

'What do they do there?' I ask.

'They are refugees.'

I throw out a careful feeler:

'What have they fled from?'

I get no answer; one woman says simply: 'They can't come back here.'

This is a pretty candid conversation for the Kadyrov kitchen, I tell myself.

'They can't get permission,' the woman continues.

'From whom?'

'From the Norwegian authorities.'

'That sounds very strange,' I say. 'Why wouldn't the Norwegian authorities give them permission to leave?'

'They can only leave after a few years. They can't visit us until they have obtained their residence papers,' she says. 'Norway doesn't allow them to come home,' the woman assures me.

The women in the kitchen believe it's time that people came home anyway. 'They can't just sit there and wait for the rest of us to rebuild the republic,' they sniff.

The day is waning and my host comes to get me. He wants me to meet the head of the family – Hoj Akhmed Kadyrov – the deceased president's eldest brother, the man with the Friday night television programme about Islam.

I am led across the courtyard to Uncle Kadyrov's chilly living room. His face is flushed after all the shouting and praying. He had prime responsibility for the family's day of remembrance.

'Just think, so many people and no trouble, no fights,' he says. 'No police, no troops. We become closer to each other in this way. There's been a stream of people here, and they were all gravitating towards God. Did you notice that? There have been people from all levels of society here, rich and poor, and no one went home empty-handed. Did you notice that people took gifts home with them? It was from our brother, peace be with him, from his fund; they gave out a lot of money today. Everyone prayed in the same circle, in the same *zikr*. Did you see how people listened to me? If I spoke – even without using the loudspeakers – everything went quiet. That's our tradition; you listen to the person in charge.'

I ask him to tell me more about the Chechen form of Sufism with mysticism and ecstasy at its heart.

'*Zikr* is our prayer. Circle prayer. It has helped us for centuries. Hadj Kunta brought it with him from his travels to Mecca and Baghdad. He was born around 1830 and knew the Koran by heart when he was ten years old. In those days there was strong opposition to the Russians. The Chechens fought courageously. We needed strength from God, and Hadj Kunta introduced us to the loud *zikr* with song and dance. But Imam Shamil, who was our leader then, preferred the gentler form of prayer. We find God through *zikr*. Sufism is independent of any nation and does not need mosques. Everything is found within the individual. That's why it has endured – through the Tsar's invasion, Stalin's oppression, deportation, wars. That's why what we have seen today –

honouring my brother's memory – is so important. Sufism is closeness and love for our fellow human beings, respect for each other, and total opposition to violence.'

'But few places in the world are more violent than Chechnya?'

'Other people have brought the violence. We're only defending ourselves. First against the Russians, then against the wahhabists.'

'How could the wahhabists get such a strong foothold if the Chechens were so united by Sufism?'

'Because our young people didn't know any better, had no education. There was widespread unemployment, people were easily influenced, and the wahhabists took advantage of that. The young people wanted to lead grand, beautiful lives, and they were bought off by the Arabs, who ruined the next generation. We thought we could get help from both God and Satan without having to change ourselves, but we were wrong. People came here under the flag of Islam and took advantage of us. They had dollars and weapons. And here in Chechnya they found the justification they needed to force their way into Russia, in order to destroy Russia. They were like Stalin, but on a different level. Those who followed them didn't know anything, didn't own anything, had no work, no money, no home. And a lot of blood got spilled. Fortunately, that's all over now. I want to educate the new generation with good, pure thoughts. Because of my fame, I'm able to reach many people. I have my own television programme, I work with the newspapers, and all my proclamations are collected and published. In any case, everything will be fine now, because we have Ramzan! He's like a son to me, and he's on the right path!'

16

War and Peace

It was a strange invitation I had received. 'The president is expecting you,' it said. The prime minister, Abdulkahir Izrailov, who lived just across the hall from me at the Astoria, said every morning: 'It may happen at any time – today, tomorrow, this afternoon, this evening. We'll let you know.'

So I had plenty of time to get to know the Green Zone. I even made a friend: Svetlana from Severodvinsk in the Arkhangelsk district was one of the soldiers who guarded the entrance to the Astoria.

"Do you want to see the beach?' she asked one day when she went off duty.

We walked down the asphalt road towards the Russian base. 'She's with me,' Svetlana said proudly when we passed the last barrier into the camp.

The 'beach' was three iron beds in a bombed-out hangar. During the day, under the blazing Caucasian sun, this was the girls' space. They took their mattresses there after duty. Armoured tanks were parked next to the beds. Here at the outer edge of the Green Zone, the listing buildings and barbed wire fences looked like bits of stage scenery that were about to collapse. Virginia creeper coiled around the cracked cement pillars.

'People in Severodvinsk will wonder where I've been when

they see how tanned I am,' beamed the blonde woman, who seemed to glow even more with every day of service in the Caucasus.

'Come on, I'll show you something,' she said, and took my hand.

Behind the ruins and the scrap heap some tall bushes grew.

'Blackberries! Try one! Aren't they good? But watch out, they turn your mouth blue and your fingers purple!'

We threw ourselves wholeheartedly into scoffing this Caucasian variety of blackberry. 'I've put on five kilos here. Soon I won't fit into my uniform! But I'll freeze them off in Severodvinsk, I'm sure,' laughed my new friend.

Svetlana's contract earned her twice as much money as the other soldiers. Putin had reinstated certain privileges for northerners, the extra pay that had disappeared under Yeltsin, and the soldiers from Arkhangelsk got monthly wages of 15,000 roubles, about £350. The tough blonde had a ten-year-old daughter and a boyfriend who was a submarine captain. She was going home soon. The train journey north took four days.

'Oh, Severodvinsk is so wonderful! I'll take you on a submarine. Would you like that? And now there's so much life in the city. It was dying under Yeltsin. No one got paid, everything went rusty. We've been saved by the Iranians, the Indians, the Chinese. They get military training from us, on condition that they buy Russian equipment. Many apartment blocks have virtually only Indians and Iranians living in them. They're really nice people. They got our city moving again. Without them, we would have had to shut down Severodvinsk completely. In the evening, the schools are full of people learning Russian!'

Svetlana wanted to show me the barracks she shared with four other young women. It was just big enough for two bunk beds along its length and one along its width. The walls were papered with magazine pictures of fashion models. A faint scent of perfume hung in the air, and above each bed dangled a net for private possessions, cosmetics, a magazine, a torch. At the end of the barracks lacy panties and bras, one red and two black, were hanging out to dry. From the doorstep you could reach the neighbouring barracks without getting your feet wet if you took big steps. It was inhabited by three young men from Lipetsk, all tank crewmen. None of them had bothered to paper the walls, but there was an enormous calendar with three naked women hanging on the end wall.

Aleksei came in and proudly offered us warm potato cakes dripping with golden fat, which he had fried on a gas ring outside the barracks.

'Eat them while they're hot, I'll fry some more,' he said. He had made the batter with mashed potatoes, eggs and flour. Dinner in the canteen, pale, quivering macaroni with a pat of butter and a can of sardines, did not satisfy Aleksei.

'You should have been here in 2001,' he said. 'Then there was plenty of action.'

'Now everything is so boring,' said Igor, the tank driver, with a yawn.

'How are things in the city?' asked Oleg. 'What's the mood?'

Russian soldiers couldn't walk about freely in the city. It was too dangerous, they said. There was a great deal of hatred simmering below the surface; many had much to avenge. Sure enough, posters all over the city showed Putin and Kadyrov shaking hands; but among the people, the abuses were not forgotten. Unarmed Russians on the street? No, it was too soon for that.

'They're wild,' said Igor. 'There will never be peace here.'

'Would you like to see a clip of Chechens slitting the throats of two Russians?' Svetlana asked suddenly. I declined. 'The Russians sit there with their hands tied behind them. Then one of them is grabbed by the hair and – swish – his throat gets slit and the blood streams out. The other man cries: "*Ne nado! Ne nado! Khochu zhit!* Stop! Don't do it! I want to live!" Then they kill him too.'

Svetlana gave me a meaningful look. 'That's how they are here. But it's different with us northerners.'

'Just as bad abuses occurred on our side,' Oleg interjected. 'I was here in 2000. Innocent Chechens got slaughtered. Civilians were caught between us and the rebels. It was dreadful.'

This was unusual coming from a Russian officer.

'Why did you choose to come here?'

'My wife hasn't got a job, we have three daughters, the youngest is two and a half, and there's no kindergarten,' Aleksei replied. 'We barely manage on my army pay. Last year my wife preserved two hundred and eighty jars of tomatoes, gherkins, mushrooms and other good things, so every day, all winter and through the spring, we had vegetables on the table. But the earth in Lipetsk is sandy and poor, so it's hard work growing food.'

'Do you want to meet our commander?' Svetlana asked suddenly.

The commander sat in a small vehicle, a kind of caravan without wheels that contained a desk, a map and a computer.

'A writer?'

I nodded.

'That's a hard job,' he said, and asked me to sit down. 'Dostoyevsky is difficult, oh so difficult to read. I like Ilf and Petrov best, do you know them? *The Twelve Chairs*. They wrote together. Absurd, satirical books. One of them worked out the structure, the other wrote the dialogue. That's clever, isn't it? Do you need a co-author?'

'I once acted in *The Wedding* by Ilf and Petrov at the University of Oslo. I had one line,' I bragged.

'Lots of people believe that Tolstoy wrote *War and Peace* with his wife, that he wrote the outline and the parts about the war, while she wrote the parts that dealt with women and everyday life. One literary critic thought that Tolstoy couldn't possibly have written all of that himself, because there's such a difference in style between the war scenes and the domestic scenes. The births, for example, how could a man—?'

'But isn't this precisely the genius of Tolstoy, that he manages to portray a woman's emotional life so well, for example in *Anna Karenina*?' I protested.

'And while he was writing he never knew what she would do next, no matter how strict a framework he'd created! I think he was completely in love with his character. What do you think?'

The commander sat with his arms crossed and, without waiting for a reply, continued:

'Today, Anna could just get a divorce, and then she could have Vronsky! She wouldn't have had to throw herself under a train. Now people get divorced very easily. No one kills themselves for love any longer.'

'Oh yes, there are still lots of people who jump from high buildings or in front of a tube train,' Svetlana declared. 'Especially men; they don't cope with love as well as women do.'

'Emotionally, women are certainly stronger, that's true,' the commander philosophised. 'Coffee?'

He brought out a tin with coffee beans rattling around in the bottom. 'This isn't espresso! It's field coffee. Grit, they call it in Brazil – the grit they find on the road. It's the stuff that has fallen off the trucks from the coffee plantations – that's what they send to the war here. Ha, ha! I hope it tastes good!'

Perhaps he had chosen the wrong career, this literature-loving commander, because he became far more taciturn when I asked about the situation in Chechnya. Yes, and hmm, he replied to my questions. We'll see. Impossible to predict. Time will tell.

'There are attacks on Russian soldiers every day,' Svetlana said to me. 'At least, that's what we find out, even if it's not reported in the newspapers. A couple of days ago two boys from Komi were killed.'

The commander set his cup down firmly on the table. The conversation was over.

'You're welcome to come again,' he said, and asked for my autograph. 'In case you become famous, ha, ha!' His thickset body shook with laughter.

It was almost midnight. I had to leave. My interview with the president might take place the next morning. I was was worried I might meet the prime minister, who lived just across from me.

Perhaps he wouldn't like me fraternising with the Russians. I fell asleep behind bullet-proof windows, to the rattle of the water pipes, and protected by three cordons.

During the night I was woken by a loud noise and a splash. I leaped up, and in the moonlight saw bits of plaster flying about. Part of the ceiling had fallen into the basin that collected the dripping water.

June arrives. The government becomes less vigilant about my supervision, and my minder is bored with me. On Russia's Constitution Day, 12 June, I am totally forgotten, and wander around the city on my own. It is the first time Russia's Constitution Day has been celebrated in Grozny.

Russian and Chechen flags fill Akhmed Kadyrov Plaza, where an inflatable stage bearing the words 'Government Committee for Youth Affairs' has been set up beside his statue.

One of my regular lunch companions from the government complex, Adlan, the prime minister's adviser, comes on stage in a dark suit and light blue tie.

'Look around you! See the mosque rising behind you! See how the city is being rebuilt! All of it thanks to Ramzan, our leader!' he shouts.

People applaud and wave small paper flags.

'We must defend Russia's unity! We are the defenders of Russia's southern front. We are united! We are strong!' cries Adlan. 'We must rally around Ramzan Kadyrov! And we must support Putin!'

Then he reads a poem. I am surprised when he says that it is by Omar Yarchev, a poet I interviewed about a year and a half ago. At that time Yarchev lived as a refugee outside Grozny. He had nailed cardboard along the walls to keep out the cold and the icy wind. In his room he had a bookcase filled with his treasures: Dante, Petrarch, Homer, Shakespeare, Pasternak, Yesenin, Pushkin.

'Ah, Pushkin,' he had cried, and began to recite:

Across the steppes the devil leads our sleigh.
Look, there he is! See him play —
Blowing, spitting on me, circling round
Until the horse falls to the ground.

'Blok, the last genius!' he had continued. 'Tsvetayeva, first-rate, and Mandelstam, poor Osip.'

His bookcase consisted of six wide shelves; once there had been glass in the doors, now only one pane remained. He had bought the bookcase in Alma-Ata, while still in exile in Kazakhstan. His love of poetry had been born with the help of the Russian librarian at his school in Kazakhstan. His parents had never owned a book. 'The Soviet era was better than now,' he said to me.

What had happened? Was it love of Russian culture that now made him write poetry for the elite? 'You have to reconcile yourself to the inevitable,' he had said to me. Was it the same fatalism that made him write a poem to Ramzan?

At the end of the tunnel, in utter darkness,
Suddenly glowed a saving flame —
Of God's will . . . and Chechnya's
Kadyrov — the young man —
Became our president.

Once he sought his fate
With his father, weapon in hand.
Today amidst the unrest
He leads us — as Allah's will decreed.

Results, not papers, matter most to him.
He can both praise and scold.
Ramzan's duty — to work for our greatest good.
Our duty — to help him do it.

So that life will be peaceful and good
And we'll sit as friends at a common table,
So that Russia will be strong
And Chechnya will be mighty!

After Yarchev's tribute, a representative of the Young Guard takes the stage.

'We are united!' he shouts. 'Our opponents are weak; some live in the past, others on another planet – in the West. Russia is one nation, and she is united. The nation stands firmly, and all right-minded youth believe Putin should stay in office. We are the President's Guard! The Young Guard! We salute Putin! Putin and Ramzan, we are ready to support your ideas!'

'The Final Countdown' rings out across the plaza. A thin Chechen with a bass guitar slung across his chest sings in an increasingly quavering voice: 'We're leaving toge-e-e-e-ether . . .!'

Standing next to me are two pretty girls wearing T-shirts with a picture of Ramzan. 'Forward Only!' the T-shirts say on the front. On the back, 'Ramzan Patriot Club'.

'Where did you get the T-shirts?' I ask.

'They handed them out at the university. All the students got one. And little flags,' they say, waving the paper flags that they are holding.

'Why are you here?'

'Why?'

'Yes . . .'

'Everybody has to be here,' they reply easily. 'If you don't come you'll be punished.'

'Punished?'

'Anyone who doesn't come is registered as absent. Our teachers go around with lists and cross off the names,' one of the girls tells me.

'You won't be expelled if you're not here,' adds the other girl when she sees the look of surprise on my face. 'You'll just get penalised. If you break the rules several times, you lose your place at the university.'

After a while they become uneasy with my questions: 'In any case, we came mainly for the concert. Let's listen.'

One speaker after another takes the stage, but the public's enthusiasm diminishes with the increasing number of poems and tributes. Eventually the Youth Palace's royal emissaries begin to complain about the audience they have summoned.

'I'm a bit surprised you're so passive!' a young man shouts from the stage. Nothing happens. He tries another tactic.

'Who is our president?'

A scattered response is heard, but it's not strong, not enthusiastic. Not the way the princes and princesses of the Youth Palace want it. The young man tries again.

'Ramzan!' comes the reply, a little louder this time.

The speaker on the stage doesn't try a third time, and lets a girl in a Ramzan shirt and Young Guard headscarf introduce the next poetry reader.

'Where are your flags?' she coaxes.

No matter how much she tries, she gets no more than a lukewarm response from the crowd.

'Look around you! Who can we thank?'

But people aren't listening any longer; most of them are talking in small groups.

'WHO IS OUR PRESIDENT?'

It's Baslan from the Youth Palace, shouting at the top of his voice.

People play along with him.

'Ramzan!'

'*Allah akbar*,' comes from the stage.

Now people have started to go home.

A group of boys is hanging around a United Russia flag with a white bear on a blue background, the emblem of Vladimir Putin's party. When I ask what they are doing here, they start to laugh.

'We don't really know,' one answers.

'Because you're patriots?' I suggest.

'Well . . .' They laugh again.

'That's what it says on your T-shirts,' I continue.

'If it says "I'm a rocker" on my T-shirt, does that make me a rocker?'

They are all wearing caps that say 'United for Ramzan'.

'To be honest, we didn't have any choice. The dean ordered us to be here. We were told that we would lose our scholarships or get lower grades if we didn't attend.'

The flag with the bear had been thrust into their hands when they arrived at the plaza.

The boys laugh when I ask what they are studying.

'It doesn't really matter,' they say. 'We're enrolled in the Oil Institute. But what will we do with a diploma? You can buy one. Everything can be bought here. A diploma means nothing if you don't have connections. In order to get a job, connections are the most important thing; money, then intelligence. That's why there are so many unintelligent people in control here. Brains mean little these days.'

'There's no freedom here,' one of the boys says loudly enough to be heard above the traditional Chechen dance music coming from the podium. 'And there's no democracy either, even if they shout about it from the stage. There is one leader, one direction, one policy, and *he* does whatever he wants.'

One of the boys takes me aside.

'I want to tell you something,' he says. He leads me away before he whispers: 'I'm a relation of Alu Alkhanov, the former president. People disappear at night. They never return. If they're critical, they lose their lives. People are afraid. In two years there will be another civil war. For the moment, Kadyrov has support, but he'll soon be a political corpse. And what will happen to him if he's overthrown? He'll have nothing left then. People are with him only because he has power and money. One of my friends was arrested, and came back with wounds all over his body. Here,' he says, pointing. 'On his wrists he had deep . . .'

'What are you telling her? Let me see your documents! And yours, too!'

A brusque man is suddenly standing between us. He is wearing civilian clothes, is tall and powerfully built. The boy I was talking to has assumed a stony expression. Out of the corner of my eye I see his friends' terrified faces as they back away. Behind the tall man in civilian clothes come ten armed men in uniform.

The man pulls out a card. He is the head of a police department in the Chechen Interior Ministry.

I take out my credentials from the Russian Foreign Ministry and the card from the Interior Ministry that allows me to visit counter-terrorist operations zones.

'Show me what you've written! What did the boys say to you?'

He grabs the notebook out of my hands.

'I don't read English,' he sniffs.

'This is Norwegian. Shall I read it for you?'

I start at the beginning of the day's notes and rattle off bits from the speeches, 'Thanks to Ramzan', 'Thanks to Putin', 'Rally around Russian unity', 'A strong Russia', and from the poem: *"Ramzan's duty – to work for our greatest good. Our duty – to help him do it"*. I read it in great detail, all the phrases I've scribbled down. Then I read everything the right-minded students had said. 'We support our president', 'We are happy to have the opportunity to praise him.'

'Shall I continue?' I interrupt myself.

He gives me an angry look.

'Where is your guard?'

'I haven't got a guard.'

'Why not?'

'Ask the people who didn't give me one.'

'And who are they?'

'I'm here at the invitation of the Chechen government.'

'And where is your group?'

'I haven't got a group.'

'Why not?'

'Because I don't like groups.'

'It's dangerous here, you need a guard.'

'President Ramzan Kadyrov says that Chechnya is the safest republic in all Russia. This is a free country, after all. Isn't it?'

The policeman standing nearest to me nods in agreement.

'You have freedom and democracy, and people can say whatever they wish; that's what they just said on the stage.'

'Yes,' says the police chief. 'We just have to make sure that people don't say the wrong thing to you. Things that aren't true. We have to make sure that people tell the truth.'

'And there is just one truth?'

'Yes, of course,' he replies. 'Surely the truth can't be two things?'

17

His Father's Son

The cars glide towards the city like a chain of silver bullets. Streaking over worn grey asphalt, they speed through pedestrian crossings, tear across intersections, thread their way inward, and reach the city centre. Oncoming drivers pull as far over to the side as possible and no one crosses the street, because traffic lights do not apply equally to everybody.

The silver bullets are the latest Zhigulis, Russia's own 'people's car'. In one of them sits Ramzan.

There are seldom fewer than thirty cars in the president's entourage. They are conspicuous for their speed, their utter disregard for personal safety, and for the drivers' audacious antics.

'You have to be able to drive as fast as a flying bullet,' says Sultan.

'To avoid getting hit, you mean?'

'Yep.'

'How fast does a bullet fly?'

'Seventy-five metres a second.'

We are whizzing along ourselves at a hundred and twenty kilometres an hour on bumpy roads, far above my comfort level. We drive through the centre of Argun.

'We always used to speed up here,' Sultan tells me. 'This is where the Islamists shot at us when they saw the government plates on our cars. The faster you drive, the less chance you have of getting hit, of course. The minimum speed for Kadyrov's cars is a hundred and thirty kilometres an hour; they can't drive slower than that. It's too dangerous. Usually they stay at around a hundred and eighty.'

When our silver-grey convoy reaches the Green Zone, the barricades had better be open. Because Ramzan doesn't stop. Some of the guards lean out of the car windows with loaded weapons. Others hop out and run alongside. Many are already at the parking place to receive the procession when it pulls up in front of the government building. Ramzan leaps out of a car. Behind and in front of him rush bodyguards, secretaries, baggage handlers, helpers and political advisers.

'Russian swine,' a bodyguard hurls at the soldiers guarding the area. He aims a big gob of spit at their feet.

'How do you respond when they say things like that?' I ask afterwards.

'What *can* I say? I'm just a soldier.'

Ramzan and his retinue run past the green-clad soldiers, past the guards in suits, and bypass the electronic entrance. They dash up a broad carpeted stairway and into a foyer that serves as a reception area for two offices. One door says *Prime Minister*; the other, *President of the Republic*.

I scurry after them. Today I have been granted an audience.

Five secretaries, each behind a desk, and a profusion of body-guards are in the foyer with me. The guards stand at the doors, lounge on the sofas, saunter along the corridors. I stand glued to my position beside a plastic palm tree. All the seats in the reception area are occupied by muscular guards who massage their legs, fiddle with their cell phones, fondle their weapons. Chechnya is a land in which men sit and women stand.

A government meeting has been called on the spur of the moment. As one of the secretaries told me, Kadyrov often didn't show up when he called a meeting. The ministers all gathered and waited for hours, but Kadyrov would have had a sudden change of heart.

'Now, instead, when we know the president is on his way we quickly summon everyone. It's easier that way. They drop everything and rush over here.'

A group of men emerge, talking loudly; the ministers and some of the guards disappear. But most of them stay. The prime minister, Abdulkahir Izrailov, calls me into the next room, where yet more bodyguards are ensconced in gold velvet armchairs or perched on office chairs. Here, too, secretaries sit at their desks gazing into space. In this room I have to turn in my handbag and empty my pockets.

The door opens and the prime minister invites me to come in. Thick oriental rugs with a pink and mint design cover the floor in the oblong room. Sunlight steals through the venetian blinds and shines on to a huge table of dark polished mahogany. On one of the longer walls, heavy curtains with a gold pattern frame the rectangular windows. On a shorter wall, hanging like crossed swords, are the red and green Chechen flag and the Russian red, white and blue.

In one corner is a massive desk on which gilt pens are laid out beside a telephone and a cactus. At the far end of the room a door is slightly ajar, leading to a small bay where a bright yellow sofa shaped like a banana curves along the wall.

The first thing I notice is the enormous portrait of the president's mother and father. His mother, who is seldom seen in public, sits there with a white scarf covering her head. In the other armchair is Ramzan's father. Stiff and severe.

Their son is leaning far back in his chair sending text messages on his cell phone when I enter. The prime minister waits nervously for him to finish, but the man in an open-collared pink shirt, blue jacket and grey trousers takes his time going through the alphabetical maze of the keypad.

I look around. Across from the text-messaging president is a sculpture made out of pearls with the words 'Jeddah Chamber of Commerce and Industry' engraved on it in gold letters. It stands on a bookcase with glass doors. I read the spines. *The Importance and*

Ideas of the Koran, encyclopaedias with volumes on artillery, tanks, aeroplane technology, radioactive artillery, submarines – a volume for each weapon in the Russian defence system. Next there's a book about Chechnya's history, then *The Big Book of Aphorisms*, *Melodies of the Mountains*, *New Handbook of Essential Knowledge*, a *Latin–Russian Dictionary of Legal Terms*, a book entitled *International Labour Migration and its Significance for Russian Foreign Trade*, and finally the Russian Constitution and a book about Islamic child-rearing.

The president presses one last key, leaps up, and says:

'Fire away! Now you can ask me about everything you want to know!'

I am invited to sit down in the chair directly across from him. I turn on my digital voice recorder. On the long wall opposite the windows hang two portraits. One is of Vladimir Putin, the other of Che Guevara.

'What is Che Guevara doing here?'

Ramzan just looks at me. He smiles a little sheepishly. Did I ask a wrong question?

'Is he your hero?'

'My hero is Putin, only Putin! He's my ideal!'

Ramzan leans forward in his chair.

'He ought to be president for life. The election laws should be changed; let him keep his position as long as he is good for Russia. If Russian citizens want Russia to become a major power again, Putin should be president. I know him well, really well, and know what he has done for our country. He loves his people. He would give his life for us.'

The most absurd political drama was taking place in Moscow during the spring of 2007. One influential politician after another begged Putin to run for a third term, despite the fact that this was not allowed under the Russian Constitution.

'The Constitution can be changed,' said parliament chairman Boris Gryzlov, leader of the president's party, United Russia.

But Putin said no. 'A constitution cannot be changed except for very important reasons,' he maintained.

One of those most insistent that Putin had to stay in office was Ramzan Kadyrov. The reason is clear: he retains power in the republic as long as the Russian president wishes; with a new president, you never know. The Chechen president was firmly put in his place by Russian muftis and imams when he told all Muslims to get down on their knees and pray to Putin that he would run for a third time. 'Muslims fall to their knees only for Allah,' said the muftis.

'We can talk endlessly about finding a new president, but we'll never find anyone as good as Putin,' asserts Ramzan Kadyrov. 'In Kazakhstan, one of the world's most developed countries, the office of president can be for life. But not in Russia, not for Putin – that's completely the wrong way round. Putin is the only one who can truly defend both us and Russia's unity. "Russia is a friend of Islam," Putin said. He said it here in Grozny . . .'

'What about you? Could you imagine being president for life?'

'Being president is a great responsibility, especially for a Muslim, because he knows that he has responsibility not only for the people but for animals, too, and on Judgement Day he must answer for everything he has done. I will be president as long as my people wish, but if someone else is one rouble better than me, I will step down – in fact, even if he is only one kopek better. These aren't just words; I come from a devout family. Many people think I'm young and unpredictable, that I have my excesses, that I exaggerate. But different times demand different things of me, and you have to show your heart. I firmly believe that.'

Ramzan Kadyrov speaks poor Russian. Not all his sentences make sense. He conjugates verbs incorrectly, he uses wrong cases, the wrong gender, and has a limited vocabulary. It is said that as a boy he could not keep up at school and did not finish secondary education. Nevertheless, he was named an honorary member of the Russian Academy of Natural Sciences in 2006 during a formal ceremony in Moscow.

'How does it feel to see so many pictures of yourself everywhere?'

Ramzan bows his head modestly.

'I don't like to see myself. It makes me uncomfortable. I don't deserve it. I'm not worthy of it. But I am proud when I see Putin and my father.'

'This is actually the only office I've visited where you aren't hanging on a wall!'

'Yes, Mother and Father are here,' Ramzan replies. 'That's enough.'

'Your father maintained, and wrote in his last book, that Chechnya should be governed by a dictator, that all power should be invested in one person. What do you think about that?'

'I'm only satisfied if I have just ninety-five or ninety-seven per cent support. Then we are where we should be. That's justice. It's law and order, democracy. Then we have everything. And those who break the law should be afraid. Now we have a balance: the courts, the parliament, the administration – all are represented. Peace and stability. I demand that my men be the people's servants. Those who can't reconcile themselves to that can't work for me. No one owns anything himself. All my men know that the cars, the offices – even the ties they wear – are not theirs, but are given to them because they are the people's servants. I have state cars, a free telephone; the state does everything so that I'm able to serve the people. So I must do everything for the people. It's really they who are the masters, and we who are the servants. I never boast about myself or about all we have accomplished. I leave that to the people.'

'How have you personally helped to form Chechnya?'

'I have fulfilled my father's dream. Chechnya is now the world's most peaceful place. Not just in Russia, but in the world. You wait: soon tourists will be streaming into Chechnya. We have so much to offer. Clean air, high mountains. What have I done? I took part in the war, I was a soldier and a defender, I fought, I got rid of people, with weapon in hand, as the prophet says. I took part as a Muslim, as a Chechen, as a soldier, as a policeman; I arrested people, I interrogated them. I served my people with joy – and to great personal satisfaction, I should add. Now we are continuing the work. I can tell you that ninety-nine per cent of the war is over, only a few insignificant bandits are left. But there are bandits everywhere, in England, in Germany, in America as well. Russia's enemies should fear me. I am for justice.'

'You have been criticised for repeated violations of human rights, both now and during the war . . .'

'Hah! I don't understand these Westerners. There they are, living far away, and they think they understand the situation better than me! I know every nook and cranny of this republic; no human rights violations take place here. Look at me, I've lost everything: my father, my relations, my friends, hundreds of my own soldiers; all that is left for me is to fight. So what do you think? Are they more concerned about my people than I am? No, they get money for it! They say they are defending this person and that person, they invent people and say something has happened to them. They just make it up. What's more, they know my name, Kadyrov, so they say: "It's Kadyrov!" But show me one person who can point to me and say that I have violated human rights. That person doesn't exist! Find me one such man! There is none. They sit there, far away, and criticise. Send them here! Then you'll see that they can't defend their accusations in front of me. They are enemies of the people, like Maskhadov. Whether they are your people or ours, let them talk. I don't care!'

'But there are cases in the European Court of Human Rights in Strasbourg where Chechen witnesses talk about your private prisons and torture chambers . . .'

'Show me *one* person who has been in a prison of mine!'

Ramzan is shouting. His arm is raised. He grips a gilt ballpoint pen.

'Let him come here and tell me about it. Send him to Tsentoroi. Let him show me the prison, and then I will happily close it.'

He throws out his hands. Suddenly he begins to guffaw. The

laughter rolls up from his stomach. He scratches the back of his neck, then puts his elbows on the table.

'We have official prisons, we have penal colonies. Why would I need my own prison? Just show me that prison!'

He looks straight at me.

'We have a criminal investigation unit. We have a court of law. It decides: guilty or not. As far as these human rights folk are concerned, I summoned all the Chechens who work for *that side* to a conference and said if anyone had questions for Kadyrov, they could just ask. That's what I said. I asked them all to come – the Memorial people, yes, all of them – and do you know what they said? "Thank you", they said. "Thank you, thank you." They thanked me because I have rebuilt the republic and grounded it in traditional Chechen values. That's what they said. "Thank you, thank you." In fact, I've rescued people who were on *that side*, those who were in the first war. Offered them amnesty.'

He assumes a mild expression.

Shamil, with whom I travelled around Chechnya a year earlier and who now heads Memorial's office in Grozny, was at the meeting with Kadyrov and has an entirely different version. He had not planned to assist, but received a telephone threat from Kadyrov's men urging him to go. During the meeting the president rose and hissed: 'I know what you're doing, and I want you to know that you don't have the right to bring shame on Chechnya!' On TV that evening a sequence where Ramzan shakes his finger threateningly at Shamil was shown. Shamil's colleagues advise him to leave Grozny, but the human rights champion says that he has a job to do.

'Some people suspect you of being behind the murder of Anna Politkovskaya. Her last article dealt specifically with abuses against Chechen citizens.'

The president rolls his eyes and smirks. He looks towards the prime minister, who is sitting with his legs crossed on a chair by the large table, and says:

'We don't kill women, we love them!'

Their laughter fills the room.

Ramzan stops laughing. The prime minister wears a blank expression. Then the young president adopts a serious tone.

'Anna Politkovskaya: she is a woman. First and foremost, she is a woman. I think people know that I can't kill a woman.'

I sit quietly. Sometimes silence is the best interview technique. It can make people continue talking. But not this time.

'She was one of your severest critics . . .'

'She had no basis for accusing me! She came here and made things up. Always wrote things against me. Always!'

He pounds his fist on the table.

'A woman like her, if she likes you, praises you, then you have to be careful; but if she's angry, then you're a man on the right track! She was used by other people, but didn't realise it herself. Everyone knew that. Those she worked for killed her themselves, and accused me. I never bothered about what she wrote, I assure you. As a woman, she should have stayed in the kitchen. What harm did she do me? None. If I had been afraid of anything or anyone, I would have stayed at home with my mother. But I know that God exists, and everything else is just gossip and nonsense! *Yerunda i kleveta!* Rubbish, slander! *Davai!* Come on! She was killed so that no one else could use her; the same with Litvinenko. Just ask Berezovsky – he killed them both. He knew them, and he killed them himself. And then they say it was Kadyrov! *Davai!* Come on! I met her, and I told her that people read her stuff like a fairytale. No, she should have stuck to housewifery.'

He twists in his chair, stretches out his elbows and cracks his knuckles.

'I know that death comes, and I'm not afraid of it. We can find God, and we have chosen the right path,' he says determinedly. He swings round in his chair, scratches himself and hunches his shoulders.

'What's so great about Europe, anyway?' he asks suddenly. 'Men and women are equal there. What's so good about that? The birth rate is low, people don't get married. The society ruins young men, they don't want to go into the army – a disaster for the country, a shame. The country will collapse completely; a boy is born and he doesn't know who his father is, who his relations are, what kind of people he comes from. That's how I see Europe. There is no patriotism. Here our traditions, our customs, are important to us. The wahhabists tried to force us into their mould, the Arabs tried, the Avars, the Turks, but we always said: We want to remain Chechens. We have everything here – justice, order, Islam. Why accept foreign things? Patriotic education is the most important thing of all. What is democracy anyway? If it leads to wickedness?

'For your people, and for the Russians, there's no tomorrow; everything is permitted, if only you can get immediate satisfaction. Like a drug addict: once, twice, three times you're satisfied, then the fourth time you're a slave. The same with prostitution; once, twice, three times, and then you're addicted. Then you need your fix every day.'

'What is woman's role in society?'

'Ah, women. I love women! A wife is holy, she must stay at home. Woman in herself is holy. Unfortunately, we see that the value of women has gone down. You can find women who sell themselves for forty or a hundred dollars; the more beautiful, the more expensive ones, for a thousand dollars, perhaps; the cheapest for a few hundred roubles. Overall a woman's price has fallen. I don't know where all these human rights champions are. Why don't they fight for women? Just picture it: men call them into their office, let's say she's tall, she's beautiful. Women are judged like cattle and sheep. But nobody cares about that, except for us here! We have preserved a woman's sacredness. I want our women to be *samie nedostupnie* – inaccessible. I want Chechen women to be the most virtuous, have the longest skirts, wear a headscarf. The way they did before. Look at Dagestan! There they have clubs, girls from Poland; women walking around the streets in shorts. It's criminal! We can't have that!'

'But that attitude doesn't tie in with the fact that you invited all the Miss World contestants to Chechnya.'

'You're right. It doesn't tie in. But they wanted to come. They asked if they could stop by here before the competition – then they could fly Moscow–Grozny–Sochi,' Ramzan explains.

Russian TV filmed the lovelies tearfully placing flowers on Akhmed Kadyrov's grave, and showed a shot of a super-sexy Miss Ukraine on a horse, chosen from Ramzan's stable. She stayed several days as the president's special guest, and the TV team showed her posing in different outfits for Ramzan as he leaned back on a sofa in his living room at home. Rumour has it that the girls received a generous payment for coming, like Mike Tyson. The famous boxer was also flown to Grozny, where he performed with Ramzan.

'No, that doesn't tie in,' he says again, referring to the visit of the Miss World contestants. 'But we also organised the Miss Chechnya competition,' he adds quickly. 'That was much better. I decided the criteria. We wanted to select the girl who was the best in the kitchen, who knew most about traditions and customs, who knew our history, who could make the finest clothes. And not least: the one who looked best; you know, some women beautify their clothes, others need clothes to beautify them! Next time we'll choose Chechnya's best housewife, the best sister, the best daughter. People will show up then, you can be sure!'

Recently the president forbade young women to own a cell phone, because you 'could receive indecent messages and pictures' on it. Chechen women had to be protected from anything like that. When it comes to the president's own modesty, pictures and video clips circulate of him in the company of scantily clad women.

'You have spoken in favour of polygamy. Why?'

'A person can have four wives. Our traditions allow that, and Islam does, too. Because of the war, there are thirty per cent more women than men here, so if every man had four wives, we would be on the right track. It would help the republic give birth to more children. But no one is required to have four wives, it depends on your own wishes, on your heart, you could say. Nevertheless: I'm for it! If I find a beautiful girl, I will gladly take a new wife myself.'

'How does this comply with Russian laws?'

'Even Putin doesn't have the right to interfere with anyone's private life. That should be directed by personal conscience. Besides, the wives don't have to be registered according to Russian law. They can be registered according to our own laws, according to Sharia.'

'I see that you have a book about child-rearing. Are you interested in that?'

'Girls especially must be brought up strictly. If my children don't set a good example, or if my wife doesn't, then what? When my wife fell ill, I took her to Hospital Number Nine here in Grozny. If I had taken her to Germany or America, as I could have, how could people believe in us? My grandfather had surgery in Gudermes, none of my relations live in foreign countries, the children go to ordinary schools. I want my children to be like Chechnya's children.'

'Many children in Chechnya lost their parents during the war. You have adopted a boy yourself, as an example for others to follow. But why have you closed the orphanages when there are still twenty thousand children without parents?'

'Twenty thousand children! What nonsense! There are no Chechen children who don't have relations. When I wanted to adopt a son, I had to look for a long time and found only a Russian boy who had been abandoned; he is now sixteen years old and lives with my brother. He's more like a brother; I'm only thirty, how wonderful that fate has given me another brother. And orphanages! They existed only so that somebody could earn money. That's why I closed them. They were like daycare centres. "I have to run my business," a woman told me when I asked why her children were in an orphanage. When women rush out to run a business, it ruins our way of thinking. The family and relations –

teips – must take care of those who are alone, be they children or old people. Anything else is an insult to the family. If I grow old, I won't go into a nursing home; no, then I'll want to see my grandchildren running around me. An old man needs his oven, his house. He has raised children, grandchildren; should we send him away? That's not our way of thinking. There aren't many old people left here now, so we have to appreciate those we have. That's why I've closed both old people's homes and the orphanages. We don't need them!'

'What was your own childhood like?'

'I don't remember much from my childhood. I was so little, after all.'

The president swivels in his chair.

'I ran around. I liked to help people; my dream was always to be helpful. When I sat down at the table I always said: "Allah, give everyone the same as I have received." My mother tells me, "That's what you always said." I never sat down at the table without saying it. But I wasn't some mummy's boy. Mama cried because I would never say that I was her son. I was always Papa's son.

'I had a hard childhood, always worked, and I always protected the weakest in class; if somebody got bullied, I defended them. I was small and slender, thin actually – true, I'm still not a big man – but I could always put up a fight, protect myself. I'm a good boxer. I've never tried cigarettes or liquor, never drunk; I've never had any weaknesses. My childhood was difficult because I always tried to live up to my father's ideals. I knew how fair-minded he was.'

'Can you tell me a little more about your relationship with your father?'

'People were envious of our close relationship. We are both by nature very strong, physically and mentally. God gave us strength. I was always at Father's side. He did everything for us, worked hard to support us, went off to work on building sites in the summer. I wanted to help him, and from the age of fourteen or fifteen I worked as his driver and bodyguard. I was with him through the first war; some called us bandits, and the gangsters called us traitors. It was difficult, there were Russians everywhere. In 1999, when the second war began, my father said: "I know I've chosen a difficult direction. If you are afraid, I can help you get a good education, and you can return when this is over." I answered: "But then I can't call myself your son." Now I'm continuing the work of a great man. I was always at his side, always.'

'Well, there was one time you were not – on 9 May 2004?'

The prime minister's foot twitches when the question is asked. Until now Abdulkahir Izrailov has been sitting calmly, with a 'Ramzan will manage this' look. Now he becomes restless.

Who actually killed Akhmed Kadyrov? The official version is that the rebel forces of Maskhadov did it. Another version, mentioned only in whispers, is that the FSB was behind it, that they wanted to get rid of a president who had proved so headstrong as time went on. The conflicts between Kadyrov and the central authorities were numerous and fierce.

The stadium, which had been completed in time for the ceremony when he was killed, was totally controlled by the security forces; all workers, all materials, were strictly guarded by soldiers and dogs, and X-rayed before they came in. The explosives were cemented into the seat, precisely the one that Kadyrov would sit on. Whoever did it would have had to bypass the security procedures. If bribes were involved, it must have required a great deal of money. Unless it was the contractor himself. The separatists didn't claim responsibility, something they are usually quick to do, even if it's only a Russian helicopter that's been shot down. This time no one said anything, except that Shamil Basayev thanked Allah that the hated leader was gone.

However, the Russians immediately attributed to the Chechens the 'honour' for the murder. Yet another mystery: why wasn't Ramzan, the personal bodyguard who never left his father's side, present on this important moment in the republic's history? Why was he asked to remain in Moscow that day?

The newly fatherless Ramzan was immediately called in to meet Vladimir Putin – on live television. Putin clenched his teeth and promised he would punish the gangsters, and then put Chechnya's fate in the hands of Kadyrov Jr.

While the prime minister fidgets in his seat, Ramzan is relaxed. He leans his elbows on the table and looks me in the eye.

'We had attended Putin's inauguration ceremony in Moscow some days earlier. We were both invited. My father as president, I as chief of staff. I had not completed all my meetings with the Russian authorities, and my father asked me to stay and finish them while he himself would leave. On 8 May I went to the airport with him. The plan was that I would return to Grozny on 10 May. I remember the plane was scheduled to leave at two-thirty. I warned him: "Be careful, it's dangerous in Grozny." I recall saying that, and he laughed: "Don't you believe Allah is in Grozny? Allah is in Grozny and in Moscow and in Sochi." We had actually talked about taking a relaxing holiday in Sochi. "Death comes when it is meant to come, and I must be with my people," he said with one foot on the steps up to the plane.'

Ramzan changes his pitch. It becomes lower, his voice is more insistent, and he weighs each word.

'I think my father foresaw his death. Do you know what he said before he boarded the plane? "Even if I were a hundred per cent sure that death awaited me in Grozny, I would go." I remember this; it was two-thirty, 8 May. And then he said, "I will never return to Moscow." The last two days he had talked about that. "This is my last trip to Moscow," he said to me, to my brother, to Mama on the telephone. Several days earlier he had said: "I'm never going to touch my beard again." "How long will it get?" I asked. "No, I'll never touch it again," was all he would say. As a religious act, I don't know. When he left Moscow he took everything with him. His suits. His books. All his things. All of them. He'd never done that before; he always kept many things in Moscow. If he weren't my father, I would have said that Allah had already singled him out. Our last evening in Moscow, he told me what I should do if he died. "If you don't do this and this and this, we will lose everything. Everything will be gone." That's how he talked. Abdulkahir, who is sitting here, is a witness. We have followed all his advice. Still. Haven't we?'

Abdulkahir nods, and a rasping sound comes from his throat.

'Late on the evening of 5 May, before we travelled to Moscow, he said: "If I am no longer with you, follow my path." My mother, who had heard what he said, came in weeping: "Why are you talking like that?" We all knew that at any time we could step on a mine, be blown up, no longer exist. He was a great man, our first president, a Chechen and a Muslim, a most worthy human being. All his dreams will be fulfilled. *Inshallah*.'

'Finished,' says the prime minister. 'Your interview is finished. You've gone far beyond your allotted time. That's it. Done. Finished.'

I stop the recorder, gather my notes, take a picture. The prime minister walks around restlessly, he can't be rid of me soon enough. I am hustled out by an armed guard who has been summoned to get me. On my way to the door I turn towards the president. He is sitting in exactly the same position as when I entered, leaning back in his chair with one foot kicking against the table, writing text messages on his cell phone.

Che Guevara watches anxiously from his place on the wall between Putin and the Kadyrov family portrait. The top sheet of a stack of white papers that was lying in front of the president when we started the interview is strewn with tiny flowers. Their smiling faces and little round petals have been drawn by the ballpoint pen that now lies discarded next to the gold penholder.

18

Tea, Old Woman?

I couldn't forget the women in the family where the men had disappeared. Sixteen-year-old Salina and her husband Hassan, whose car had been found burned out on a roadside. Tamara, who prayed her son would return alive from prison in Arkhangelsk. A year and a half had passed since I had visited them. I had tried to go back several times, but never found anyone willing to take me.

'It's too dangerous, they are being watched. *There is something about that family,*' everyone said.

Tamara's story was not uncommon, I discovered. Once I met someone I could trust from the same village and asked if he had any news of the family.

'Which family?'

'You know, the woman who has lost four sons . . .'

'Which one?'

'What do you mean, which one?'

'There are many women in the village who have lost four sons.'

Summer comes and then autumn, and another winter turns into spring without my having visited them. Finally, in the summer of the second year, Zaira agrees to go back with me.

I sit in the back seat of an old car on the road out of Grozny wearing a fluttering pink summer dress from the bazaar made with two layers of material and shimmering white silk flowers. Around my head I have knotted a delicate scarf in a shade of pink that just about matches my dress – but only just: that's how it should be. On my ears I'm wearing gold teardrop earrings, and my eyebrows are drawn in sharp arches. The eyeshadow is green; the kohl, black. My high-heeled shoes have flowers and a pink tassel at the front; they clash, but only slightly, with the dress and the scarf.

I look down modestly when the soldiers peer in at the road-block. Only the driver's papers get checked.

We drive to the banned house. Zaira knocks. There is no one on the street. The gate is opened and a few words are exchanged. She waves to me and I slip out of the car, which drives away.

'I don't know if you remember,' I say. 'I was here the winter of last year . . .'

'Of course I remember,' says Tamara, and embraces me. Then I recall: *Those who have contact with these people are the enemy, too. Those who weep at their funerals are themselves outcasts.* Of course she remembers.

The fruit trees clustered near the house were laden with snow the last time I was here. Now they are weighed down with peaches. An abundance of yellow-green plums hangs on a crooked tree further back in the yard, near the house where the women were gathered to pray when Hassan disappeared. Down in the garden the same cow moos on its tether and trudges around a robust walnut tree. The garden consists of neat patches of earth where onions, cabbages and dill have sprung up from the dark soil.

On the back porch where grapevines provide some cooling shade, two older women sit looking at me suspiciously. They are the sisters of Tamara's deceased husband; one of them is Hassan's mother. On the table between them are a pot of tea and a plate of fresh potato pancakes folded over thick slices of homemade cheese. One woman lifts the cover keeping the pancakes warm and offers us some. The other has already brought cups. I sit down beside Tamara on an old bed they use as a sofa.

'Iznaur is out of prison,' Tamara says quietly.

I smile at her. That's good news. She doesn't return my smile.

'He got out this winter. He's at work now, has a job as a carpenter. He learned to work with wood up there in Arkhangelsk. Ouf, the way they treated him! He will tell you himself when he comes home. He's free. He's free. But I'm just so afraid it's not over yet . . .'

'What about Hassan? Has he come back?'

The three women sit silent and dejected.

'They found him just after you were last here, perhaps a week or two later,' Tamara says. 'They had already found the car. Hassan was discovered not too far away. One leg was cut off, also an arm, and one eye had been poked out. He had a bullet hole in his forehead.'

'Do you know——'

'It was, of course, *them*,' says Tamara. 'His sister-in-law still hasn't been found.'

'What about Salina? How is she?'

'She doesn't live here any longer; she has gone home to her family.'

'Her family? Her whole family had been killed . . .'

'Nevertheless, she doesn't live here any more.'

'What about her boys?'

'Her sons are here. They belong to us.'

'What happened?'

Tamara gives me a look that says: Don't ask any more about that.

'Can I meet her?' I ask.

'No,' says Tamara. 'You can't meet her.'

'You shouldn't babble so much,' one of the women with the stern faces says to Tamara in Chechen.

'*Ya ustala molchat,*' replies Tamara in Russian. 'I'm tired of keeping silent, exhausted with keeping silent.'

'Just before they took Hassan – in fact just before you were here –

they took me, and my daughter as well.'

'You?'

'Yes, I couldn't tell you this last time because I didn't know anything about the man who was with you. And back then, Iznaur was still in prison.'

'Where did they take you?'

'They came early in the morning, dragged us out of the house in just our nightclothes. Fatima's sons were screaming, but the men ignored them. They shoved us into a car and drove away. In the car they hit us. "Who do you know? Where are the rebels? Who are you hiding?" As they hit us they asked about men I had never heard of. They drove us towards Tsentoroi and stopped the car in the woods.'

Zaira stares open-mouthed.

'To Tsentoroi?'

Tsentoroi is the home of the Kadyrov clan.

'A bigger car was parked there,' Tamara continues. 'In it sat five men with their hands tied behind them and their jackets over their heads like hoods. We were thrown into the car. The men who had taken us there said: "The car is full of explosives which will soon be detonated. If you want to save yourself, you must tell us where the rebels are hiding." None of us said a word. Fatima and I didn't know anything, after all. I was sure my last hour had come. Fatima wept for her sons; she was convinced she would never see them again. After a while the men came back and said that we had a few last minutes to tell them what we knew. Then they walked off, as if to get away before the car was blown up. We saw everything; neither Fatima nor I were blindfolded. Two hours later we were let out. "This is a warning," they said after driving us home in the same car they had picked us up in. They drove us right up to our gate. I have no idea what happened to the men tied up in the car.'

Tamara switches between Russian and Chechen as she speaks. Zaira translates when the older woman slips into her mother tongue. She also interprets when Tamara's two sisters-in-law keep repeating the same thing: 'You must be careful, Tamara. Haven't you lost enough already?'

But Tamara has made up her mind. She is in danger if she keeps silent, and she is in danger if she speaks. Now she has decided to do the latter.

'Who were they?' I ask.

'*Them*,' Tamara says emphatically.

The chickens cluck around us. Their shadows have lengthened.

'The Kadyrovtsi,' Tamara continues. 'The president's men.'

The dry heat that made the plains almost desert-like has let up a little. Tamara continues her story. Some weeks later the men came back. This time they let Fatima stay at home and took only the older woman. Once again they drove her to the grove near Tsentoroi. Suddenly they came to high fences. The car drove through a guarded entrance.

'It was like arriving in hell. I was thrown out of the car and pushed along by men with automatic weapons. I heard screams and moaning around me without knowing where they came from.'

The two sisters-in-law sit silently. Their lips are pursed in a look that says they think Tamara has gone too far. That's enough now, their faces say.

'I was shoved towards something that looked like a battle trench, a long rampart. I saw only the top of it. First from a distance, then closer. Boards or planks had been laid over it so you could walk from one side to the other. I was ordered to cross it. I'll never forget the sight that met me when I looked down. Corpse upon corpse lay there. Bloody, beaten, without teeth, without eyes. One of them, one of the corpses – or maybe he was alive – looked at me. I dream about that look and wake up screaming. I was led into the area inside the rampart. From there you couldn't escape without falling into the trench, because the planks across it were guarded by men with automatic weapons. In the middle of this area was a rack made from poles and pipes on which three men were hanging. An electric current flowing through the pipes was being turned on and off. On and off. We could tell by the screams when the electricity was connected.'

'What did they want with you?'

'The same as the first time. They wanted me to tell them where the rebels were. But I don't know anything. I just said to them: "You've taken all my sons now; I'm the only one left. If you want me, then kill me straight away."'

'Did they hit you?'

'No, they didn't touch me. They set out a little table and a chair in front of the rack where the men were being tortured. They told me to sit down there. Then they set out tea, sweetened cream and a piece of bread, about this big.'

She holds out the palm of her hand.

'"Tea, old woman," they said. I just shook my head. "What's wrong with you, Baba? Don't you want a drink?" I would rather die than drink tea in front of those men being tortured to death. Or in front of the corpses in the trench.'

'How many corpses did you see?'

'They lay higgledy-piggledy. Many dozens. The trenches were of red brick, with high metal edges. I don't know why they were built like vats; maybe so that they could pour acid in them. I've heard something like that.'

She continues speaking as if in a trance. Even though she is looking right at us, her eyes are still back there.

'Kadyrov's men strolled around laughing loudly. Music blared from loudspeakers, Chechen pop music. Tables laden with food were set out: platters with big chunks of meat, bread, soft drinks. They relaxed and ate before getting up to torment the men on the rack again. Two women took care of the food and clearing the tables. One of them sat calmly peeling potatoes. In the midst of hell. When I refused to drink the tea, I was ordered to clear the things away and wash the dishes. I did so. I then thought that the two women were prisoners too, but no, they were in fact paid to work there. "How can you do that?" I exclaimed. I wasn't afraid of anything then. I thought it was the end anyway. The prisoners only had themselves to blame, the younger woman replied: "*Ne nado bylo vlest kyda ne nado.* They shouldn't have got mixed up in things that didn't concern them." I was shocked. She was ice-cold. What's happened to us? How did we become so evil? Never, never in our history have we tormented each other as we do today. It's no longer the Russians against the Chechens. It's Chechen against Chechen. A neighbour was also taken prisoner and interrogated. She had just given birth and milk was pouring from her breasts. She never got out of there, I've learned. But I don't know what they did with her.'

Tears run down Tamara's cheeks. She continues:

'It started to get dark, and I would never have got out of there either if it hadn't been for a man who suddenly called out: "Isn't that Iznaur's mother?" I don't know who he was, but I think he saved me. He talked to someone, and after a while they drove me home.

'But they can come back any time. For myself I'm not afraid, but I'm terrified of what could happen with Iznaur. I know who came after me, who took his brothers, who took him. I know who they are. But I don't say that to him. I've refused to tell him. And I'm so afraid of the day he will try to take revenge, and be killed himself . . . my last son. No, I'll never tell him who they are.'

The door opens and a young man enters.

'Iznaur!' exclaims his mother, and her expression softens into a smile.

The boy – because he isn't much more than a young boy – is handsome, with a mass of dark curls and a gentle expression. We introduce ourselves, and he tells us to remain seated. His mother has her arm around him. 'When he came home he was so thin, just skin and bone, and now – my strongman is back!'

Iznaur disappeared in 2000 and returned in 2007. He is marked for life.

They pounded a nail into one of his shoulders. All the way in. With a hammer.

They drove a pencil into his chest. The lead is still there.

They pulled flesh from his chest with tongs. Deep hollows remain.

'The Russians. To get me to talk,' says Iznaur.

This was a family I chanced upon when I selected a name from a Red Cross list of people who had sons in a Russian prison. The family I chose proved to have a story that has been difficult to write about. Had I picked a different name on the list I would have found a different story. Behind the names and addresses scribbled on a piece of paper at the Red Cross are other family histories.

This one turned out to be that of Tamara and her lost sons. Salina and her murdered husband.

I left the family for the last time that summer evening, but still keep up with them, because Iznaur is one of the few people who have chosen to go public with their stories. He is an important witness in the case against Lieutenant Sergei Lapin, better known as *The Cadet*, who carried out 'counter-terrorist' activities on behalf of the Russian government as an 'authorised agent in the fight against terrorism and organised crime'. It is rare for a person to be held accountable for abuses in Chechnya. Few people dare to accuse anyone; the consequences are too great. But the family of one of the young men whom The Cadet tortured to death has not given up. Lawyers from international human rights organisations have made it possible for the family to pursue the case and to endure the pressure from the authorities.

The Cadet was notorious for his cruelty. It was he who hammered the nail into Iznaur's shoulder. He who drove a pencil into the boy's chest. He who pulled out his flesh with tongs.

Now his deeds have caught up with him through a legal system for which he had only the greatest contempt. When one of his victims protested that he was innocent and wanted to speak to a lawyer, electric wires were fastened to an ear and to a finger, and they in turn were connected to a telephone. When he dialled, the electric current was activated. The procedure was referred to as *zvonok advokatu* – calling a lawyer.

Iznaur has chosen to be a public witness. Iznaur is his mother's son.

19

While Putin Watches

Summer holidays were just around the corner, and Hadijat had begun to plan for autumn long ago. Several of the children were going to enter class one, and the cupboard where they kept their school things was already overflowing. She gasped for air. Although it was only June, the thermometer had crept up towards an unheard-of forty degrees. There wasn't a breath of wind, not even the smallest cloud in sight. A damp, stagnant haze hung over the children's home without giving the slightest relief from the sun that blazed down from a bright blue sky. She would ask Zaur to put up new shelves. The materials were in the store room. All they needed were nails.

At the market, the produce gasped in the heat. The first yellow melons were already ripe; the skins had cracked and their heavy sweetness followed people along the row of stalls displaying large crates of plump apricots. Fruit ripened with each passing hour and its fragrance blended with the smell of cigarette smoke, of rusty iron, paint and flypaper. In the dusty bazaar at Rosa Luxemburg Street you found the best prices, even if you only needed a box of nails.

Zaur had gone to the market with his friend Said, and after shopping they hustled on to a crowded bus. They were lucky, each managing to flop down into an empty seat just before the bus left. The clammy plastic upholstery stuck to their bodies, and there didn't seem to be any air to breathe. A smell of petrol spread through the bus. Some people tried to open the windows. Dust danced in the light coming through the door, which could no longer be shut. Suddenly, the light was replaced by dark shadows. Three men were standing in the doorway.

'Document check,' they said, pointing at Zaur and Said. The boys had no documents with them; they were only making a quick trip to the market, after all.

'Then you will have to come along to the office,' said the men, who were dressed in civilian clothing.

'We can go and get our papers,' Zaur managed to say before his T-shirt was pulled over his head, his hands yanked behind his back and cuffed. They were pushed off the bus. Said shouted his address to the other passengers: 'Tell Mama!' No one stood up. No one tried to stop what was happening. And no one went to notify.

One of the men had his hands in Zaur's pocket.

'What's there I can take out myself,' said Zaur, but the man just pulled out his cell phone, wallet, some pieces of paper and threw everything into a waiting car. The boys were shoved into the car, too.

Zaur had noticed them as he came into the market — three silver-grey Zhiguli 110s, the cars of the Kadyrovtsi. They were parked on the outer edge between the pavement and the dried mud, standing out from the others.

The men forced the boys' heads between their knees, and they sat like that as they were hit on the back of the head and neck and on their backs. Feeling sick from the speed with which the car was cornering, Zaur tried to work out where they were being taken. He did his best to guess where the car was going by the stops and turns it made, but it was difficult without being able to see. Hunched over with his back and neck exposed, he was defence-less against the blows of fists and something hard, some sort of club, he assumed.

During the ride, one of the men telephoned somebody and asked: 'Should we take them to *the place*?'

'I'm just an ordinary citizen,' Zaur shouted between blows. He was sure he was going to be killed and tossed into a rubbish bag to be found later on a roadside, or simply disappear. Like so many before him.

When the car stopped and they were shoved out, his T-shirt slipped from his head and he recognised a tall metal door near the MVD buildings – the Russian Interior Ministry. He knew there was a prison there. They were led into a corridor and pushed forward. The men did not allow them to lift their heads, to look up, to look around. If they moved their heads the slightest bit, they were hit. From a small opening in his shirt, Zaur could see only brown linoleum.

They were taken to separate rooms. They were still handcuffed, but the men pulled the T-shirts down from their faces. The room where Zaur was taken contained a desk with a computer, two chairs, a safe, a bed, and a shelf with four books. Above the safe hung three portraits – Vladimir Putin flanked by Kadyrov Jr and Kadyrov Sr. Two small flags, Chechen and Russian, stood on the desk. All the men in the room were armed, and they were all Chechens. One of them picked up the telephone and dialled a number. He described Zaur's appearance in detail.

'Tall, yes, good build, beard, long hair, brown eyes, big hands and feet, silver ring, watch.'

The man took a picture of Zaur on his cell phone and sent it as MMS. He got an answer saying they had got the right man, and came towards Zaur.

'We brought you here so that you could speak freely,' he said, and clapped him on the shoulder.

'This must be a mistake,' Zaur managed to say.

'Where is *Shturmovik*?'

The man's voice was as hard as steel.

'I don't know any *Shturmovik*.'

A blow to the nape of his neck.

'Where is he?'

'I don't know who you're talking about.'

A blow to the back of his head.

'Don't lie!'

'I don't know . . .'

A blow to his temples. His ears rang. They hit his neck, his forehead at the hairline, his wrists, ankles, behind his knees, his back.

'Out with it!'

'I don't know who you're talking about. I've never heard of him. Never met, never seen. I don't know if he's dead or alive,' gulped Zaur.

Blow after blow.

They continued to shout about *Shturmovik*, which translates as Fighter Plane or Stormer, and about the Pirate and *Moryak* – the Sailor. They were all call names for known rebels who once had fought with Ramzan Kadyrov, but later changed sides and assembled their own forces. But Zaur didn't know that. He had never heard of them. Zaur also didn't know whether the men knew who he was, or if they had just taken two boys from the bazaar at random.

'This is the FSB,' thought Zaur. They weren't big and muscular like Kadyrov's personal bodyguards who trained at the Ramzan Boxing Club or like men from OMON – the riot police. These were slim and well dressed, in the latest jeans and T-shirts, with clean-shaven faces and short haircuts, in their thirties, some a little older. They talked, or yelled, in relatively well-bred Chechen. Despite the room's official appearance, with portraits of one dead and two ruling presidents, there was no interrogation protocol, no arrest warrant.

'I know some of Ramzan's people,' Zaur ventured. 'You can call them; I can give you the number!'

One of the neighbours down the street, an old classmate of Zaur's, had contact with Ramzan Kadyrov. He might stand up for him, Zaur thought desperately.

'*Nam Ramzan do lampochki*,' replied the interrogators, and laughed. 'We couldn't care less about Ramzan! Look, we've got Ramzan, too, he's hanging over there. We're friends of his, too, ha ha!'

A blow. To the kidneys. Another blow. To the head. Another blow. To the ribs.

'Should we get the wires?' one of the men asked the others.

A man went to get the instrument of torture, but returned saying it was being used, that they had to wait a bit.

'Then we'll use the old method,' they laughed, and hit even harder. Some men left and new ones came in. Zaur could not keep track.

'You know we'll kill you if you don't tell us where the Stormer is . . .'

'But I have no idea—'

A blow.

'—who he is!'

Another blow.

'Do you know what an electric shock feels like? You shudder and burn, then you get thrown forward about three metres. If we're feeling kind, we place you away from the wall; if we're not, you stand right up next to it, with your face in that corner. No three metres there, you can see. Nice, eh?'

Once Zaur fainted from the pain, but they just slapped him until he regained consciousness and continued to beat him. One man took a rest and lay down on the bed with the club lying on the floor. He wiped the sweat from his forehead. 'This damned heat,' he said. 'It's roasting in here. Can somebody get something to drink?'

The man on the bed was the worst, the one who talked the nastiest, who hit the hardest.

'When we kill you, will anybody look for you? Will anyone avenge you?'

'Yes!' shouted Zaur.

'Ha, do you think anyone will find you?' laughed the sweating man.

*

Zaur stops. It's not easy for him to recount all this. I ask for a number of details that he doesn't understand are necessary in order for me to be able to reconstruct the story.

'Exactly what did you see in the room? What did the men look like? What were they wearing? How did you say he was lying on the bed?'

We are sitting out on the shadowy covered veranda between Hadijat's bedroom and the boys' side. Three weeks have passed since the kidnapping. Down in the yard the children run around kicking a ragged beach ball that has been taped together. It has ripped apart almost everywhere, and they constantly have to stop and blow it up again.

'Everything changed that day,' Zaur says, looking at me sadly.

'They hit so it felt as if my head would explode, everything turned red, and I fell down; I fell several times, and those men — they know where to hit. They can destroy a person in no time. Just then I had only one wish: to see the world one more time. There was a window in the room, it faced a brick wall, there were dogs in the backyard. All my life I'd heard about people who were taken away, tortured, who disappeared. But that it should happen to me . . .'

'Take off your ring,' ordered the interrogator. 'Why are you wearing it?'

Both boys were wearing a silver ring with a small jewel. 'The Prophet wore a ring, on his little finger; the Prophet liked that kind of thing, so I have one too,' Zaur had told me the year before when I asked him about the ring with the small purple stone. People said it was a sign that you were a wahhabist.

'And your watch, who gave you that?'

They pointed at the Casio stopwatch.

'I bought it myself, in the bazaar.'

'No, you got it from the Stormer! The rebels use watches like that.'

'I bought it myself, for seven hundred roubles.'

'Why?'

'Because I think it's nice!'

Zaur didn't want to say that he had bought it to signal the five daily prayer times. 'It's very practical in that way,' he once told me.

'You're lying. Who gave you the watch?'

Hit. Kick. More blows.

'I bought it myself!'

Another blow.

'The rebels gave it to you!'

'No!'

'We have proof that you . . .'

His head is banged. His neck burns. His back stings.

'. . . are recruited by the rebels. By the Stormer. By the Sailor. By the Pirate.'

Then they laughed.

Zaur didn't recognise any of the names. And could only shout no, no, no.

'The word still echoes in my head,' he says.

They kept beating him on the same parts of his body the whole time. How many they were, where they were from, Zaur did not know. But the torture took place on official premises of the Chechen government, carried out by men paid by the same authorities, who in turn are funded directly by the Russian treasury.

The abuse occurred on 25 June 2007, the same day that Ramzan Kadyrov opened the new hippodrome in Grozny. Two and a half months after he had been sworn in as President of Chechnya and had promised, with his hand on the Constitution, to stabilise the republic and respect Russia's laws. Ramzan Kadyrov was personally appointed by Vladimir Putin. Russia's president is also the only person who can remove him from office.

'What do you think about Putin?'

'I respect and honour Putin,' replied Zaur.

'And Ramzan?'

'I support Ramzan in everything.'

'We're warning you, don't be friends with those who aren't friends with Ramzan,' the men threatened. 'Don't follow those who don't follow him. Putin helps us. Things aren't like before; the Russians are with us now.'

'Are you afraid of the FSB?' they asked.

Zaur wanted to say that he feared only Allah, but answered: 'Why should I be afraid of the FSB? I haven't done anything wrong, and have no reason to fear the FSB.'

'Right answer,' they said, and laughed.

Another man came in and ordered: 'Keep beating him. Harder. Lock him up! Kill him if he doesn't cooperate.'

'I thought about all those who disappear without trace. Who are killed for no reason. I wanted just one thing. I wanted to leave, to start life all over again.'

Zaur looks down. 'It wasn't necessarily us they were after,' he continues. 'They see someone they think looks suspicious, watch what he buys, where he goes, who he's with, and not least, what he's wearing. Does he look like a rebel? Does he look like an Islamist? Does he look like a resistance fighter? Said and I were wearing jeans and T-shirts, but we had beards and long hair.'

Long hair is one of the signs that you lean towards wahhabism, which Kadyrov has declared is his main enemy.

'The Prophet had long hair,' Zaur continues in his rather slow, morose manner. 'That's why I had it, too.

'I think they probably knew who we were. It's their job to know what's going on. That's the only way Kadyrov can hang on to power. By spreading fear that makes people stay within the fold, look like everyone else, act like everyone else. They wanted to take somebody that day, in order to do their job, to report that they captured this person or that person, to give the impression they were accomplishing something, and not least, to create fear in people. The way they hit showed that they had done it hundreds of times before. They liked it, they enjoyed giving beatings, and they knew where to hit so that it would be the most painful without leaving marks. They laughed. They drank. They hit. They had fun.'

Zaur hesitates.

'I saw through the window that the sun was setting. The man who had been lying on the bed came and stood close to me. "We can make an agreement," he said, looking me straight in the eye. I shuddered.'

'We'll let you go, if you agree to be an informer.'

'At the time, all I thought about was getting away. I don't remember what I answered, but suddenly I was leaning over the desk and writing down what they told me to write. I had to write the promise – the promise to be an informer – myself. They dictated it. It was terrible. It *is* so terrible. And dishonourable. On that paper it says that I will be on the lookout for rebels, that I promise to inform on people, that I will contact the authorities if I find out anything about the rebels.'

He pauses.

'If I hadn't signed that paper, I wouldn't be here now. But I swear to Allah! I won't inform on anyone! I only wrote that to get out. I won't do their filthy work! And that paper, that paper, they won't be able to use it against me again. It's just to show that they are doing their job, they have bosses too, that the paper is a proof that they recruit people.'

Zaur trembles. 'Now everything is written down,' he says. 'I'm on their database. As an enlisted informer.'

The tone in the interrogation room had changed.

There was one more thing.

'You've seen us,' said one of the men. 'What are you going to do about that?'

'I'm going to keep my mouth shut.'

'Yes, that's wise. If you don't, we will come and get you, little boy. Don't think you can hide from us.'

*

'It lasted just one afternoon,' says Zaur. 'Between lunch and dinner. They tortured me between lunch and dinner. And everything has changed.'

After the boys were driven back and shoved out in front of their gate, Said left Chechnya. Zaur didn't leave the house. For the first couple of weeks he lay in bed in severe pain with bruises all over his body and face. There were large, tender lumps on the back of his head. He remembers almost nothing from those first days. Pictures of the bruises were taken, as proof, should he ever need it, but he hasn't dared to let a doctor examine him.

'The first few days I was in so much pain that I couldn't even kneel to pray,' he says.

Now he sleeps with his clothes on, fearful that they will come and get him again.

'I've got to get out of here,' says Zaur. 'When they have you on file, they will come again. They will come again. But next time they won't get me. If they come before I've left Chechnya, I'll run away. Out the back window by the bathroom, down the roof, over into the neighbour's backyard. But I'm not quite sure how I'll get out of there; the fence has some sharp spikes on which you could impale yourself. I have to get rid of them somehow, make an opening that I can creep through. But Luiza, my wife, says there's no point in running away; then they will just think I'm guilty of something. And shoot.'

'Is there anyone you can complain to? Report to? Memorial? Human rights groups?'

'Pah! How can they help me? No, it's better to just disappear.'

'But according to what you say, this happened in a Russian government building. Can you report the men who tortured you? You have the pictures, after all – can you send them to a lawyer?'

Zaur shakes his head.

'This isn't Germany, where if you write a report it gets delivered. This is Russia. Here things operate by different rules.'

The muezzin from a nearby mosque calls to prayer. Zaur struggles to his feet.

'Allah saved me,' he says, and goes to pray.

Zaur, his wife and their two-year-old daughter chose to leave Grozny in the autumn of 2007, and now live outside the republic.

20

Honour

One subject constantly crops up in Chechen conversation. Honour.

A soldier's honour. A nation's honour. A leader's honour. A woman's honour. It's the latter that riles people most. Honour killings are widespread. Very widespread. When I ask the women sitting around the table one evening, they all know of numerous instances – neighbours, acquaintances, relations.

'Not all the children here have become orphans because of the war,' says Hadijat, and reels off the names of those who have lost their mothers in honour killings.

'It's terrible,' she says. 'But there are many who accept it. Honour is important.'

'It acts as a warning,' says Malika. 'So no one will follow in the footsteps of these cheap girls.'

'I'd like to talk with a person who killed someone that way,' I say. 'To try to understand the rationale behind it.'

'We can certainly arrange that,' says Hadijat.

'Arrange? When I can barely get permission to go outside the gate?'

The afternoon is drawing in. Hadijat excuses herself, and I continue drinking tea with Malika and Madina. Malika is sad. The brother-in-law who disappeared a few weeks earlier came back, but died immediately afterwards. His whole body broke out in a terrible rash, and he was dead within a few hours. Malika is sure he was poisoned. He had told her that they pricked him with something.

Hadijat comes downstairs again, and asks me to come up to her room. 'Bring your tea with you,' she says. On the stairs, she stops. 'I've found what you wanted,' she says.

'What do you mean?'

'Someone who killed his sister.'

I stand open-mouthed.

'You can meet him on one condition. That you don't reproach him.'

'I promise.'

We enter her room. I go burning hot, then ice-cold, when I see who is sitting there. Her son Abdul. Quiet, taciturn Abdul. Who has just got married, who met his wife on a pilgrimage. Who is afraid he won't be paid on the building site, but doesn't dare say anything. Who always walked two steps behind the other boys. Who is soon to be a father.

'Yes,' says Hadijat. 'Here you have one.'

She goes out, leaving the two of us. What can I say? The interview suddenly feels impossible. I had simply mentioned that I'd like to talk to someone who had murdered for the sake of honour. And now here is Abdul. Parts of his story I already know. He was almost a teenager when the war broke out. One year into the war, he buried the charred remains of his parents after a rocket hit the gas cylinder in the kitchen as they sat drinking tea after dinner. Abdul had been out with some friends at the time. He saw the flames shoot up and ran home. Planes and helicopters were flying overhead. The house had become a sea of flames before he reached it. As he stood there, the roof caved in; all that was left were a few walls. Whether his mother and father had been hit by the rocket or killed by the explosion, he did not know. It was impossible to tell from their remains.

For the first few months the children had lived with neighbours.

They collected bottles and metal, then began sniffing glue. One day his brother disappeared. Abdul never saw him again. His sister went to live with other relations. Abdul was twelve when he, like Adam, became a messenger for the rebels.

This much he had told me. Now, in Hadijat's room, he would tell me the rest.

Abdul speaks in a low monotone. He twists the palms of his hands together. In the flickering light from the gas flame he appears even paler than usual; his reddish hair looks almost black against the shadows on the ceiling.

Brother and sister lost contact with each other when he was living with the rebels, but after a year he heard that she had been seen with men who were not relations. He didn't believe it, but began to search for her. He found her after a couple of years, took her home and threatened her. He was fifteen now, she was two years older; but he was stronger. He tied her to a chair with a rope, and fastened her legs with a long chain and a hook.

'I demanded that she confess. She wouldn't. Quite the opposite: she swore on salt and bread that she had never done anything **wrong**, that she would never do anything wrong, and that she would respect me as the head of the family now that our parents were dead. I untied her, and before I had even turned round she ran off and was gone. Later I heard several stories about her. I searched for her for three years. I made enquiries, and travelled around Chechnya by bus.

He shifts his position and rests his hands on the chair.

'Actually, I liked those trips; I always took a seat in the back row, and I'd sit there, watching the trees fly past. Then I found her. A neighbour from Grozny had seen her in a village and told me she lived there. She sold petrol on a little street. That morning I started out with renewed hope. I borrowed a car. By lunchtime I reached the village. I found the mosque where it was supposed to be, and counted the houses according to the neighbour's description: to the left, first, second, third house. And there, there she was, on the street with a petrol can. My heart nearly stopped; I had been so fond of her, remembered how she had taken care of me when I was little. Now I was eighteen. I already had a beard, like a true Muslim; she was about twenty. A man was sitting next to her. She got up, and wanted to give me a hug. "My little brother!" she cried. I must have looked threatening, because the man drew back. I took my sister's hand and said, "Let's go home."

'"Where?" she asked.

'"To see some relations," I answered. "Where we lived before. I'll drive you back here afterwards."

'She came with me. The look on my face probably made it impossible to do otherwise. She sat beside me in the front seat. The whole time I thought: Should I do it? Not do it? Kill? Not kill? If I don't kill her, I will have to go through my whole life filled with shame. I will have to endure having people speak disapprovingly about her, and about me. He who can't manage his sisters, who can't protect his sisters, is not a man. That's how I thought. I couldn't continue to live with this sister. After all, I had nothing to counter the accusations with, nothing I could use to defend myself.'

Abdul looks at me. 'Why do you think the neighbour told me where she was? If it wasn't so that I would . . .?'

He continues:

'The road was full of holes, so we couldn't drive fast, only forty kilometres an hour, maybe. It had started to get dark. I drove on to a small road leading into a grove of trees. I had planned where I should turn off. By a bombed-out factory and a big rubbish dump. I pretended that the car swerved into a ditch. Then I asked her to get out and push. "Let's try together," I said. I had a pistol in my belt; I always carried a weapon then. She stood to my left and pushed. It had grown dark, the moon was shining, and I pulled the pistol from my belt with my right hand, aimed and fired. I hit her in the arm. She screamed and started to run.

'"Why do you want to kill me?" she shouted as she ran.

'I shot her again.

'I shot her three times in the back, and she sank to the ground. As she lay there, I shot her in the stomach. She looked at me. Her eyes were open, huge. Blood came out of her mouth. She lay with her arms outstretched, just the way she had fallen; she couldn't move any more. Her face quivered. She stared at me. It seemed as if she wanted to say something, but she couldn't.

'I stood over her, and shot her one last time. In the middle of her face. To make sure that she couldn't survive.'

He looks at me as if he's finished the story.

'What did you do with her body?'

'She was already lying in the ditch, so I dug a deeper hole and covered it with earth and grass.'

Abdul looks straight ahead.

'Did you ever go back there?'

'No.'

'Do you think anyone found her?'

'I'm sure some dogs found her and chewed at her. I didn't cover her up especially well.'

He sits in silence for a moment, then continues:

'I've seen her in dreams. I walk across a field, and she comes towards me. She has a hole in her forehead, with a sticking plaster over it. "Didn't you die?" I ask. "Death could not conquer me," she replies. *Smert ne mogla menya pobedit.* She is wearing a white T-shirt and a light-coloured skirt, the same skirt she was wearing when I killed her. In the dream her clothes are spotless, not bloody as they were when I buried her.'

Abdul clenches his fists so that the knuckles turn white.

'I didn't sleep all night. Didn't think. Didn't feel. Just saw my sister before me.'

Only now does he start to cry.

I let him weep. What can I say? I can't comfort him, have no words for this. I remember Hadijat's one condition.

Abdul's shoulders are hunched. He sobs quietly.

'Why are you crying?'

'It's a long time since I talked about this. I've only talked about it twice. Once to Malik, Hadijat and the oldest brothers here. Then to my wife, half a year into our marriage.'

'*After* you got married?'

'Yes.'

'What did she say?'

'She just asked why I did it.'

'What did you answer?'

'I did it so that others wouldn't point at me and despise me. I did it so that I could hold my head high. By killing her, I knew that I *could* protect my sister. I hadn't planned to tell my wife. Didn't want to. But when she told me about her fate and all the difficulties she had gone through – her father became disabled fighting in Afghanistan, was imprisoned, lost all his fingers, died as a prisoner. When she had shared her sorrow with me, I told her this.'

Abdul sniffles, and falls quiet again.

'Your sister, what did she look like?'

'She had light hair. Like yours, a little darker,' he says. 'Or like mine, a little lighter. Her hair came to her shoulders, it was wavy, and she had deep blue eyes. She was pretty.'

He is far away; then he straightens up and says coldly:

'To be honest, I don't remember her very well. She doesn't exist for me. I have no sister. Remember, I offered her everything. I cried in front of her. I asked her to live a respectable life. I got on my knees and asked her to act honourably. I said I could take care of her, find a husband for her. But she didn't want that. She chose the outcome herself. If I hadn't killed her, everyone would have said, "Look at him, he can't even manage to kill his sister."

Abdul looks straight at me.

'I want to live like an ordinary person, be a respected citizen. I want to live according to Sharia. The woman must subject herself to the man, the wife to her spouse, the sister to her brother.'

'But how could you know that what people said about her was true? Maybe they were just rumours?'

'The rumours were murderous enough. And just think, if

someone who didn't know she was my sister had started to talk about her *that way*. As if she were a cheap woman and everyone could say whatever they pleased about her. Imagine if someone didn't know I was her brother and started to talk disapprovingly about her. How could I have got over it? I'm proud that I did it. I am proud. And I walk with my head held high.'

Abdul has to go home. It has grown late. He lives on a farm outside the city, with an honourable wife, a child on the way and a sister who haunts him at night.

21

The Fist

The wind howls through the streets of Moscow. Snowdrifts tower like mountain ridges along the pavements. At the foot of the soft mounds lie gleaming pools of clear blue water. It has snowed for several days. Day and night, white wisps have drifted down to cover the streets and pavements, cling to people's coats and dance on their fur hats. The snow banks are too wide to step over and too soft to walk along; you need to look for openings. When your foot thinks it's on safe ground and dares to take a step, it sinks down into the icy water beneath.

The fronts have changed in spring's battle against winter. The past week, a proud March sun fought its way out, only to take cover again from the snowstorm. This morning, an icy wind is on the offensive. It tosses the snowflakes wildly; they fly about as if they are weightless and will never reach the ground, but finally become powder in the drifts or drown in the pools of water. As the day goes on, the morning's snow crystals will be transformed into slush and the clear pools into muddy brown water.

It is one of the first days of March 2006. Two pointed suede boots are making their way past the snowy obstacles near the Studencheskaya metro station. They belong to the singer Liza Umarova. Her eyes, like those of the other strugglers, are focused on the ground; she doesn't want to end up on her back, or on her knees in a puddle. Liza, who usually dresses in black, wears a purple headscarf with pink overtones this morning and walks like a woman used to getting attention. Sometimes a delight, sometimes a nuisance, but always a matter of course. She has dark eyes and curly black hair. Her face is beautiful, but gaunt; soon it will be an old woman's face. The lines etched by the last few years have made it hard, a little sad, a little mysterious.

Liza is not walking alone. She would have preferred to be accompanied by someone in her family, but since she has no family in Moscow she asked Apti to help her. Apti, or Oleg, as he calls himself in Russia, was more than willing. The short, stocky man walks quickly, almost skipping, beside Liza. He has red hair and ruddy, freckled skin. For the occasion he is wearing a freshly ironed pink shirt that makes him look like a banker.

Apti is a historian. A historian without a job, but nevertheless with numerous uniquely constructed theories which he energetically disseminates. Tramping through the slush he tells Liza about his sensational new hypothesis that will transform the world's understanding of history and religion; namely, that the Chechens are directly descended from the prophet Mohammed, via his son-in-law, Ali. According to Apti, Ali fought in the Caucasus and is buried in the mountains.

Apti's voice hammers in her ear like a piston, but Liza hardly pays any attention to it. Six months have passed since the event that forces her to spend yet another day in court. She's tired of it. Both she and Murat forgave the three boys long ago.

On the opposite side of the courthouse the Ivanovs walk briskly from the Kutuzovskaya metro station. Olga and Ivan are of average height and have grey eyes, pallid winter skin and blond hair covered by a cap and scarf. They are wearing clothes from an ordinary manufacturer and solid winter boots. The man has a handsome square face; his only blemish is a row of uneven teeth. An eye tooth in his upper jaw has gone, giving him an ambiguous expression when he smiles, as if someone had set a trap in the regular features. The woman is slightly overweight, has a round, ordinary face, and wears discreet make-up with grey eyeshadow.

They walk through the drifting snow feeling that the world is unfair, that it's contrary to nature and against all principles to be on their way to a court hearing in which their youngest son is a defendant, and that Sergei has been innocently drawn into this disgusting case. After all, their son never said that he was a fascist sympathiser. Both of his grandfathers fought against Hitler in the Second World War.

Walking through the same revolving door of the metro station is Boris Gorbenko. Two metres tall, with broad shoulders and strong legs, he tramps along in the loose snow without bothering about the lurking water traps. He has a slight stoop now, but, even so, he towers a head above most of the other people. Wisps of dark blond hair stick out at the back of his neck under his fur hat. His eyes are deep-set. One front tooth is broken; only the root remains. He has big, chunky hands. The network of grooves and furrows in his palms and on his fingers are black with oil that can't be washed off after a working life as a mechanic. Walking beside him in heavy boots is his eldest son, also wearing rough working clothes. He too is about two metres tall.

A few steps behind their snowy backs, Boris Gorbenko's mother-in-law, Antonina Grigorevna, grandmother of the second defendant, struggles forward in the icy domain. She barely comes up to the men's chests, but is even broader, and puffs along with a rolling gait. Her coat is tight across her back and chest, a thin crocheted scarf is tied under her chin. Perhaps it's the exertion that makes her lips tremble slightly.

Conversation among the three has come to a standstill.

Ouf, what weather it is this Friday! The wind howls, the snow blows sideways, people shiver with cold, cars collide, the airports are closed, and children are kept home from school when Liza and Apti, Olga and Ivan, and three generations of Gorbenkos reach the Dorogomilovski court of law. It is modestly situated in a rear courtyard between tall buildings and a fenced-in playground with some rusty swings. The only colour in the drab complex is the Russian flag at the entrance. It means there is someone here who exercises power.

After a security check, they all enter Courtroom 203 and sit down among the members of the public. Artur, the third friend accused in the case, is already seated on a chair with his back to the spectators. According to Gorbenko, Artur had the good fortune of not being held in custody because of his father's contacts. The Ivanovs greets Liza Umarova briefly, but ignore Apti. Grandmother Antonina gives everyone a friendly greeting, while the Gorbenkos sit with their arms crossed on their chests and blank expressions on their faces.

This is the case: when the second war in Chechnya began, Liza fled with her three children to Moscow, where they live in a two-room apartment on the outskirts of the city. The children started school and made friends, but like most Chechen children had to endure bullying and abusive language. They were called 'terrorists' and 'gangsters'. After the terrorist attack on the children's school in Beslan in 2004 it was especially difficult to be Chechens in the Russian capital. Violence against people from the Caucasus exploded. For a young boy with typical North Caucasus features, like her son Murat, it was particularly bad. Liza had long thought the fifteen-year-old needed to develop a few muscles in his thin body, that he should begin training in a combat sport, just to be on the safe side. As soon as school started the previous year, she found a gym near Fili Park and took the boy there. On their way back through the park they met three drunken young men who grabbed Murat.

'What nationality are you?' one shouted, holding the boy by the collar. When Murat didn't answer, three pairs of fists hit him in the face.

'Russia is for Russians!' they yelled, and kept hitting. Liza shouted for help, but the park lay dark and silent. The one who had started everything, a fellow two metres tall, pulled up his T-shirt. Tattooed on his chest was a large swastika dangling in the beak of an eagle, the Russian eagle.

'This is what we ought to do with the two of you,' he shouted, pointing at the swastika. 'You can't live here,' he declared as they continued to beat Murat.

Liza screamed louder, and, when the young men let go, she and Murat saw their chance to run. Murat was bleeding from the nose and mouth, but they didn't even think of going to the police.

An estimated fifty thousand racial attacks occur in Russia every year. The number is increasing. Few people dare to report the assaults. The police often sympathise more with the attacker than with the victim. Only a few hundred incidents are recorded each year, along with fifty racially motivated murders. The perpetrators are seldom prosecuted; a conviction is even rarer. Most assaults are by young men. One out of two cases related to fear of foreigners is held behind closed doors because the defendant is under eighteen years old.

People from the Caucasus in general, and from Chechnya in particular, top the list of hate figures and have the lowest reputation among ordinary Russians. Chechens have problems registering in Russian cities, enrolling children at school, getting jobs, finding places to live.

So Liza did nothing about the incident. But the next victim did — a man with a hooked nose and dark eyes who 'looked like he was Jewish', as the boys would later tell the judge.

He described the attack to the police like this: 'I was on my way home with my wife and daughter. Three young men ran towards us. One pushed me, and soon all three started punching me. After I was knocked down, they used their feet. Between the blows and kicks one asked me my name, and I answered Pavel Semyonovich. "So you're Russian?" he said in amazement, and stopped with his hand in mid-air. "We thought you were Jewish! He's white!" he shouted, and went down on his knees in front of me and begged forgiveness. Then they staggered away.'

The young men had forgotten something important. Aleksei

Gorbenko's bag was left behind; in it was his student card with his full address, and notebooks with swastikas in the margins and racist slogans.

Pavel Semyonovich went straight to the police, who dutifully recorded the incident, but took no further action. The man went to the local casualty department where he got written verification of large bruises on his legs and the small of his back, as well as effusions and swelling on his face.

When Liza and her son finally got home after a long trip on the metro and then a rickety local bus, the telephone rang. It was her friend Nadya inviting her to come over. When Liza described the assault, Nadya, who was a journalist for the paper *Gazeta*, sensed a good story and convinced Liza to report the attack and consent to an interview.

A few days later the headline read: 'I Want to Sing for Skinheads'. Even though Liza Umarova was completely unknown in Russia, she was famous in Chechnya. She had never made a CD, but pirated recordings of her songs were played everywhere.

When Liza reported the attack and the newspaper article appeared, the police in Fili district went back to the case of Pavel Semyonovich, and there was all the information they needed. Ten days later, early in the morning, the police rang on the doorbell at the homes of Aleksei and Sergei and their incredulous parents. Artur was picked up some hours later during his first morning class. Police interrupted the professor at the lectern, handcuffed Artur and escorted him out of the room.

The three young men were questioned individually. Artur was able to call his father, who arranged for a lawyer, and he was released from custody. His friends remained in detention. The charge was clear: incitement to national, racial and religious hatred. The so-called racism clause, Article 282 in the Constitution – an Article that had seldom been applied.

At first Liza had been happy that they were going to be brought to trial. What would stop them, otherwise?

But now the young men had been in custody for almost six months, and the case was at a standstill. It was inconvenient to have to go to court so often. And it was unpleasant meeting the parents.

As people crowded together in the rows of seats this chilly March day, two guards dragged a couple of pot plants across the linoleum. Their dry foliage made the room look even more dismal. A white grille on the windows created a sunburst design. Radiators under the windows were covered with boards that had lost several screws, so some of them hung crookedly while others were missing completely. The light switches on the wall were almost black from years of greasy fingertips.

The lawyers took their places at a small table at the front of the room, and the judge seated himself at his desk on a platform facing the spectators. Above the judge's chair hung the Russian flag and a gold eagle.

Behind the lawyers was a cage with grey bars and steel netting that created a low ceiling. Inside the cage was a bench.

The doors to the corridor opened and a group of policemen approached. One of them was handcuffed to a pale young man, whom he led into the cage. The cuffs were clicked open and attached to a pole by the bars. Then the policeman left the cage and closed the door. The young man sat with his head down and his hands lying loosely in his lap, from time to time stealing glances at the rows of spectators. His mother waved, almost without raising her hand. His father sent him a stern 'just wait till you get out' look. But why was Sergei sitting alone? Where was Aleksei?

The judge looked out over the assembly with an arrogant expression and read from a piece of paper: 'Aleksei Gorbenko is in quarantine after an outbreak of meningitis in the prison.'

A gasp went through the audience.

'The court will reconvene in two weeks,' said the judge, and rose from his chair.

The cage door was opened, the handcuffs were put on again,

and locked. Sergei was led out of the cage handcuffed to the guard who had escorted him in. The group turned down the corridor and disappeared.

'Meningitis!' exclaimed Antonina Grigorevna, aghast.

The people around her looked at her gravely. Contagious diseases are rife in Russian prisons, and meningitis can kill you. Inmates die of illnesses like tuberculosis or from sudden epidemics.

The ill-assorted group said a somewhat disconcerted farewell. Liza and the Ivanovs still maintained a chilly politeness. The babushka crossed herself and said she wanted to stop by at a convent in Taganka, while the Gorbenko men ignored everyone. The thing that brought them together, the event of six months earlier, gave them nothing in common.

The door of the courthouse slammed shut behind the last members of the public. They huddled more snugly into their winter coats and trudged back to the metro stations they had come from, while the wind whistled around their ears.

The Gorbenko family live near the Akademik Yangele metro station, where a forest of tall concrete structures sprang up during the 1970s. Lovely birch trees have been planted in front of the buildings, and a network of paths connects their entrances. Once you get away from the metro, a gradual calm descends. You are shielded from the noise of traffic by the ever increasing number of buildings sprawling across the flat landscape. Soon you can hear birds twittering and the sound of your footsteps creaking in the snow. Although the apartment blocks hold thousands of families, there's hardly anyone to be seen. Because this is a dormitory community; people's homes are here, not their lives. About seven in the morning the area swarms with people who trudge along the paths in the winter darkness, crowd into trams and then elbow their way to the metro, where they stand squashed, sweating in their winter coats. The same happens at about six in the evening. In the middle of the day there are plenty of seats on the metro and the paths are empty. Moreover, today is Sunday, and few people are out among the concrete colossuses.

In a kitchen on the tenth floor of one building Galya Gorbenko is frying *blini*. The stack of golden pancakes grows; she has put a little baking powder into the batter so they will be light and airy. Galya sets out salmon and sour cream, turns yet another pancake in the pan, and in between sets the table. The oilcloth on the table has a three-dimensional design in shimmering shades of silver with plums, cherries and flowers floating above it. The kitchen cupboards are decorated with stickers from the Soviet era. Labels from vodka bottles are glued to one cupboard. Others are pink, in glaring contrast to the orange-flowered wallpaper. Dried flowers, potted plants, knick-knacks and plastic figures hang, lie, stand everywhere in the kitchen.

Boris Gorbenko shows me around the living room and asks me to look at the books.

'Pushkin's collected works, Tolstoy's collected works. Here is Bulgakov. Look, here is Karamzin's world history, Solovyev's philosophy, and here, *Myths of the World* and *Legends from the Bible*. Yes, legends. Note the word. The Bible is all fabrication, there's no logical coherence to it. We're atheists in this house,' he asserts, while his wife mumbles something to the effect that you can never know really.

In the son's room there are more shelves of books, series about explorers, *Children's World History*, *Children's Atlas*, *Children's Physics and Chemistry*. One bookshelf near the ceiling is filled with soft drink and beer cans.

'He started to collect them as soon as cans came to the Soviet Union, and he's kept it up. As soon as new brands came on the market, he wanted to have them,' says the father.

A huge poster of Bambi hangs on the wall. Boris picks up a couple of dumb-bells lying in a corner.

'Feel these! Can you lift them? No? Our son was so strong that if he had hit Murat, he would have killed him with a single blow.

That's how strong he was! And the boy only got a few bruises! It couldn't possibly have been our Aleksei.'

It's the anniversary of Stalin's death, which this year falls on the last day of *Maslenitsa* – Shrovetide – when you're supposed to gorge yourself on pancakes before the fasting begins.

The fifth of September the previous year had been a perfectly ordinary day, apart from the fact that Aleksei had been paid. He had taken two of his friends and some bottles of beer to Fili Park, where they sat and drank. They had got up to go and sit somewhere else when they saw a dark-haired woman and her dark-haired son. From this point on Liza's and Aleksei's stories differ.

According to Aleksei's parents, Murat jostled their son and shouted: 'Russian swine!'

'Was our son supposed to just stand there and take that? Put his head down and keep walking? Should we be afraid to respond, in our own country? Even if we're insulted?'

Boris Gorbenko barely has space enough in the little kitchen, where we are sharing a bench nailed to the wall. Galya sits with her back to the window.

'Our son asked, "What are you doing here if you don't like us? Go home!" That was all. He came home and ate a late dinner with us. We didn't notice anything special, except that he'd been drinking a little – but that's normal, after all. One morning the police came. "Does Aleksei Borisovich Gorbenko live here?" they asked. I said yes. "He is under arrest," they said. "What have you done?" I whispered to him, terrified, but he just rolled his eyes. The policeman said Aleksei was going to be asked a few questions, and would be released quickly. Had I known he wouldn't come back, I would have gone along; but I let them take him and went to work. When I came home, I telephoned the police; they said he was being held in custody. It was several days before they let me see him. And you know what? They stole his cell phone, and he had six hundred roubles in his pocket – in fact, almost seven hundred – and they took his keys, too, so we've changed the locks. When I reported this to the police they just said: "Send your complaint to the Kremlin"!'

Aleksei's mother is short and stout, with a cheerful face, clear skin and blue eyes. She is wearing a turquoise tennis shirt, and over it a baking apron with a pattern of stars and garlands. She has a pudding-basin haircut and the curls dance in her face as she says indignantly:

'Oy, oy, oy, he's got so thin. He's lost forty kilos! He was big, he practised karate and aikido. Now he's as thin as a rake, but before, he was strong; he inherited my biceps. Look!' she cries, gripping her plump wrists. 'His were even bigger than mine!'

The parents also find it painful that Aleksei has been singled out as the ringleader. There were three of them there, after all. Galya and Boris are certain they are right. The two other boys have bribed their way out of it. And now they all blame one another. Artur, who evaded custody, is the worst, they think. When Galya went over to him during the trial he just whispered: 'Papa paid.'

'Look at him now. He's continuing his studies, while our Aleksei sits in jail!'

Aleksei had been studying history at a teacher training college and would have completed his degree by the summer.

'They were expecting him at the elementary school over there,' says Galya, pointing to a small building, the only low one among the high-rises. 'Now he won't be able to finish. You can draw a big cross over his future, like this,' she says, tracing an X in the air. 'Just because he pushed that little boy!'

Aleksei, or Lyosha or Alyosha, as his parents call him, already had a cross on himself, a swastika tattooed on his chest. He sympathised with *Slavyanski Soyuz*, an organisation with the suggestive initials SS. Their watchword is 'Russia for Russians'. The members dress like tough guys and are often shaven-headed, like Aleksei.

His parents play down the connection.

'Lyosha had short hair because that was modern. Don't you

remember when the Beatles were so popular? Everyone had long hair then; in fact, Boris had long hair when we met. It didn't mean anything except that he was following the fashion. And as far as the swastika goes, he was drunk, and when he woke up, somebody had tattooed it on him. Both of his grandfathers fought against fascism in the Second World War. His grandmother, too. Last year they got a card from President Putin in which he thanked them for what they had contributed sixty years ago. Aleksei's grandfather was a paratrooper and fought in one of the most prestigious regiments in the Soviet army. He was very thin, and blind, and had had his leg amputated. He died just after he got that card.

'When we were working at the dacha last year Aleksei kept his shirt on, but as it got warmer and warmer, he decided to take it off, and showed us the tattoo. "Now you can no longer go to Jewish doctors" was his father's only comment.

'He just wanted to be like them. Belong. He wanted people to be afraid of him,' Galya continues. 'And they were. I remember I went to buy a watermelon from an Azerbaijani; yes, only Azerbaijanis sell watermelons. When he was about to hand me one, he saw Lyosha, who was standing a little behind me. Then he swapped the melon for a different one, and when we came home we found we had a delicious, juicy, red watermelon – not a pale one like I usually got. You see? They were afraid of him. Alyosha wants people to be afraid of him, but he has such a good, kind face. He used to stand in front of the mirror and practise looking scary; he wrinkled his brow, thrust out his chin, stared with an ugly look in his eyes,' says Galya, and grimaces.

She shows me the piece of jewellery she wears around her neck. It's like a swastika, but has three arms instead of four.

'That's the fire god Peron, from before the time of Christ,' she explains. 'I got it from Lyosha; he said it would protect me. The swastika is actually an old Celtic symbol, and I think that was what Lyosha was thinking about when he got tattooed. He's no Nazi or racist or skinhead.'

'But when he shouted "Russia for Russians"?'

'Who else should Russia be for?' Boris interjects. 'For pygmies?'

Galya nods energetically.

'For darkies?' Boris continues.

Galya gives me a penetrating look.

'Yes, for whom, if not for Russians?'

'Now he could get five years because he dared to express his opinions!' Boris thunders in the tiny kitchen. 'And as if that weren't enough, he could lose his life; he could be killed for those words. Now he's quarantined because of meningitis. Other parts of the prison are raging with tuberculosis. Our son isn't serving time like Khodorkovski, who gets a private room.'

Galya has been sitting with her head in her hands, but now she straightens up and urges me to have another golden pancake with salmon and sour cream.

'Let's say it straight out,' says Boris. 'We don't like Chechens. Not before and not now. We know our history and know how criminal they are, how they never accepted Russian rule, but continued to live as wild men, *dikary*. Of course people should have equal rights, but the Chechens never give in. They fight against everyone, they live in bandit territory, they take revenge on everyone, they govern according to their traditions of blood feud. In 1944 Stalin did the only right thing: he deported the entire nation to Siberia. Do you know why? Because the Chechens shot us in the back. They collaborated with the Nazis. They blew up two apartment blocks not far from here. Do you remember? Two hundred people were killed. Where will they stop? Maybe it was Umarova's clan that blew up those blocks.'

Boris has focused his hate on the Chechen woman. The Russian who first reported his own experience to the police is seldom mentioned.

'When Alyosha realised that the man wasn't a Jew, he went down on his knees and apologised. He's a wonderful fellow, such a good boy. Actually, he liked to sit at home and play computer games; we bought a lot of games for him, so he would stay at home,' sighs Galya. 'He always liked to fight, and I told him, ever since he was a little boy: "Try to explain with words, Alyosha. With words, not by hitting."'

The parents are allowed to send Aleksei food once a month and they pack up biscuits, sugar, tea, apples, nuts, raisins and onions. 'Bring more food next time,' he had asked his grandmother who, after numerous trips to the prison, was finally allowed a visit with the help of her 'Second World War Veteran' certificate.

'It's fine to send the cheaper things, but send more of them; there are many of us,' Aleksei had said.

The many are not always among his best friends. Anyone who doesn't obey *The Oldest* is beaten up or punished some other way. There are forty men and twenty-four hard bunks in Aleksei's cell, so the inmates take turns sleeping; the longer you have been in prison, the longer you get to lie in bed.

The parents have received telephone calls from a tearful Aleksei. 'Meet in front of this metro station, look for a blonde woman in a grey jacket. Ask her if she's waiting for Boris, and if she answers, "No, I'm waiting for Vanya", then give her an envelope with two thousand roubles.'

His mother has been four times.

'So now, because of this Umarova, our Aleksei is mixing with gangsters! His friends say that he asks them for money, too. He told them he couldn't ask us for any more. Boris has lost his job; the factory downsized, so they threw out the oldest workers. And all because Alyosha bumped into a Chechen!

'During the Soviet era, all nationalities were friends. Everything was fine then,' Galya continues. 'Every morning we said hello to our fellow students, those from both Afghanistan and Mozambique.'

'It was Lenin and Stalin who started all this,' says Boris. 'They created the republics. Before that, there was one governor for the northern regions and one for the southern regions. Vladimir Ilyich and Josef Vissarionovich drew the borders for the territories.

Brezhnev strengthened the Soviet Union, Khrushchev gave away the Crimea, and Gorbachev ruined everything. He shoved us into the mud, took away our pride. Before, the Cossacks in the south protected us from the Chechens. Grozny was built by Cossacks, the border was the Terek River. Now the Chechens have crossed the river and are sneaking in all over.'

The telephone rings.

'Oy, my child! How are you?'

Galya's voice quavers.

Boris fixes his eyes on his wife's face.

'Do you have everything you need? Toilet paper? Underwear? Do you have enough? Are you unhappy? I was so frightened when I heard about the meningitis. When is the quarantine over? We're sitting here eating pancakes; it's Shrovetide, you know. Yes, of course I can take in your trousers. Don't you get any food? Oh, your voice sounds so . . . well, it's good to hear it in any case. Are things any better than last time? Lyosha, you can't fool me, you know . . .'

Galya hangs up. Their conversation had suddenly been cut off. Her eyes fill with tears.

'We Russians are very patient,' she says. 'It takes a lot to make us lose our composure. Our boy wears a size forty-seven shoe; he could have killed that Murat with just one finger. Bruises and a nosebleed?'

'Maybe he slipped and fell on the ice – or no, on the asphalt maybe,' says Boris. He takes out a bottle of Russian champagne and dusts it off. It appears to have been saved for a special occasion, but he opens it. Galya watches anxiously. The champagne is sweet and mild and warm.

'We aren't fascists,' Boris reiterates. 'But who are the Jews anyway? They wandered around in the desert for forty years so they would forget where they came from. Then they started to kill the local people and moved into their houses. I'm against Israel. The Jews got their Jewish republic in Siberia. They could live there! And this friend of Umarova who goes around spouting his ideas – that Ivan the Terrible was a Muslim? that the Chechens somehow descend from a fine Arab family? I said to him: "Fine families usually live in fine places, so if you people are so superior, you'd be from Istanbul, or at least Damascus. And what did you get? Some black mountains where nothing grows"!'

The warm champagne froths in the glass.

'Chechens are sly, deceitful, treacherous . . . there's probably a man behind her, because a woman from there could never operate like that on her own,' Boris asserts. 'And why does everything go so badly down there? Because of the clan system. They don't hire experts to run the factories or the administration, they hire members of the clan instead, unskilled uncles and cousins and brothers. Is it any wonder there's trouble? Do you know what the Egyptians did to get rid of the Jews? They imposed double taxation on them. Wasn't that smart? That's what we ought to do with the Chechens, impose double taxation. Then they'd disappear!

'And that woman, Umarova, who says she's a singer – I've never heard her sing. Spare us her wailing about freedom; she can go back to Chechnya with her songs! This whole case is fabricated by that songbird; she's using it as publicity, in order to promote herself. That's why my son has now lost his freedom, forfeited his education, and lives with forty others in a room with twenty beds. Why does she absolutely have to sing in Moscow? Why here in Moscow, if she thinks it's so bad living among Russians? Besides, it was she who provoked my son; she shouted: "Russian swine"! Is it any wonder that he got angry? No. Let them live and build in their own land. No one is stopping them. Leave us in peace.

'These Muslims are all idiots; they didn't understand that the cartoons of Mohammed were just that – cartoons. As a matter of fact, I thought they were very good. Mohammed with a bomb on his head, that's exactly the way they are! They're idiots, but dangerous idiots! And our son was the only one who dared to speak the truth. He'll become a national hero! And I can say to myself: "I'm the father of a well-brought-up son."'

*

A dusty silence settles on the kitchen after the champagne has been drunk. As always every Sunday, the Gorbenkos visit Babushka Antonina, who lives a few buildings away.

We seat ourselves around a table in the modest living room. The grandmother takes a photograph of her grandson from the sideboard and presses it to her breast. 'Oh, he's such a good boy, so helpful, so kind.'

The attack on the Chechens she calls a boyish prank. The swastika is worse. She first learned about that when it appeared in the newspaper. 'I'll save money so that he can have it removed. I can hardly bear to think about it. Just imagine, a swastika . . . How can he ever go to the sea? Swim?'

The grandmother sighs. What went wrong?

'Yesterday I telephoned Politkovskaya,' she says suddenly.

'What did she say?' Galya asks.

'*She*? No, I was the one who talked. I asked why she called my grandson a fascist. Why did she write that he spread national hate? I told her that he had attended the wedding of a childhood friend who was Jewish, and that he wasn't a fascist. I told her that I was a veteran of the Great War for the Fatherland. That I'd got a medal. That my husband had defended Moscow. That both my father and my grandfather were arrested in 1937. That I was ten years old when they took Papa. How frightened we were! Papa was sent to prison camp. Now Alyosha is in prison camp. Papa was a Party man, but was called an enemy of the people. Now Alyosha is called an enemy of the people. Papa was rehabilitated. Alyosha must be rehabilitated, too. What's more, I said that I have a Jewish neighbour. She's eight-two years old, lives right above me. That's just fine. It was a nasty article this Anna Politkovskaya wrote about Alyosha; I told her that. Then I hung up. She didn't get a chance to say anything.'

Her son-in-law drums his fingers on the table. 'Useless,' he says. 'Useless.'

Antonina snorts.

'I was at the convent yesterday,' she says. 'The priest told me that now it's the Russians who are being persecuted. *Gonenie na russkikh*. But he asked me not to give up. "We Russians endure everything," he said.'

Antonina often takes the metro and then a tram to the convent of St Matryona, who watches over prisoners. She rises heavily and goes and gets a prayer book she bought at the convent. Leaning her hands on the table, she slowly sits down on her chair again. Then the nearly eighty-year-old woman reads loudly and clearly from the prayers about atonement, purification and forgiveness.

'A random collection of words,' Boris says contemptuously.

'Be quiet,' says Antonina.

'A collection of words,' he repeats.

'Show respect,' shouts the grandmother, and aims a blow at him.

Boris and his mother-in-law have, over many years, learned to put up with each other, but are continually fighting.

'Myths, stories, childish prattle,' Boris continues.

'Now just you calm down!'

'Calm down both of you,' hisses Galya. 'Let's watch TV!'

And with TV, the discussion ends.

At the other end of the city, just as far out but on the north end near the Altufyevo metro station, the Ivanov family live in a three-room apartment on the sixteenth floor.

'Before, we could see all the way to the airport towers at Sheremetyevo. Just look how they're building, they've ruined our view! But at least the new buildings shield us from the noise of the traffic from the ring road,' says Ivan Ivanov, Sergei's father.

In the living room, which also serves as the parents' bedroom, are a soft sofa and a couple of armchairs. Each of the two sons has a bedroom of his own; in one, the bed is made up perfectly. 'Well, this is Sergei's room,' says his father, and closes the door. In the kitchen Olga Ivanova serves tea and chocolate buns.

Ivan brings out some photographs. 'See, they trained here,

these are from Murmansk, and this is from a bicycle trip to the Crimea; here we are at Yalta, this is from Odessa. We biked, took with us everything we needed. My boys are strong. For two years in a row Sergei has competed in the Super-100, a one-hundred-kilometre ski race. He did it in five hours and came in twenty-first. Not bad for someone who isn't a professional. You've got the Vasalopp, that's tougher perhaps, even if it's only ninety kilometres, because it's classic skiing. At the Super race you can skate. I prefer to skate because then I don't have to wax my skis and it's faster! What was it you said you did the Vasalopp in? Seven hours? Not bad. Look, there's Yelena Välbe, six times world champion. Next to my son, you see? There's Julia Chepalova. She got silver in the thirty kilometres at the Olympics in Turin, and the gold in the relay; she did the third lap, got the best time of anyone.

'The past few years Sergei has been strong in dog racing. Last year he won silver in the men's class; I came in seventh. The year before he won in the junior class. You can see in these pictures — see, there he is starting. Even if we were never rich in the Soviet Union, we were always strong in sport. Not that everything was good then, but people all had the same opportunities. School, training, sport. Everyone was able to have a go at things. Don't recall that we lacked anything.'

After going through the pictures, Ivan pauses. The FSB officer runs his hand through his thick blond hair. He looks only a young man himself. Olga and Ivan had their children when they were in their early twenties. The same age as their sons are now.

Ivan wonders whether there was anything he could have done differently. But Sergei had never said he was a Nazi or that he disliked foreigners. And he wasn't a neglected child. On the contrary, he was pampered. Ivan had spent most of his free time with his two sons from the time they were children. He took them on trips to the woods and fields, taught them to ski, went along to training camps. When price limits were removed without a corresponding increase in wages during the early nineties, and money was tight for the family, Ivan worked weekends on the black market to scrape together enough roubles for the boys' sports equipment. Despite the fact that this was strictly forbidden for army officers. He had a degree in engineering and did repairs for people in their homes – washing machines, fans, ovens. So the boys wouldn't lack for anything.

It was a great disappointment when the oldest son, Misha, quit active sport as a sixteen-year-old. But Sergei continued. He and his father had already planned their dog- racing season.

Ivan purses his lips.

One week before the fateful blows, Sergei started an agricultural course at a college.

'That evening, yes. Three good friends. Drank a little. They were celebrating a birthday.'

Sergei had been upset when he came home, at about midnight. He had eaten a little and had some tea with them, but they got no answer when they asked what had happened.

'They were walking on a narrow path. And they brushed against each other,' Olga explains. 'You know, for example on the bus, they sit there talking in every imaginable language, usually loudly. It's not exactly pleasant, or polite. Often I feel uneasy, and think they're saying something negative about me. What with everything that goes on in Chechnya – the attacks on Russian soldiers, the terror, kidnappings, assaults. We don't want the conflict to move here, of course, and with all the Chechens that come . . .'

'This Article 282, what do we really need it for?' asks Ivan. 'In the Soviet Union we had even more nationalities living together. We didn't need it then. I think it was introduced because of pressure from all these funds and organisations that work for all sorts of human rights. But what are they actually doing? In order to get money, they need cases to refer to, and they get a lot of cases through Article 282. For example: a Ukrainian starts a quarrel with a Russian. The Russian says, "You damned Ukrainian, go back where you came from!" That makes the Ukrainian angry, and he can accuse the Russian of violating Article 282. If they were both Russians, nobody would be convicted. In Russia it's rare that anyone gets punished for fights, even if someone is hurt. But if one of them is a foreigner, he can wave Article 282 and the Russian gets served a summons. Is that fair?'

The parents speak with one voice. They are an average couple as regards appearance, home, work, background and opinions.

'When Olga was three, her father died from wounds he got in the Second World War, my grandfather died at the front – also his brother, my uncle – all in the same war. There isn't a family in Russia that hasn't been harmed by fascism,' snaps Ivan. 'Our country is vast. We asked Germans to come and live here, we asked the French to come. And now we're called racists! We who invited everyone to come here! I hope the same thing happens with Article 282 as with Gorbachev's grapevines. Do you remember? In his eagerness to get rid of drunkenness, Gorbachev ordered all the grapevines to be pulled up. What happened? The wine industry was devastated, while the vodka industry thrived, along with moonshine and smuggling. People drank perfume, industrial alcohol, antifreeze. Gorbachev ate humble pie and admitted that it was a mistake to destroy the grapevines. We hope that the same will happen with Article 282, that Putin will regret it and get rid of it.'

'When our son went to prison everybody knew which Article he was prosecuted under, and in his cell there were many inmates from the Caucasus . . .

'They telephone us and say: "Your son has lost at cards. He owes such and such. It won't be very pleasant for him if you don't pay up." We can't do anything except pay. Use our savings. Borrow money,' sighs Ivan. 'They even gave me their licence plate number. I could have gone straight to the police. But they knew their power. The first three times it was people from the Caucasus – at least, they didn't have Slavic features. The last couple of times they were nicely dressed men, Russians; probably it was the prison guards who extorted money from us.'

'Liza Umarova gave me a book for Sergei,' says Olga. 'But we don't have permission to take books. So I read it myself instead. *Sedoi Kavkaz* it was called. To be honest, I got a little irritated. The whole book is about how the Chechens have suffered for centuries. As if *we* haven't suffered? As if the Russians haven't suffered? Everyone suffered in the eighteenth and nineteenth centuries – in the last century, too. Everyone suffered during the Second World War. What makes the Chechens feel they are so special? Yes, it was an OK book, as far as it goes, but there's got to be a limit to all the whining. Going on and on about the hard life of these poor mountain people. After all, both Pushkin and Lermontov wrote about that. As if our lives were any easier? No, the Chechens are harsh people. In their language there's no word for *miloserdie* – compassion,' Olga asserts.

'Poor Aleksei. He was called a skinhead in the newspaper! We had workers from Georgia here, and I never saw him react against them. He would have, if he were a fascist. I know the boys were interested in Aryan things, at least Alyosha was. But why do the accusations always go in just one direction? Why is it never reported when dark people attack the light ones?'

It has grown late; Olga's face has become even greyer. Ivan looks sad.

'Well, Lenin called the prison a university,' he just says.

While his skiing friends speed among the birch trees under a sparkling March sun, Sergei sits in a musty cell in a prison on the outskirts of Moscow. A small air vent is his only access to spring. One hour each day the inmates are taken to the open-air area on the top of the building. It has a corrugated-iron surface and is railed off. He has been in custody for six months, and from the very first day he tried to learn the survival tactics of prison life.

'When you enter your cell for the first time you must put down your bag at the door so that *starshi* – The Oldest – can go through it and take what he wants,' explained one of the experienced prisoners.

The position of The Oldest isn't to do with age, but with prison experience, criminal history and leadership qualities. He is chosen by his fellow inmates, or he selects himself, and stands or falls depending on whether he is obeyed or not. The hierarchy goes according to what kind of crime the person has committed, and already during the first ten days Sergei had become an expert on Articles. The most prestige went to those charged with simple theft – Article 158. There were several levels within the theft clause; a pickpocket stood high on the list because picking pockets required basic criminal cunning. Breaking into an apartment was also good. Then came assault and robbery. It should be quick and effective; preferably, no one should get hurt. After theft came murder. At the very bottom came those imprisoned for rape. They got the hardest tasks and were hounded most severely. Somewhere along the way came drug dealing. But where did Article 282, the racism clause, come?

'That depends on the cell,' said the experienced prisoner. 'If you've got many from the Caucasus, you'll have a hard time; if most of them are Russians, you'll be a hero.'

After a couple of weeks Sergei was moved to the cell he would occupy for the rest of his time in prison. Twenty-five heads looked up when he was led in and shown to a bunk by the lavatory, the worst sleeping place in the cell. The guard left the cell, slammed the door behind him, turned the key, and Sergei was left to the vultures. He put his bag down by the door and asked: 'Who's The Oldest here?'

The men pointed to a dark-skinned man with a beaky nose and huge biceps sitting on the bed under the air vent, the choicest place in the cell.

'Which Article?' he asked.

'Two eighty-two.'

'What did you do?'

'Got in a fight.'

'Who with?' asked the man with the beaky nose.

He's clearly from the Caucasus, Sergei said to himself, and trembled inwardly. He was lost.

'There was an argument, then a few blows, and then I, or rather, we – there are three of us – were reported.'

Three men against a woman and a child. That would not have high status. He tried to change the story, to save himself, thinking that he had landed up in the worst possible cell. Dark, penetrating eyes turned towards him.

'But why the racism clause?' asked the man with the beaky nose.

'I don't know . . .'

'Oh?'

'Well, they were Chechens . . .'

'That's bad,' said the man, and Sergei flinched. He had failed the first test. He felt they were hissing at him. His legs shook. He looked towards the rat-grey walls. The cell was silent. The air nauseating. The Oldest said to the others: 'Don't touch him. In here, we're all equally unlucky.'

Sergei had been given a chance. A chance he had better not abuse.

The Oldest was from Georgia, and even if he was from the Caucasus he was no friend of the Chechens. Georgians are Christian, and Beak Nose thought the Chechens gave the whole region a bad reputation with their terrorist activities. Just five of the two dozen prisoners in Sergei's cell were Russian, the rest were from the Caucasus or Central Asia. The prison was like a village, where each cell was a house with its own rules. In the bunk above Sergei, the one with a view of the lavatory, lay a rapist. The bunks of the thieves and murderers were closest to The Oldest.

Sergei kept to himself during the first days, which he spent waiting for them to end. The inmates were woken up at eight o'clock; then came cell inspection, breakfast at ten, exercise at eleven, lunch at two and dinner at seven. The food was terrible: sticky porridge, thin soup with shreds of something, or potatoes and soya meat. Food parcels from home broke the monotony. First the parcel went to The Oldest, then to the person to whom it had been sent, and then to the other men – you put it on the table so everyone could help himself. The unwritten rules maintained a certain balance. Even if The Oldest helped himself first, he couldn't be too greedy; that would cause grumbling among the others. The same moderation held true for the recipient of the parcel. If he hid certain treats, it was regarded as impolite and he would be ostracised as punishment.

The worst crime among the criminals was being a stool pigeon. If anyone was caught as an informant, the cell brothers showed no mercy. Sergei saw several get beaten up. The Oldest did it himself or designated someone to dole out the punishment. No blood could flow, so they hit in places where it wouldn't be seen – on the temples and the back of the head, where bruises were hidden by hair. All the same, the solidarity was better than in the army, where sadistic officers can wreak whatever havoc they wish on soldiers during basic training, while documents saying 'Cause of death: Suicide' were sent to the parents. In prison, you had to have grounds for a beating. You could set matters straight, as you would with a mate.

It was The Oldest who was responsible for extorting money – 'so that nothing happens to Sergei in prison', as he said to Olga in his thick Georgian accent.

As time went on, Sergei adjusted to prison life. He started to smoke, something he had never done before, and he became a good card player. During the Olympics in Turin they got a TV. Sergei sat glued to the television. When his old training comrade Yevgeni Dementyev won the gold in the thirty kilometres he was jubilant. Yevgeni, who was a couple of years older than him, had always been outstanding – big, fast, strong. 'As a fifteen-year-old he was already competing with the seniors,' Sergei boasted to his cell mates. He remembered his friend's raw humour, as untamed as the place Yevgeni was from, the furthest east you could go in Russia.

As for Sergei himself, his muscles vanished, the exercise area on the roof was no more than twenty square metres and it drove him crazy walking in a circle. Of course, he could have done exercises in the cell, but the air was suffocating there, and he would have been intimidated by the others watching him. So he gave up the idea once and for all.

Liza Umarova sits with headphones, a stack of paper and a drawer of index cards in the music section of the huge Lenin Library near the Kremlin. She is looking for Chechen folksongs. When she finds the titles of records she wants to hear, she writes them down and gives the names to the librarian, who brings the records from the archives in their sleeves so that Liza can write down the song tracks. The first sleeve contains Czech, not Chechen, folksongs.

'Yes, yes, that is certainly catalogued incorrectly,' mumbles the librarian. Bach's symphonies stream into the speakers from the next record. 'Oy, what's happened here?' whispers the librarian, and recatalogues Bach. The next record is Bach as well. The librarian becomes flustered and Liza indignant. Have all the Chechen records been removed from the music section?

The fourth record is a genuine Chechen recording. It's from the Soviet era, and most of the tracks are marches with titles such as: 'I Love the Chechen–Ingush Republic!' Or choral music about the happy Soviet days in the Caucasus.

Two records have what Liza is looking for: Chechen accordion-playing. One track features the musician with whom Liza wants to collaborate on her recording. On her dream of a recording. Liza is an actress, in fact. After graduating from drama school in Grozny she got married, and her husband never allowed her to act either in films or on the stage. She was to be a housewife, and she gave birth to three children before the war began and her husband left them. She started writing songs during the war.

'The words come first, then the music,' she says.

One bitterly cold winter day she took the bus from Grozny to Nalchik, the capital city of the neighbouring republic Kabardino-

Balkaria, with a hundred dollars in her handbag, to record some songs she had written. Mountains of ruins, piles of junk instead of houses, collapsed roofs, the remnants of walls – this was the landscape along the bus route.

'For the hundredth time, I thought: What horrible things surround us. The extreme has become everyday. But isn't our city a hero? A hero that is still fighting, still alive? I wrote down the words in my diary, and then the melody came, accompanied by the rattling of the bus. When I reached the studio in Nalchik the technician asked which song we should record first. "Grozny – My Hero!" I answered.'

'I can't find that on the list,' said the technician.

'No, I wrote it on the way.'

First she gave the cassettes to friends and acquaintances; they copied the music and passed it on to others. The song about Grozny was played in the market, in the bazaars, on radio stations. Some day this will be our city's anthem, people said.

Hero City – *Gorod Geroi* – meant something special in the earlier Soviet Union. It is a title awarded to cities that have been severely tested, such as Leningrad during the Second World War blockade and Stalingrad for resisting the Germans.

'The song deals with what Chechens experience every day: a whole republic is humiliated, a whole population is forced to keep still. But it also deals with a nation that does not give up.'

> *Although your streets are gone*
> *And our childhood lies in ruins,*
> *Collapsed, destroyed, deleted,*
> *We are proud, our capital, of you,*
> *Grozny – Hero City!*
> *You did not fail, you did not yield, you did not fall.*

Once she was stopped at the Kavkaz roadblock on the main highway out of Chechnya, where so many had disappeared. When she showed her passport, the soldier stood there amazed.

'Are you that Liza Umarova?' he asked. 'The singer?'

Liza was afraid that she would be punished for her songs.

'No, that's somebody else,' she replied, and added: 'Surely *she* doesn't ride in a crowded bus – at least in a Mercedes.'

The soldier nodded. 'In a Mercedes, of course,' he agreed.

But Liza doesn't earn one kopek from her music. She lives on the books and magazines she sells for a small publishing house in Moscow, and what her brother sends her from Kazakhstan. She writes her songs at her kitchen table.

'That's where I wrote the song "Russian Mothers". I was washing clothes and weeping, and suddenly I thought: our tears are the same, the Chechen mothers' and the Russian mothers'. The verses just came to me. I left my scrubbing and went to the kitchen to write. Then I went back to the bathroom to finish the washing.'

She writes sad, patriotic songs. Some call them primitive and say her music is simple. Others say that the songs sound like falling buildings, that they are raw, immediate. Tough, like the brutalised people who continue to live in Grozny. Her most famous song is '*Garmonist*' – 'The Accordion Player'.

'There was a man in the market who played old songs on an accordion, songs that my mother remembered. One day he wasn't there, and some market women told me he had been killed by a bomb. So I wrote the song about him.

'There's indifference all across Russia. That's why I wrote the song, "Stand Up, Russia". It's dedicated to everyone living in Russia, both Chechens and Russians. My words are meant for everyone: "People! Stop and think! Cry out that war must end"!'

Liza refuses to perform for the Chechen diaspora in Moscow, which includes not a few rich businessmen. She has been offered two or three thousand dollars for an evening.

'I ask: "Have you heard my songs?" If they say yes, I say: "Then you can't have understood what I'm singing about. Listen again to 'Stand up, Russia'! The first line is for you: 'Canary Islands, casinos and clubs, while there is war in Chechnya'." Then they usually hang up. Some ask me who I think I am. But if the Chechens in Moscow don't care about what happens to their country, how can we demand that others do?'

Liza, who has turned forty-four, has still not given up hope of making a CD, but Chechen artists have no status in Russian recording companies. So while she dreams of a contract, she plans a cover. She imagines pictures of bomb-blasted ruins, children peering out from between them, old men with stooped shoulders at their sons' graves. Finally, she chooses a monument of old gravestones with an enormous hand holding a sword. The monument was put up under Maskhadov during Chechnya's brief independence from Moscow and is dedicated to the war victims. She wants to have a blood-red background, and shows it proudly to a friend.

'Liza, Liza. What are you thinking of? Where will you sell this?'

'Here. In Moscow.'

'To Russians?'

'Yes . . .'

'No store will take it. It looks like something terrorists would listen to.'

'I can sell it myself. I can stand outside the mosques and sell it.'

'But you want Russians to listen to your music.'

'Yes.'

'You have to be gentler, not vindictive. Gentler.'

Liza looks at her friend sceptically.

'What if you made a cover with only your eyes, for example? That would be so beautiful, gentle and yet mystical. What do you think?'

It would not be her music that made the Russian press write about Liza. The attention came with the attack.

'It's not safe for you among Russians!' wrote one.

'Get out!' wrote another. One young woman almost showed some understanding: 'I realise that you need publicity, but do you have to do it by ruining other people's lives? After all, it's not just these young men who suffer because of your actions, but also their parents, friends and sweethearts . . .'

The greatest threat came from Slavyanski Soyuz – whose ideas Aleksei supports. They wrote her exact address on their website: 'Liza Umarova lives on the first floor and she not only has a son, but also two young daughters. She often leaves them at home alone. Liza and her children live completely on their own, with no man in the house . . .'

She regrets reporting the incident.

'I don't think the Soviet prison system can improve anyone. The best punishment for the young men would have been some hours with me. I could have explained to them what the Caucasus is, what Islam is. I could have taken them to a mosque, taken them to see how Muslims live, and then I'm sure they would have changed their opinion. In spite of everything, it's ignorance that made them act as they did,' she said to the judge at the first court hearing, and suggested the case be closed with a reconciliation.

But the legal system wants it otherwise, and when Alyosha comes out of quarantine everyone meets again in the courtroom. Summer has come, and now it's no longer snowflakes that swirl in the air, but Stalin's curse – greyish, cotton-like pollen from the poplars that Stalin ordered to be planted along Moscow's avenues. It tickles your nose, sticks in your throat and adheres to perspiring cheeks.

There are only two rows of public benches, and they are entirely filled. At each court hearing, the same friends troop in with their bags and cell phones; one boy always has the same large plastic bottle of green tea.

Alyosha's grandmother is here, dressed in black, in mourning for her husband who died nearly a year ago. Ivan, in a light blue shirt and blue V-neck sweater, holds a sports bag on his knees.

The third defendant, Artur Antonov, who has not been held in custody, sits on a chair in front of the public. He looks straight ahead, never turns round. His parents have not been present during the court hearings. He too had a shaven head before, but he has let his hair grow.

Boris Gorbenko flicks through a book entitled *One Hundred Big Secrets*. 'Did anyone know that, due to the moon's influence, each day is 0.00164 seconds shorter than the last?' he asks into thin air. No one replies.

'Some million years ago there were four hundred days in the year,' he continues. 'No one is listening, because it's only the father of a fascist talking.' He laughs dryly and goes on:

'Under the Romans there were only ten months; *deka* means ten, and *dekabr* – December – was the tenth month. October, the eighth month; November, the ninth. But then Julius Caesar ruined everything. He created July, and Augustus created August – just imagine, in the middle of the year, in the midst of the best season. So they had to calculate the days all over again. Therefore, it's clear that Jesus' birthday is not 24 December; they had a completely different calendar then. I'm an atheist, so it doesn't matter to me, but what's right is right.'

Then the two prisoners arrive. They shuffle across the floor in shoes without shoelaces. Sergei wears a blue college sweater with 'Salt Lake City' in white letters on the arm and 'RUSSIA' on the back, a copy of the 2002 Russian Olympic team uniforms. Aleksei has on a faded red checked shirt. The two friends are handcuffed to each other and to two policemen. Only when they are in the cage are they unlinked from each other. They shake their hands a little before placing them limply in their laps. Both sit with heads bowed, smiling a little sheepishly, like two boys caught doing something at school who can't take the punishment completely seriously because the rest of the class is watching.

Artur gives his testimony first.

'We were walking in Fili Park. About nine, nine-thirty. A woman and a young boy came along. Alyosha went over and asked them: "Who are you?" We tried to restrain him, but he's stronger than us. Then there was a man who pushed me. I thought he was trying to hit me, and hit back. My friends came to help me. I didn't see that the man was with his wife and daughter.'

'Who hit?' asks the judge.

'I didn't see anyone get hit.'

'That's rubbish!' shouts Pavel Semyonovich. 'I didn't push him. And he hit me hard!'

'I've asked for forgiveness,' Artur continues meekly. 'We're students, we're all studying to be teachers, we aren't Nazis or gangsters.'

The man who was attacked shakes his head.

'The wife and daughter also say that you hit him,' says the judge.

'Women react more emotionally . . .'

'Are you saying that they're mistaken? Yes or no.'

'They were in shock . . .'

'Well, OK, the women were in shock. What about the man?'

'Well . . .'

'Did you hit him?'

'Yes, but he's exaggerating. We were all a little drunk. Maybe we said something about dark people.'

'Why would you do that?'

'They had dark hair; we saw they weren't Slavic.'

'Are you pure Russian yourself?'

'Yes.'

'What did they look like?'

'They definitely appeared to be from the Caucasus.'

The other two defendants give similar testimonies.

'We met at five in the afternoon, drank four or five bottles of beer,' Sergei begins, with a quick glance at his father, who doesn't meet his gaze. He coughs, begins again; but his voice fails him.

'I was going to meet a girl later that evening; otherwise, I would rather have gone home. We met a woman and a child, and then Artur pushed this man, hit him in the face, and I remember a woman shouting: "Aren't you afraid of God's punishment?" Then I went home.'

'Any passers-by?'

'No.'

'Did you hit anyone?'

'Well . . .'

Through the cracked windowpanes in their rotting frames comes the chug and clatter of an excavator starting up. The judge casts an angry look in the direction of the window.

'Did you say anything yourself?'

'Maybe I said, "Russia for Russians" or something like that.'

Sergei is allowed to sit down again; he leans forwards with his head in his hands, his elbows resting on his knees.

Then it is Aleksei's turn; he swallows. Galya bites her nails, Boris sits with his hands meekly in his lap listening to his son's testimony.

When the man started to run, it was Aleksei who chased him.

'But it was just so I could apologise. Then we talked a little about God,' says Aleksei. His lips twitch, as if he has a tic. 'He looked like the father of a childhood friend of mine who was Jewish; that's why I thought he was Jewish.'

His grandmother listens attentively as he speaks. Then comes the worst part for her – the swastika.

'Do you know what it means?'

'Yes.'

'What does it mean?'

'It's an ancient Celtic symbol.'

'But what does it mean?'

'It's a sun sign.'

'You, a history teacher of the future! You ought to be the first to know what those behind the swastika inflicted on Russia. There wasn't a single family that didn't suffer. Why did you get that tattoo?'

Aleksei draws a deep breath.

'I support the national socialists, and Russians are threatened. We're being chased out of our own country. Especially by people from the Caucasus. We have many of them in Moscow. I could clearly see that Liza and her son were from there. Russia is for Russians. Moscow for Muscovites.'

His father's knuckles turn white.

'I was very depressed at the time. My girlfriend had broken up with me. I wanted to commit suicide. Wanted to throw myself in front of a car, so she'd be sorry. But patriotism helped me.'

Galya looks sternly at her son from behind white-rimmed glasses.

Once again, the judge rejects any kind of reconciliation. He believes that the crime wasn't committed against individuals but against the state, against the Russian Constitution. The Constitution has been violated. Ergo the victims' forgiveness and the attackers' remorse mean nothing. He wants to test the little-used racism clause, and now it is Liza's turn.

'Why did they approach you?'

'Well, they were drunk, they wanted to bother us a little.'

'But why you specifically?'

'It was dark, after all.'

'It sounds as if you want to say something more. Go ahead and say it!'

'I say that they were drunk.'

'But why did they specifically choose the two of you?'

'Because that's what happens in our country,' Liza replies quietly.

A couple of weeks later. The prosecutor states his demands:

'Gorbenko. Guilty. Three years.'

Gorbenko swallows. The audience gasps.

'Ivanov. Guilty. Two and a half years.'

Ivanov looks down.

'Antonov. Guilty. Two and a half years.'

Antonov closes his eyes and lowers his head. The only sound is of a branch tapping against the windowpane.

Aleksei Gorbenko's lawyer, a burly, overweight fellow, is the first defence attorney to speak.

'This case has been highly politicised. The judge had his mind made up in advance. It creates publicity that gives the impression Russia is doing something to fight xenophobia. Those who pay for this publicity are three young men who have already apologised.'

'They have already paid for it!' shouts Boris Gorbenko from the public benches.

'Silence! Silence!' says the judge, looking sternly at Gorbenko.

'They have apologised, and both parties involved have forgiven them and asked that the case be closed,' continues the lawyer.

'"Bestial abuse", the prosecutor called it. I think the worst blow Gorbenko inflicted on the victims was when he said there is no God. That was the worst offence that evening, insulting the victim's religion. But is it illegal? No. And why ruin the young men morally, which is what three years in prison will do? My client has poor eyesight, and that was not considered in the sentence. Sometimes things go wrong in life. The months they have already been in prison – it's more than half a year now – is more than enough punishment.'

Sergei's defence counsel, a buxom woman with bleached hair and heavy make-up, speaks next.

'No one has denied the facts,' says the swaying figure in a skin-tight skirt and boots with sky-high heels. 'But aren't these young men themselves victims of an unhealthy nationalism? It's important to fight against extremism, but haven't these three already learned their lesson? A violation of the Constitution? No, someone has created a fable here. Your Honour, the young men have no prior criminal records. Even a few years in prison could ruin their lives.'

'They're already ruined,' shouts Boris Gorbenko. 'People aren't rubbish!'

He gets a final warning from the judge.

'And where are all the people that were supposedly influenced by these young men? The reason for using the racism clause, after all, is that racial hatred has been spread,' the woman continues. 'It is rather these young men who have been influenced, like sheep, by what appears in the media,' she concludes, and points at the three with long pink fingernails.

Then it is the defendants' turn to speak.

'I am very sorry and I apologise,' says Sergei tearfully. His voice is unsteady. 'I'm not xenophobic. I was just drunk.'

'I promise that it will never happen again,' says Aleksei, and sits down. Artur says the same.

The prosecutor's demands are accepted.

When the case goes to appeal – in the Moscow municipal court – Artur's punishment is quashed. Aleksei gets one year, and Sergei's sentence is reduced to nine months. On 16 June 2006 he is released.

His father refuses to come to the prison. It is Olga who is standing outside when Sergei saunters through the prison doors. She rushes towards him.

'My boy!'

They indulge themselves by taking a taxi home.

'Hello, *sinulya*. Hello, son,' the father says sternly, without giving him a hug, without smiling.

'Hello, Papa,' Sergei says meekly.

They stand there in silence. The father purses his lips. The son looks at the floor. Ivan goes into the living room, and Sergei slumps down in the kitchen, where Olga is warming up the homecoming dinner she has prepared.

Ivan comes to the kitchen door.

'Is it better here than in prison?'

'Yes,' whispers Sergei.

'Then you'd better use your brain next time.'

Sergei nods.

'I've got a job for you tomorrow. I've agreed to haul gravel at a dacha site all weekend. I promised you'd be there too.'

'But I'd planned to see my friends tomorrow. And besides, I'm worn out. I want to relax a little.'

'You've been resting for nine months!'

'But Papa—'

'I've ordered the gravel. I'm going to lay a road over to a dacha. I need you.'

'I'd really like to be with my friends tomorrow.'

'You have a debt to repay, do you know that?'

The meal is soon ready and Olga begs them not to quarrel. Several of Sergei's friends are already at the door. Everyone is invited to the table, and the festive meal – a plate of fried potatoes, Olga's bottled tomatoes and a piece of chicken for each person – is quickly eaten. Ivan takes out a bottle of champagne. Sergei smiles timidly. His father pours a glass for everyone, but skips Sergei's.

'What about the guest of honour?' Olga asks her husband.

'That boy will never drink again,' says the father, and clenches his jaws.

No one says a word about the prison throughout the meal, there is feverish conversation about everything else imaginable. About bottled tomatoes, summer at the dacha, dog races. Ivan talks about last winter's dog races. Olga caresses her son. Gives him the last potatoes. His father ignores him.

After the meal Sergei slips away with his friends. Ivan remains sitting in the kitchen.

'Where have I gone wrong? Where have I gone wrong?'

During the summer Alyosha is also released from prison, and the following year the two boys scrape by. Neither of them is accepted for new courses; they are unemployed until they get jobs as casual labourers. Galya tells me that Alyosha is completely changed since his time in prison.

'They took a boy from me,' she says. 'And I don't know what I've got back.'

The telephone line crackles.

'He won't talk, won't say anything. I don't know what happened to him there. He just wants to forget everything, he says. Doesn't visit Babushka any more. He's brusque and surly.'

The crackling continues. Galya says something about crime and punishment. About deserving punishment.

'What?' I shout back.

'Everyone will be punished. Liza will be punished for this. Anna Politkovskaya has already been punished.'

'What do you mean?'

'You remember the nasty article she wrote about Alyosha? Saying he was a fascist. What she wrote about the Russian people! She degraded us. Now she's gone.'

'Do you mean that you support . . .'

'I'm just saying that everyone gets their punishment,' Galya interrupts. 'From God or Allah or whatever they call him.'

22

For the Fatherland

The bang is the last thing he remembers. Not the flash, not the pain. The bang. It was soon New Year, and the fields were at last all white. Snow covered the slopes and mountain tops, the road was frozen mud. Deep tyre tracks from heavy vehicles had created uneven patterns in the dark earth. Frost and thaw had dug grooves under the asphalt and cracked the grey surface. Sometimes the men had to pick their way around large holes. In the ditches, dry rushes thrust through the snow; the walnut trees, whose nuts they had gorged themselves on all autumn, stood black and naked.

He had been in the army for a year and a half. The first time away from home. The first time he had gone anywhere except to his grandparents' village, where during the summer he helped his grandfather chop wood, carry water, weed the field and care for the tomatoes, the potatoes, the beans. The first time on his own. Although he had made some friends – there was Pasha, there was Vlada – he felt quite alone. He had never been talkative, never taken up much space. Up here in the mountains he mostly kept to himself.

They had left the camp in Borzoi – 'the wolf' – and headed across the mountain after breakfast. They were checking the road to Tsentoroi, Kadyrov's village, for landmines. It wasn't cold, around zero perhaps; a raw mist made the air damp. They were on foot, and began to tire; sweat mingled with the mist, the small talk ended. Behind them, armoured vehicles rolled along beneath the walnut trees. It was twenty minutes past three when it exploded.

Two weeks later. New Year's Eve 2004. Klaudia Mikhailovna finally has some time off. The day before, after she got home from work, she cleaned the whole apartment until it shone. Now she would just rest. Not think about the sewage plant, where she cleaned the gratings so no waste would collect and clog the pipes. She would celebrate the last day of the year alone.

Her New Year's dinner was in the refrigerator. She had prepared two dishes, winter salads: one with cooked carrots, peas and mayonnaise; one with pickled cabbage and onions. Finally she would have a couple of glasses of vodka. Just for herself. For the new year. The small celebration would not carry over into the new year itself; by midnight she would be asleep. On New Year's Day at seven in the morning she had to be at the plant.

The telephone rang.

She hurried to it, thinking it was her oldest son wanting to wish her a happy New Year. Or maybe her youngest, whom she hadn't heard from for several months . . . she had received only three letters, the last one in August.

'Yes?'

'Is that Klaudia Mikhailovna?'

'Yes.'

'Your son is severely injured. He is at the military hospital in Rostov.'

Head injuries, the woman said. Serious, she added. Stepped on a landmine, she explained. Nothing more. She introduced herself as a Sister of Mercy from a church in Rostov, a volunteer who cared for the soldiers, fed them, watched over them. Klaudia's head was spinning. Nikolai had been there for more than two weeks, the woman said. Why hadn't anyone called her before? It was Nikolai who had given the Sister of Mercy the number when he regained consciousness after the coma. A coma? 'I think perhaps you should come,' the woman on the other end told her.

Klaudia telephoned the local military commission in Ulyanovsk, her son's home district. The tone reverberated in the receiver before it changed to short pips. She looked at the clock and tried again. No answer. Even though it was only early afternoon, it had started to get dark. The snow looked grey in the twilight. The military commander had probably taken the day off. It was New Year's Eve, after all.

Now everything happened quickly. She packed a few things, gathered up what little money she had, and went begging from people she knew in neighbouring blocks. Just before the evening train to Moscow departed, she stood at the ticket office and bought a third-class ticket. The carriage had no compartments, only some fifty bunks on two levels, filled with travellers who were going to celebrate New Year's Eve on the train. On the bunk next to her was a woman from the Urals who shared food and vodka with her. After sixteen rattling, sleepless hours Klaudia Mikhailovna, in a daze, got off the train at the Kazan station in Moscow. From there she took the metro as far east as it went, and after that a bus to Domodedovo airport. Here she waited half a day for the plane to Rostov.

Before daybreak on 2 January, she arrived at the southern Russian town, that for thousands of parents has such sad associations. This is where Russian mothers and fathers go when the army calls them to identify their sons, where the dead and severely wounded are flown in from Chechnya. Here are the morgues, where parents point out their sons before they are sent home in sealed zinc coffins. The Russian army is sparing with numbers, but at least fifteen thousand young men are said to have been killed in action in Chechnya during the past decade. Three times as many have been wounded.

Klaudia Mikhailovna can walk past the morgue; she is going

to the hospital. In the darkness, before the first rays of light appear in the sky, she stands outside the grey stone building. It is snowing. At the reception desk she is directed to the neuro-surgical unit, a five-storey building a short distance away. She leaves footprints in the fresh snow. In through the main entrance, up a stairway, down a corridor. A nurse shows her a door. She opens it.

He is lying with his face to the wall. She recognises the thin back, the narrow shoulders, the bandaged hand resting on his hip. His head is also swathed in bandages. She doesn't want to frighten him, he may be sleeping, and whispers as she approaches: 'Zhurik, my Zhurik. Mama is here . . .'

He turns slowly. She can't see his face behind the blood-stained bandages. He can't see her, either. His eyelids are glued shut behind the surgical dressing, which is soaked with deep red stains.

'Am I going home now?'

He had been walking on the left-hand side of the road. Just behind the mine detector. Alert and watchful, carrying a loaded auto-matic weapon, he had scanned the area in between the walnut trees and towards the scattered groves of oak and beech. Mine detectors should look down into the ditches, on the roadsides, at the cracked asphalt. His task was to look up, to protect the convoy from attack.

Despite the fact that the Russians and their supporters had con-trol over most of Chechnya, there were still attacks on the patrols, and mines could be laid just before they passed. Preferably by children and young boys, it was said; they could hide in the terrain more easily.

For some reason, only one of the patrol members had detec-tors this December day. They missed the trip-wire. One soldier stepped over it. Nikolai, who was looking towards the moun-tainside as ordered, was the one to set off the explosion. The mine operated as intended – it was designed to detonate at chest and head height in order to cause the greatest possible injury.

Numerous fragments, large and small, penetrated Nikolai's skull.

Three days after the explosion he woke up. He couldn't open his eyes; they were sewn shut behind the bandage. He heard someone beside him.

'Where am I?'

'In the military hospital.'

'Why?'

'You stepped on a landmine.'

He had felt his body; his legs were there, his feet were there, his toes were there. But on his left hand only the little finger remained.

Then he fell asleep again.

'Blind,' the doctor said to Klaudia Mikhailovna the first day. Most of the fragments had been taken out, but one had gone through his skull and buried itself in his brain. It will have to stay there, the doctor said. If they tried to remove it surgically, even the tiniest movement could damage the nervous system, then there was a danger that Nikolai would be paralysed. But he might well live for twenty years with the fragment lodged in his head, the surgeon concluded, looking intently at the X-rays.

'And what then?' Klaudia wondered.

'What do you mean?' asked the doctor.

'After twenty years, when he's forty, what then?'

'Oh, he probably won't get to be that old,' replied the surgeon, and put the X-rays away.

In the months that followed, it was Nikolai's mother who cared for him. Fed him, washed him, comforted him, held him, listened to him.

'It's good you came,' the Sister of Mercy had said. 'Now you can take over his care.'

Otherwise, there were just some soldiers assigned to look after the patients. If you wanted proper care, you had to pay cash, a hundred roubles a day. Klaudia sat by her son's bed day and night. No one from the military had contacted her yet.

'They don't need him any longer,' she thought bitterly. 'He doesn't exist for them any more.'

She remembered when her older son neglected to report for the army physical. They had telephoned. They came to the door. They threatened. After two days they found him at his grandparents' home. When it was a matter of getting boys into the military, they tried everything. When a soldier was no longer useful, they didn't even bother to make the call to the number on the first page of his army papers. Parent or guardian: Mother, name, address, telephone. Father, deceased.

Klaudia would think these thoughts over and over again in the weeks that followed. *My nikomu ne nuzhny.* No one needs us. We are redundant.

She had cried when Nikolai was drafted into the army. She'd heard about boys who had been sent straight to Chechnya after basic training and who'd come home in zinc coffins. Or maimed. Or with grenade shock. Some returned home like different people. They lashed out, screamed, drank. Like the neighbour across the hall. He had gone mad in Afghanistan. Since he'd come home in 1989, all hell had broken loose, every night.

During the Soviet era, two years in the military had been a matter of course. Now it was something most young people tried to avoid. Military service was for those who didn't have money to buy their way out, for peasant boys. When Nikolai was drafted, the war in Chechnya had been going on almost as long as the catastrophic campaign in Afghanistan in the eighties.

'You can get a deferment,' his mother had said. 'You haven't finished your schooling yet.'

Nikolai had hesitated. The next day his mother took the bus to the vocational school he attended and asked for written confirmation that he had not yet taken his final exams. She got it, and gave it to Nikolai so that he could show it at the army physical.

'Besides, you have no father, so you don't have to serve in Chechnya,' she added before she let him out of the door.

When he returned home, he had already enlisted.

'Didn't you show them the statement from your school?'

The son shook his head.

'Why not?'

'If they hadn't taken me now, they would have taken me in six months,' he said. 'Besides, I don't have anything against being a soldier. Then I don't have to think.'

'But your education, your training. What about that?'

'Now I don't have to take those exams.'

Nikolai had never done well at school, and hated exams. In class one he had already begun to fall behind, but that school year his father stood over him and made sure he went over his homework once more or did his sums again until they were correct. When Nikolai was ten days into class two, his father drowned. On a fishing trip in a little rowing boat on the Volga with his cousin and Sergei, Klaudia's son from a previous marriage. Sergei was the only one who managed to swim ashore. Thus Nikolai lost his father, and, in her grief, his mother demanded nothing of him. He barely made it through secondary school and finished with twos and threes, marks comfortably below average. After secondary school he began a two-year training course to become a welder.

Towards the end of 2003 Nikolai's entire regiment was sent from Perm in Siberia to Borzoi in Chechnya. By then he had been given three hours of target practice. At the new base he was assigned the position of *strelok* – marksman. In Perm he had received training as a mechanic, but they didn't need mechanics in Borzoi.

'Send some warm socks. Something sweet. And a pair of good gloves,' he wrote in his first letter. His mother knitted socks out of thick yarn, bought a pair of lined leather gloves and posted them off along with chocolate from the Red October factory. The package was returned; you were not allowed to send anything except letters to Chechnya because of new anti-terrorism laws.

The barracks were ice-cold, he wrote. Socks didn't dry overnight. Shoes went mouldy. The sheets were damp. They spent long days outside. They stood guard, they marched. One day he collapsed and lay in the field hospital for six weeks. Pneumonia. His mother didn't find out until he wrote about it himself, months after he had recovered. Everything she had found out too late. Including this: an officer had come to the hospital and asked Nikolai to sign up for an additional three years' service.

The army had problems getting enough soldiers to serve in Chechnya. After Nikolai enlisted a new law was passed that prevented them from being sent there for their first tour of duty. The military needed more men on contract. When the company commander asked for volunteers, no one responded. That had to change.

Still in poor health after his illness, Nikolai was sent back to serve as a marksman. He now weighed forty-eight kilos. He was beaten up. Threatened. Bullied by the officers. Soldiers who didn't sign up would be sent to the mountains, where the toughest battles were fought, the officers said.

'Dear Mama, don't worry, everything is fine here. No matter how bad you think it is, I've signed up for another three years. It's too late to do anything about it. I'll earn money. And don't be afraid. It's safe here, and I'll do everything I can to come home as soon as possible.'

For an entire year I had stayed in contact with Nikolai and his mother by telephone.

I saw them through the window before the train stopped. A pale young man with sunglasses and a baseball cap pulled down over his face, arm in arm with a stout elderly woman in a fur coat. When I hopped down from the high steps of the carriage, the mother waved to me and nudged her son. He turned his head in my direction as I walked along the platform, and when I got close he held out his hand. We smiled at each other. The face behind the sunglasses had angry red scars; some teeth were missing.

'Welcome to Ulyanovsk,' he said.

'Off we go. Turn round,' his mother said gently.

Nikolai turned round.

'To the left.'

His feet shuffled forward on the uneven platform.

'Here comes a snowdrift. Let's go round it.'

We were about the only ones left at the station.

'There's a puddle here. Take a long step,' his mother continued.

Nikolai lifted his foot.

'We're going up a step here.'

He adjusted the length of his stride.

'Now to the right.'

Nikolai kept a firm grip on his mother's arm.

'Stop here, we're going to cross the street.'

He waited.

'Here's the car, get in.'

His elder brother Sergei drove us to where Nikolai and his mother lived. We crossed the Volga, which lay frozen beneath us. The snow had blown into ice waves, and the white surface glittered. People were fishing down there. The bridge was several kilometres long. Sergei pointed out the spot where a vessel a few inches too high had crashed into the iron span and sunk some years before. Hundreds of people had drowned.

Nikolai and his mother lived on the other side of the river, at the far edge of the city. Snowdrifts rose like mountains in the gaps between the high-rises; each day they melted a little, but then froze again towards evening. A sea of icy water reached up to the car doors.

'Hardly anyone has shovelled the snow away this winter, so when all this melts we'll have to swim!' laughed Klaudia.

'You've got to understand. I haven't had a father since I was eight years old.'

We are sitting in their tiny kitchen on the outskirts of the city by the Volga, while the snow outside sparkles in the bright February sunshine. From the window on the sixteenth floor you can't tell that spring is coming; you see only tower after tower of grey concrete standing lifeless against the sky.

Nikolai has fumbled his way to his stool by the kitchen table. He lights a cigarette.

'I thought it would be good for me to live among men. Why shouldn't I fight for the fatherland, like a man? For the first time in my life I would earn money. Send money to Mama. Be a help. To the fatherland, too. Those were my two reasons. To fight for the fatherland, and to earn money. If we didn't sign up, we'd be beaten until we could neither hold a pen nor think clearly. The commander probably had a quota he needed to fill. For the sake of his own career. *Dobrovolno prinuditelno*. Voluntary coercion.'

Nikolai breaks out into grating laughter.

'Voluntary coercion,' he says several times, and clears his throat. 'Who wants to lose three years in the mountains? And perhaps lose his life?'

He takes a last drag from his cigarette, inhales deeply, stubs it out. For a long time he sits there pressing the stub into the ashtray, until it's flattened.

'I've never had money. I've grown up without money. Fifteen thousand roubles was more than I could earn at any job at home. I had no work experience, and you need contacts to get a job. How would I find such contacts? I didn't know anyone. Then I'd have a month's holiday each year, and after ten years' service you have the right to get a flat, we were told. You could get loans, free travel.'

Nikolai had asked that his pay be sent home to his mother. He only needed a few roubles for cigarettes and chocolate. But his first pay was taken by one of the officers, another took his next, and he doesn't know what happened to the third. The officers told Nikolai they had taken a small 'loan' from his pay. As time went on, he also had to spend more and more on 'equipment'. Soldiers had to buy their own white camouflage uniforms for winter. And warm boots. Or they could wear summer boots and freeze. During the autumn he also needed money for food to supplement the meagre army fare. Nevertheless, Nikolai says:

'If I hadn't become blind, I would probably have stayed in the army. What else could I have done?'

He puts drops in his eyes, which often become dry and itchy. He rubs them frequently.

The stitches in his eyelids are obvious. One pupil, barely visible behind a narrow opening, is criss-crossed by a network of pink nerves. The other has disappeared behind the lid, which has no eyelashes. A jagged red scar shoots downwards from the upper edge of each lid. In the left eye you can still see a blue crescent.

'Before, you could see both irises,' his mother says. 'Now the whole eye has sort of turned round and drawn inward. Like Nikolai himself.'

He is taciturn. It takes time to tell the story. Now and then he stumbles over the words. 'He didn't do that before,' says his mother. Suddenly he can stop in the middle of a sentence and just sit there. 'He never did that before,' says his mother. Nervous twitches cross his face. His hands are never still. He tugs at the skin of his throat, pulls the hairs of his eyebrows, scrapes his nails on his face. 'He never did that before,' says his mother. He interrupts these gestures by slapping his arm or shoulder with his good hand, then his fingers continue their feverish activity.

He lights a new cigarette and exhales the smoke between his teeth. The teeth are far apart; three were knocked out in the accident. There has never been any talk of getting new ones. His left hand is completely destroyed; feeling in his right hand is also diminished. The explosion damaged his fingers so badly he has never learned Braille.

The bits of metal that were not removed immediately have worked their way out with time. Some have wandered and come out. His jaw has grown crooked. He has frequent headaches – severe pain in his forehead, especially. A fluid-filled cyst has developed in his temple. Between his eyebrows is a crooked hollow. He has a few wisps of hair on one side of his head; the rest of his skull is covered with nasty-looking scars.

Nikolai has not heard a word from his regiment since the accident. Not one letter, not one telephone call.

'You know what we call someone who steps on a landmine? A single-usage soldier. When the mine detector didn't do its job, I became of one-time use.'

He hasn't heard from any of his fellow soldiers, either. 'They have their own things to think about,' says Nikolai.

Nor has anyone returned his personal belongings. 'My things had probably already been stolen before I was flown out. After all, everyone knew I would never come back,' he laughs.

In the spring Nikolai was sent home from Moscow, the capital he had never seen and now would never see. He was going home for good.

It was a quiet time. He adjusted to the darkness, and his mother was finally able to pull herself together enough to fill out the application form for a veteran's pension. A formality, she thought. But when she went to the military commission in Ulyanovsk she was told he had no right to anything at all.

'He was blinded in the army!' Klaudia exclaimed.

'According to our documents, he is still serving in Chechnya.'

'But he's been in the Ministry of Defence hospital in Moscow all spring!'

'According to our information, he is still in Chechnya.'

'He was wounded before the New Year. He stepped on a landmine.'

'There's nothing about that in our documents.'

The next day Klaudia brought the medical report from the military hospital in Moscow: 'Cracked skull . . . titanium plate inserted . . . plastic replacement in skull . . . brain injury . . . severe bruising . . . bleeding . . . significant damage to central nervous system . . . foreign body in left temple . . . injury to both pupils . . . has led to total blindness . . .'

'That doesn't help,' said the bureaucrat wearily. 'Officially he is still serving in Chechnya. Therefore he cannot get a pension.'

The next day Klaudia took Nikolai along, first on a number forty-one bus, then on tram number eight, to show the war commission his totally blind eyes.

'In any case,' said the bureaucrat, not the least bit placated, 'until we get confirmation that he is discharged from the army, he is still in Chechnya.'

For an entire year Klaudia tramped from one office to another, to the local military commission, to the district military commission, to the regional military headquarters. The Ministry of Defence in Moscow received letters in neat housewifely handwriting, the district governor received letters, members of parliament received telephone calls. When she telephoned Nikolai's regiment in Chechnya she was told that the commander was not in, so no one could answer her questions. 'Call back later,' they said each time. After a while they no longer said that when they heard it was her. She was a nuisance.

'*Chuzhoe gore komu nuzhno?* Who needs another person's sorrow?' sighs Klaudia. 'Now he's redundant, no one needs him. No one! No one has bothered to update his records. When he wouldn't sign up for three more years of military service, they threatened him, flattered him, and finally bought him – or swindled him; he saw nothing of the money they promised him. But now! Now he no longer exists for them!'

On the documents Nikolai has four different birth dates. His mother holds them up and points. The medical evacuation papers have the correct date, 12 November 1984. The first medical report says 12 June. At the Ministry of Defence in Moscow he has become two years younger, and at the district hospital for war veterans they are out by a month.

'Nothing is accurate. Carelessness!' says Klaudia. 'A life – what's that, after all?'

A year and a half after the accident, in July 2006, the letter they were waiting for finally came. After a long series of paragraphs it states clearly: 'The soldier is *not fit* for duty and is *discharged. "Osvobozhdenie".*' The word has a double meaning in Russian. It means discharged, freed, released, but also dismissed, removed.

For Nikolai it meant a veteran's pension.

Or partial pension. After a detailed report he was placed in a group of 'second-degree invalids' with 'certain health problems, but partially fit for employment'. Point fourteen stated that he did not need a guide. Able to work? Him? Without a guide?

In order to get a full veteran's pension they had to document that he was a first-degree invalid. Several months later, after renewed efforts, Nikolai's mother finally got him registered as a first-degree invalid, with the right to claim the highest pension. A total of 6600 roubles – around £140 a month.

'Three thousand eight hundred and seventy-seven roubles as a war veteran. Plus eighteen hundred as a war invalid, and then a thousand from Putin.'

'From Putin?'

'Yes.'

'How come from Putin?'

'He's the one who gives it.'

'He was also the one who started the second war in Chechnya,' I counter.

'Putin is good. He holds our country together,' says Nikolai. He stretches his arms in the air, flexes them, lets them fall, and searches for his packet of cigarettes.

'Do you ever think about who's to blame for you sitting here in the darkness?'

'Fate. It's determined in advance,' he replies.

Since he came home two years ago, he has never been out alone. The whole day he waits for his mother to come home. Then in the early evening they take a little walk around the block.

'But perhaps you could go out alone with a white stick?'

'A stick! I want to stay alive!'

'Yes . . .'

'Haven't you heard about the crime in Ulyanovsk? The gangs! Every block has its own gang. That's their territory. People can be killed right outside their front doors! If they see a fellow tottering around with a stick, it's like an invitation to beat him up. They prefer to attack defenceless people. Hit them till they lie twisting on the ground, then rob them. This part of the city is full of trouble, violence, jailbirds, ne'er-do-wells, unemployed. If you so much as brush someone with your shoulder it's enough to get you punched on the jaw.'

We're sitting in the living room. It's a grey morning. Klaudia has gone to the sewage plant. A cold draught wafts in through the mouldering balcony door.

We run out of words. My head is empty. I have no more questions. Should I perhaps tell him something? About what, then? About my life? My travels? People I've met? The clock on the wall ticks insistently. I wonder if the batteries can be removed. On the chest of drawers is a photograph of Nikolai in uniform, taken on one of his first days in the army. He stares gravely into the camera.

'What do you miss the most?'

'Seeing, of course.'

'Yes. Of course.'

The ticking takes over again, and I stare out at the pale grey sky. I look at Nikolai and it feels like an assault.

'In addition to eyesight, what have you lost by becoming blind?'

'Freedom.'

'I understand. Of course.'

Of course I don't.

Nikolai gets up, goes over to the stereo and puts on a CD of army songs. We sit there listening to tunes like 'Russia', 'Two Helicopters over Mozdok', 'Men at Work', 'No Better Paratroopers', 'War Comrades', 'Medals Can't Be Sold', and 'Because We Are Russians'. Nikolai sings along. He knows all the words. I've heard him hum a song about a soldier who comes home in a zinc coffin. He plays it now. Turns up the volume. Sings at the top of his voice. About heroic deeds. Courage. Russia. Sometimes he yells the songs, sometimes he mumbles them. I sit there following the pattern of the pink and white flowered wallpaper. The designs merge into each other; here and there a seam or a tear interrupts them. In some places they are discoloured by damp. On the wall hangs a picture of a birch tree with white bark and autumn leaves; it is reflected in a lake surrounded by snow-covered mountains with a bright blue sky overhead.

'Have you seen *9th Company*?' Nikolai asks.

We sit down to watch the film. That is to say, Nikolai listens. He has heard the movie many times before. It's about a group of soldiers who meet at basic training in Krasnoyarsk and then are sent to Afghanistan. Nikolai tells me what's going to happen before it does. 'He's going to get shot now.' 'The convoy will be attacked.' 'Soon he's going to step on a mine.' Towards the end the elite troop, the 9th Company, has received orders to hold a hill, no matter what it costs. It's New Year's Eve and the soldiers are celebrating. At dawn they are surrounded by Afghans, who slaughter the drunken Russians. One soldier sends desperate calls for help, but gets no response. The company is practically wiped out. Only a couple of the men are left, and as they lie there writhing in pain, a car drives up. An officer tells them the war is over. The Soviet Union is withdrawing. They are going home. At that point, the main character goes mad.

'No one goes free,' says Nikolai.

'What do you mean?'

I get no reply.

Towards evening we are sitting on the hard stools at the kitchen table again. The elder son Sergei and his wife Ivana have come for a visit. Klaudia is feeding Nikolai whole sardines. They are small and slippery and almost impossible to pick up with a fork, especially if you can't see them. When Nikolai tries to catch them in his fingers they just slip out, so his mother puts them on the fork, one after another, and asks him to open his mouth. Since the accident Nikolai can only eat food that has been mashed, or sardines, which can be swallowed whole.

In between, we toast with vodka: to our meeting, to meeting again, to the future.

The trip to Chechnya was Nikolai's first. 'When I landed in Chechnya I thought, "Oy, what beautiful mountains!" I'd never been outside Ulyanovsk district before, never seen mountains, never seen the sea. Now I'll never get to see the sea. But I've seen mountains. High, snow-covered, proud. The place we were stationed is called Borzoi, which means "ox", I think. Oh, how I hate that place! About thirty houses, a school, a mosque, a café, a marketplace. No one did anything to us there, they were too afraid, but I remember the hate in their eyes, even the children glared at us. Chechens are wild, like animals. They have no civilisation, they think only of killing. I hate them. Why do they come here? They sneak across the border. With belts full of explosives. They want to kill us. This is our country. The government needs to close the borders. If we hadn't let them come here, we wouldn't have had terrorist attacks.'

'But it was the Russians who invaded Chechnya in the first place,' I say.

No reply.

Sergei, who until now has been watching television in the living room, comes in. Ivana has been drinking vodka with us, and goes to ask her husband to show us a clip on his cell phone. It shows a pale man sitting with his hands bound behind his back in front of a group of Islamic soldiers who are reading from the Koran. Suddenly one of them grabs the man's hair, a hand holding a knife darts out, the prisoner's throat is slashed. Blood streams out. The body collapses. All over in seconds. The decapitated head is placed on top of the body lying on the floor. The fighters cheer.

'That's Muslims for you,' says Sergei. 'If we don't fight them now, they will slaughter us.'

Ivana wants to watch the clip one more time, and her husband plays it again.

'Barbarians,' says Klaudia's daughter-in-law.

Nikolai smiles.

'Do you remember the clip where some soldiers from the military intelligence service cut a smile on a couple of Chechens? From ear to ear!' he shouts, and draws his hand like a knife across his face. 'That was so cool!'

'Yes, they deserved that,' says his brother.

'But then the Russians are equally barbaric,' I venture.

'We're just avenging all the brothers we have lost,' Nikolai replies sharply.

'You have lost and they have lost. A hundred thousand Chechens have been killed during the war, most of them civilians, among them many children,' I object.

'None of them are just children. In Chechnya even the children know how to use an automatic weapon. There they are all rebels. It's the children who lay the landmines. I bet that when I lay bleeding on the road, they ran to the commandant and got their money. It made no difference whether I was killed or only wounded, as long as I was unable to fight, as long as the Russian army had copped it. They kill whoever they want, but when we kill anyone we're charged and put in prison.'

'When did that happen?'

'It happened to a paratrooper; he shot his way into a building and killed a family. He was charged, and sentenced to twenty years' imprisonment. Twenty years! Because he defended the fatherland!'

'But if he killed defenceless civilians—'

'Civilians! What are civilians? Inside every Chechen is a fighter. There are no peaceful people in that place.'

'But a defenceless family—'

'We have mothers, too,' says Nikolai.

Klaudia has been silent during the conversation.

'Son, it's your turn to make a toast.'

'You know what we should do?' Nikolai says into thin air. 'Drop a bomb. A bomb that would wipe out all of Chechnya.'

'What about the people who live there?'

'What about them? *Netu cheloveka, netu problemy*. If the person disappears the problem disappears, as Stalin said. The Chechens are evil from the inside. They are evil in their souls. They're like wolves, and live according to the laws of that beast. Once, we discovered that some Chechens who worked at our compound had laid landmines in the area. Those Chechens are no longer alive! They were punished on the spot. With Chechens, it's best to kill them immediately, otherwise they shoot you in the back.'

The daughter-in-law looks at me with big blue eyes.

'They have hot blood, you see,' she explains. Ivana looks like a Barbie doll, slender, graceful and not much more than one and a half metres tall.

'Red-hot. War seethes in them right from birth.'

She smiles behind heavy make-up. She wants so much for us to agree, to condemn someone together, to bond with each other.

Nikolai changes wars and begins talking about the heroic soldiers from 9th Company in Afghanistan.

'Do you know how many died in that war?' I ask.

'Fifteen thousand,' he replies readily. The official number of Soviet soldiers killed.

'I mean Afghans, civilians.'

'There are no civilians.'

'One and a half million Afghans,' I tell him. 'One and a half million people in ten years. And there are still six million landmines from the time of the Soviet occupation.'

'But they attacked first!'

'They attacked first?! Afghanistan was invaded under Brezhnev because the Soviet Union wanted to control the country!'

'As if the USSR didn't have enough land,' sighs Klaudia.

'No, they attacked first, just like the Chechens,' Nikolai insists.

'Like the Chechens? They were invaded first by the Russian troops. Yeltsin ordered . . .'

'You need a shave,' Klaudia interrupts.

'Yes, you see best, I guess,' he smiles.

It is my turn to propose a toast.

What shall I say? What can we drink to now? Nikolai's health? Peace in the world?

'May all go well,' I say.

We raise our glasses. But nothing will change. Everything will remain the same.

Nikolai is about to light a cigarette, but now his mother objects. A grey blanket of smoke hangs over the kitchen after the intense discussion. 'Out,' she says. 'Out on to the balcony.'

I follow Nikolai out to the balcony. He opens the windows that enclose it. We stand there feeling the wind waft over us. A mild February wind.

'Sometimes I wonder how I can live the rest of my life without seeing,' Nikolai says quietly. 'What kind of life is that? Can I cope with it? Will I be able to stand it? A life chained to Mama. I'll never have my own family. Who wants a blind boyfriend? Who needs me?'

There is darkness all around us. Most of the lights in the neighbouring buildings have been turned off. It's almost midnight. A pale moon hangs in the sky.

23

Minus and Plus

The two men and the woman in the compartment had already changed.

'Shall we go out so that you can change?' asked one of the men.

I shook my head, a little embarrassed.

It had been ten years since I'd last travelled by train in Russia. I'd forgotten that passengers always bring along a tracksuit to put on before the train leaves, and arrange their clothes neatly on a hanger above each bunk, ready to slip into before arrival and repack the tracksuits. By then they could be marked by all sorts of stains. A drop of vodka, dark tea, something homemade, something pickled, greasy finger marks. I hadn't brought a tracksuit, so I sat there in the clothes I'd worn at Nikolai's and Klaudia's home. *I am different* was written all over me.

I had already been reminded of the code of conduct on the trip from Moscow: people greet each other politely at the beginning of the journey, then pretend they don't notice each other, busying themselves with their own things. For a while. Glance at a newspaper. Look out of the window. Arrange their clothes. Rummage in their bags, whose contents may determine the fate of the trip.

The train jolted and snorted. I gazed out of the window at the drab industrial city. Thought about Nikolai, and about all those who had come home from the Caucasus with injuries or traumas. 'The Chechen syndrome', they called it – soldiers who turned to violence when they came home, or who were mentally paralysed, like Nikolai. The dark grey outlines of Ulyanovsk at dusk slowly disappeared behind us. Only a shining mirror image of ourselves remained in the dark window. We might just as well pull down the blind. The trip to Moscow would take all night.

Our tickets and passports were handed in, and we each received a sheet, a pillow and a blanket. A solicitous, buxom stewardess served piping-hot tea in glasses with tin holders. Lemon? One, or two, lumps of sugar?

The eldest of my fellow passengers – a bald man in his sixties, well fed and bespectacled, wearing a blue Terylene tracksuit – took out one metal food container after another. His travelling companion – a pear-shaped man of around thirty in a white shirt and black Adidas tracksuit bottoms whose dark hair was slicked to the side to hide incipient baldness – took out a large piece of meat which he cut into thick slices.

The older man removed the metal lids carefully so as not to spill. Aubergine in tomato sauce. *Pelmeni* stuffed with meat. Pickled gherkins with chopped dill. Mushrooms in garlic.

'That's my wife,' laughed the man. 'She was afraid I'd go hungry in Moscow. The prices are mad there. So she spent a whole day cooking and stirring. All I packed myself was the vodka!'

He laid out forks and spoons on the remaining corner of the table. The pieces of meat rested on a board. A loaf of bread was held up in the air and sliced.

'You should taste this! Help yourselves! Have another piece. Don't be shy! There's plenty!'

The men were mathematics professors from Ulyanovsk on their way to a conference in Moscow. The older one proved to be the younger man's teacher, but he made it clear that his former student had delved far deeper into the mysteries of mathematics than he had. His colleague protested vehemently.

'We have the best mathematics education in the world,' they agreed. 'The best teachers. The hardest-working pupils. The brightest students. And still, still, you can't get admitted to foreign universities with our exams! Even though we have the highest professional level in the world. Now we have to adapt our teaching to a lower standard, in order to bring it in line with Europe and America. It's absurd!'

I nodded politely, as did our fourth fellow traveller.

The woman – beautiful and well groomed, wearing purple tights and a glittering top that emphasised her good figure – was a secretary in a private dairy. She was going to Moscow to look for a job. And for a chance to exchange her two-room flat in Ulyanovsk for a one-room flat in Moscow.

'The prices are mad,' she sighed, echoing the professor's wife in her kitchen. 'I dream of living in Moscow,' she continued, and waved away the mathematician's offer of vodka. 'Here there's no future. It's a backwater. Moscow, on the other hand – isn't it a beautiful city? That's where I want to live.'

In contrast to the woman, the two men were very satisfied with life in Ulyanovsk.

'It is where Lenin was born. Did you know that?' the portly man informed me. 'Vladimir Ilyich's last name was Ulyanov.'

'What brought you to our city?' asked the older professor.

I told them about Nikolai.

It grew silent.

The younger mathematics professor gave me a searching look.

'Don't you have enough dispossessed people in your own country without coming looking for ours?'

Three pairs of eyes were turned on me.

'But do you think it's right that he just sits there without getting any help?' I asked in return.

'I think that, in any case, you shouldn't come here and dig around in all that.'

'But he's fought for his country . . .'

'Yes. And a soldier should keep quiet.'

'Well, he should get help anyway,' the beautiful secretary interjected.

'Pooh,' replied the younger man, and looked at me.

'That book of yours,' said the older professor. 'Will it be negative or positive?'

I was at a loss for words. I didn't want to say negative even if, well, you might say it could become a little negative.

The dairy secretary came to my rescue.

'You mathematicians, can you only think in pluses and minuses? Negative or positive!'

'The book is about those who have been destroyed in the war. Who have been violated. Who, yes, have been dispossessed,' I tried to explain.

'But why do you have to come here to write about that? Can't you pick on your own country?' the younger professor asked, rolling his eyes.

'What *right* do you have to criticise us?' the older man broke in. '*Who* gave you that right?'

'I don't think journalists should focus on the negative,' the younger man continued. 'You ought to write about positive things. About things that go well.'

'That would be the way it was in the Soviet era,' I retorted.

'And what's wrong with that? We were respected then. No one came and told us how we should govern our country, what our society should be like; we were a superpower then, we were strong, we were feared! Now the West thinks it can say whatever it likes to us, do whatever it wishes here. Who gave you that right?'

The older professor stares dreamily into space. 'Just think, back then a single one of our nuclear submarines could have blown up half the USA!'

He went on at great length about rockets, conquering space, great Soviet scientists, everything his country had given to the world.

'Do you mean that newspapers and television should report only happy stories?'

'At least there ought to be a balance,' said the younger man.

The mathematicians were completely in tune with the Russian authorities. Not long after our conversation on the train, one of the largest news bureaux received an order that at least half of what they broadcast was to be of a positive nature.

I wanted to explain how the war in Chechnya had ruined so many lives. Taken away Nikolai's eyesight. Timur's childhood. In Chechnya . . .

'Chechnya! What are you going there for?' interrupted the younger professor.

'They're all gangsters. Smoke them out! Punish them harshly!' said the older. 'Stalin did the only right thing when he sent them into exile. I have an acquaintance who lived in Chechnya when the Chechens were deported; then it was quiet and peaceful. But Nikita let them come back. They should have stayed in Kazakhstan where there was plenty of space for all of them. Why would they come back? Stalin knew how to keep order!'

'Stalin was a fine leader,' the younger man agreed. 'But Putin is a patriot, too.'

'Yes, he's good. But unfortunately, he goes along with the West too often.'

'I cried when Brezhnev died,' the secretary interjected.

'Stability is the most important thing,' said the older scholar. 'Order and stability.'

A homemade apple cake was placed on the table.

Not only was I so clearly different, I hadn't followed the rule that on a train journey everyone contributes. I'd turned down Klaudia's offer of some food; my backpack held nothing more than a bottle of water. I had betrayed the collective values. Had been too preoccupied with *my own* trip.

We toned the conversation down. After all, we were going to share a compartment for the whole night. Still, the unpleasant atmosphere was hard to dispel. Even with a mouth full of tea and apple cake, a certain sourness hung in the air.

The older man tried to smooth things over:

'When you write about Russia, you must find at least as much positive as negative. Otherwise it won't be correct. It must be equal. Minus and plus. Equal zero.'

He gave me a thoughtful look from his seat opposite.

'So what do you like about Russia?'

'Me?'

'Yes, you.'

'Well, the literature, the music,' I said, and couldn't come up with anything else. What had happened to me? Once I searched for the Russian soul with fascination and uncontrollable curiosity. On my travels around the empire in third class I was filled with enthusiasm and amazement. Had I become too negative? Disappointed?

With my stomach full of the professors' food and my head aching from the conversation, I said goodnight and lay down in my bunk to read. I had brought a worn copy of *The Master and Margarita*.

The older professor got up.

'Phenomenal. It's phenomenal,' he said. 'I've read it five times. It's the best book I know.'

The professor and I had the same favourite book.

I lay awake in the dark and thought that I should travel more often by train.

24

The Little Wolf and the Thief

Which road would you choose: the one that is overgrown with grass and flowers, or the one that is full of trash and tyre tracks?

Correct answer: where people walk (throw away trash) and cars drive (tyre tracks) there is the least danger of landmines.

– INFORMATION LEAFLET FOR SCHOOLCHILDREN

It started one sunny day. A storm, dark as lead, blew in. As if carried into the yard on sudden gusts of wind, it crept under clothing, cast shadows on faces, made features contract, foreheads darken and pupils turn black. The women's smiles were swept away, and they continued their tasks in silence. Malika stirred the porridge vigorously, so that it wouldn't burn. Seda cut potatoes with a sharp, angry knife. Luiza scolded the older children. It was time they tidied up their shelves. Madina brushed the little girls' hair until their scalps tingled. Zaur was depressed. He sat upstairs trying to get the slow computer to work. Adam was sleeping after coming off night duty. Abdul, as usual, said nothing.

Only the youngest children noticed nothing, and continued to play. The older ones hunched their shoulders and stared at the ground. A ball bounced weakly a few last times as children formed quiet groups in the yard and waited in fear for the squall.

But the sun still blazed down, the sky was bright blue, the heat sticky. Under the sheet of plastic stretched between the garage and the kitchen you could find a bit of shade, but it wasn't enough to let you cool off. Flowers drooped towards the barren earth. The garden had been transformed to grit and dust, the grass was brittle. Only the melons enjoyed the heat, and the washing dried in minutes. The Caucasian summer day was absolutely still.

The sudden change in the weather was only in their minds.

Problems had piled up at the children's home recently. After Zaur and Said were apprehended, Hadijat and Luiza were sick with worry. *When they have taken you once, they always come again.* The boys had to leave Chechnya.

One morning Malika didn't come to work. She usually spent every second night in Belgatoi with her husband and father. She would leave the children's home after dinner and return on bus number six at dawn the next day. But this morning she didn't come, and it wasn't until breakfast should have been on the table that the telephone rang.

'My nephew has disappeared. They came and got him last night.'

Hadijat stood with the receiver in her hand. Another one. In the same family. Men in dark uniforms. Beards like the president's.

'Papa does nothing but cry,' said Malika when she arrived. 'He can't take any more. He's lost so much. Two sons, Mama, and now again . . .'

In addition, Hadijat had received a disturbing letter from the mayor's office saying that the flat they owned near Dynamo Stadium, where Madina lived with some of the youngest children, was in danger of being repossessed. The new authorities believed the title-deed was invalid. Hadijat had three days to prove otherwise.

Something terrifying was happening in Grozny. Uniformed men came to people's doors with orders to evict the occupants. The story was everywhere the same: the leases, signed during Maskhadov's government, from 1996 to 1999, were invalid. They were issued by a state that did not exist, because the Kadyrov regime did not recognise Ichekeria – independent Chechnya. There were widespread tales of people being thrown out of their flats, only to have others with close connections to the elite move in.

When Hadijat had gone to the mayor's office two days earlier, the secretary barely glanced at the title deed before saying it was invalid.

Madina brought some disturbing news: she discovered that the mayor's brother lived in the flat next door. If you tore down a wall . . .? The mayor himself owned three flats next door. One week earlier uniformed men had gone there and broken into the flat of a woman who had been ordered to leave. They dumped her and her four children in the yard, along with her furniture and other belongings. Before leaving they broke the door and windows, so that no one could live there. The flat was going to be completely renovated anyway for its new owner.

The greatest concern at the children's home was money. Prices had rocketed after the authorities began massive building projects around the city. But as Chechnya disappeared from the media, help from abroad dried up. Hadijat dreamed of building a bakery; bread got more and more expensive, and they needed so much. Also, in the bakery, children who couldn't keep up at school could learn a trade. But the budget they had fixed for the past year no longer applied. Bricks cost twice as much, the price of nails had trebled; cement, cables, wires – everything had shot up. Even water cost twice as much as a year ago. The children's home didn't have running water; they had to buy water in large tanks.

Furthermore, Hadijat now had responsibility for additional children. When Ramzan Kadyrov decided that all state orphanages in Chechnya should be closed – because 'in Islam it is your duty to take care of your relatives, and all children have relatives' – many children were sent back to people who either could not or would not take care of them. Once again the streets and rubbish dumps became filled with children.

Many from the orphanages were brought to Hadijat. Her house hadn't been closed down because it was registered as a private home and did not receive public financial support. But she couldn't take all of them. She had neither the space nor the means – for bread, for soup, for soap, for school bags, for everyone.

Workers in the orphanages suddenly lost their jobs. Often they became homeless, too; many of them were single women who received room and board in addition to wages. Two Russian women knocked on Hadijat's door one day and offered to help in exchange for food until they found something else. They had worked at the orphanage in Gudermes. Both were named Galya and both had grey hair dyed a fiery red. One was stout and close to pension age, the other a little younger and a little thinner. The women had been born in Chechnya during the years when no Chechens were living there because they had all been deported to Central Asia. They had never learned the local language, but both had sons who, despite being Russian, spoke Chechen without an accent and had fought with the rebels when the war started. They had each lost one son in the conflict. The younger Galya was the mother of two sons. The one who hadn't been killed in the war had worked as a policeman. A couple of years earlier, after they had eaten dinner, he had said goodbye, gone to the top of the apartment block and jumped.

'The pressure had become too great,' Galya told the other women with tear-filled eyes.

This particular morning Hadijat was up early. At dawn she was already in the kitchen with Malika, gulping down tea. Today was the deadline, and she wanted to be the first in the queue at the mayor's office. Her legs hurt and felt heavy. These days, when she made her way from office to office with letters and documents, her feet swelled so badly that her shoes no longer fitted. She took medication for high blood pressure, but had forgotten the dosage; so each time she had more pain in her heart, or head, or feet, she swallowed some blood pressure pills.

Just as the sun had appeared, promising another hot and suffocating day, Luiza entered the kitchen with a gloomy expression. 'Nothing,' she said when they asked what was wrong. She didn't want to upset Hadijat before the important meeting at the mayor's office.

Hadijat hurried out with the precious papers to catch the bus for the city centre.

Meanwhile, the storm was brewing.

It was late afternoon when she returned, sweating and panting. The other women lowered their eyes; the corners of their mouths turned down. Hadijat took a deep breath and put her hands on her hips:

'What's wrong with you? Has something happened?'

Children who had come outside to give her a hug scurried away and disappeared. The older ones had already retreated. The dark cloud had settled heavily over the yard; people shivered in the blazing sun.

One child was absent. She was in the girls' bedroom, getting dressed up. This afternoon she was going back to the part of the city where she had lived before. She took off the faded light blue dress, made from different flowered materials, that she had worn the whole week. For the most part, the children wore clothing that had been donated abroad and sent via Lithuania. Liana wore a T-shirt under the dress because it had thin straps, and Hadijat didn't allow them. But now everything was coming off. She would surprise them with how nice she could look.

Twelve beds were lined up in the room. On her upper bunk she had laid out another dress. Bright red. It had a full skirt with ruffles, a ruched waist and short puffed sleeves. If she twirled round and looked down, the dress reminded her of a rose.

She hadn't been back to Zavodskoi since she and Timur had been taken from there a year ago. The reason they were going back was that Hadijat needed to get their documents, which their uncle still had. Only then could Hadijat and Malik be registered as guardians for Liana and her brother. When Hadijat came home, they would leave. Liana would show the way: the apartment block, the entrance, the neighbours, the brats. Her aunt and uncle. She would show them that she had become another person. The girl from the previous spring was gone!

Standing in front of the window, she brushed her hair until it shone. The strands danced around her head, flew up, then settled down after the brushing. She tried to fix her fringe, which she had cut herself a few days ago. It was only a few centimetres long, and stuck out, all spiky, from her silky mane. She had been reprimanded afterwards. 'Why do you want a fringe? You who have the nicest hair of anyone!' Hadijat had scolded, but then given her a hug when she saw that Liana was close to tears. 'It's your hair, you can decide what to do with it.' Liana agreed that perhaps it didn't look so nice with a crew cut in front. She gazed gravely at the pale face in the mirror. Maybe she should ask Hadijat if she could wear the gold earrings this afternoon?

As the girls got older, they were given earrings. It was like a coming-of-age. The earrings were theirs alone, and were kept in the glass cabinet in Hadijat's room. Everything else was shared. You wore your clothes until you grew out of them. Then they were passed down to the smaller children, while you inherited clothes from the older ones. The same was true of shoes, school bags, school books.

Each child got his or her own shelf when they started school. On her shelf Liana had her belongings: a shiny little black handbag she had received from Hadijat, in which lay a key ring with a tiny soft monkey, a small coloured-glass picture of a cosy house with a blue, blue sky overhead, a metal bauble that had fallen off a zip, a pen that wrote with rose-coloured ink, two teddy bear stickers, pearl nail polish and the label from the red dress – two bits of paper with a plastic thread through them and the name of the dress written in English letters. She had cut off the labels and kept them. They were from her own new dress that no one had used before her. Hadijat had bought it just for her. She had never worn it. Until now.

Today she would show them. Standing there in her pants, she was just pulling the rustling dress over her head when Seda threw open the door and hissed: 'Go down to the kitchen!'

It was Luiza who had finally said it out loud:

'The bread money for the whole week has gone.'

Hadijat had only managed a weak '*What?*' before she dropped into a chair under the plastic sheet in the yard. Her face quivered, her lips trembled; all she wanted to do was cry.

The other women stood around her looking tired and discouraged.

'Yes, we probably know who . . .'

Hadijat hid her face in her hands.

None of the other women had wanted to confront the children. Even if everything pointed to the same child.

'Get her.'

Seda came into the kitchen with Liana; the girl's eyes were downcast, her jaw jutting out, her arms hanging at her sides.

'Have you taken the bread money?'

Hadijat's voice reverberated across the dining room, out into the yard, down into the cellar.

Liana shook her head.

'Do you dare, do you *dare* to lie to me?'

Liana shook her head.

'Look at me! Have you taken the bread money?'

Liana did not raise her eyes. She had drawn back, one elbow leaning against the kitchen unit, as if her whole body were being held up by that elbow.

'Get the others,' Hadijat commanded. Seda ran out again and

returned with the children, hustled them into the kitchen for judgement to be passed. Only their shuffling steps across the tiles could be heard. They looked down, each one more conscience-stricken than the next. No shouting or pointing. No malicious glances.

'I want the guilty one to come forward!' said Hadijat.

The children drew back against the wall. Nobody moved. Liana was asked to move away from the kitchen unit she was clinging to. Her newly washed, newly brushed hair hid her face. She stood there in the red dress, alone, in the middle of the floor, one arm hanging straight down while the other clutched her elbow like a vice.

'I'm asking you for the last time; you have a chance to tell me yourself. Did you take the money?'

Liana shook her head again. Her eyes were focused on the scratches on the floor. The floor and walls were tiled, and the Russian peasant-style ceiling was the prettiest in the house. Its light birch, darker oak and black walnut created an intricate pattern of leaves. Now the fluorescent lights shone cold and white.

Liana slumped further, her head grew heavier, her arms longer, her back more bent. She stood as if glued to the tiles she often swept.

Then came the questioning of witnesses.

That morning each of the children had been given an ice-cream cone. Liana had bought them from the kiosk at the end of the street. They were the most expensive ones, sprinkled with choco-late and wrapped in shiny foil. The older girls had asked where she had got the money. When she said that she had got it from Malika, they accepted the ice cream. 'Eat fast, eat fast! Eat it all up!' Liana had urged the younger children. She had stuffed the cones into them so fast they had ice cream and chocolate sprinkles smeared on their faces and dripping from their chins. Then Liana had bought chocolate bars, Snickers and Bounty, and slipped round a corner. There she gobbled up one bar after another. All this, according to the children's accounts. Those who had gone round the corner after her had also got a taste of the expensive imported chocolate.

The lace curtains fluttered lightly in the breeze. It was getting dark outside. Hadijat was on the point of tears. She turned to the older girls.

'You're almost fifteen years old! You should have known the money wasn't hers!' she cried. 'But you happily eat stolen ice cream. That makes you just as bad as she is. Don't you get enough food here? Is there anything you lack? All the bread money! Eight hundred roubles! Do you think I can just put another eight hundred roubles in the bread box? Don't you get sweets? Didn't Malika spend a whole week making apricot jam for the winter? Didn't you get a taste? Don't you get sugar in your tea?'

Then she turned to Liana in the middle of the room.

'Where is the rest of the money?'

Silence.

'How dare you not answer me?'

Liana continued to stare at the floor. Her face had become mottled. Red patches spread over her cheeks, under her eyes, down towards her throat. But she did not move, did not change her position, just slowly shrank inwardly.

'Where have you hidden it?'

She looked up with wet eyes.

'I don't need your tears!' yelled Hadijat. 'Where is the rest of the money? You can't have bought eight hundred roubles' worth of ice cream! What are we going to do with you?'

Hadijat looked around in despair.

'She should be severely punished,' said the older Galya, and slapped herself on the palm of one hand.

'Send her back to her uncle! That's where she belongs,' hissed the younger Galya – the woman who had lost two sons, one shot through the neck, the other crushed on the asphalt.

The Chechen women said nothing.

*

Liana had never been punished for her stealing. Everyone had felt sorry for her and tried to be kind to her. She would surely learn, now that she was in a good home, they thought. But this time Hadijat would not let her off. Eight hundred roubles was a lot of money.

'Give me the money!' Hadijat commanded.

'I've given it away,' replied Liana in a barely audible whisper.

'Given it away? Given away the bread money? To whom?'

Liana pointed.

'To him. To him. And to him.'

Now it was the boys who were at a loss for words. Two of them were brothers who had come from an orphanage in Kurchaloi that had been shut down. They had been thin as a rake, their knees had stuck out from their legs like clubs; but now, after a month here, they had put a little meat on their bones. The boys each pulled out ten roubles Liana had given them. They didn't know about her stealing.

'I see,' said Hadijat. 'The rest!'

'I gave a hundred to Naid,' said Liana.

'What?' Twelve-year-old Naid protested loudly. 'That's not true, that's not true! I didn't get any money from you.'

'Yes!'

'No!'

'Yes!'

Naid was almost in tears. Small, freckled Naid, who had lived in the flat next door to Timur and Liana and who had been beaten daily, just as they were. He had come with them a year ago. At the time he had been so battered and bruised that he couldn't sit down. This year he finished class four with a certificate – the best in his class.

'I didn't get any money from you. Why are you lying?' Naid sobbed.

Liana turned away from him.

'And then I gave a hundred roubles to Marha and Aishat.'

Marha and Aishat had received the money, but had gone straight to Malika with it. They had guessed it was stolen.

'Don't you see what you are doing?' said Hadijat. 'Not only do you steal, you make sure others get involved, too. You teach the children to eat stolen treats, standing there stuffing ice cream into the little ones: eat fast, eat fast, eat it all up, so no one sees you! What are you doing? You're ruining them! Then you give away some of the money so you'll have accomplices!'

Liana stood like a statue. The red ruffled dress with the ruched waist suddenly seemed several sizes too large, and hung loosely around her.

'There are still almost six hundred roubles missing! Give them to me!'

'Give them to her!' the two Galyas echoed.

Liana just stood there, and Hadijat declared that no one would be leaving the kitchen until the money was handed back. Nobody said a word. The glaring overhead light and the unpleasant atmosphere made everyone look grimy. One of Malik's friends was in the yard and had followed the confrontation through the open window. He was the one who would drive Hadijat and Liana to Zavodskoi, that was the plan. Now, he leaned over the windowsill.

'Cut off her hair!' he rasped. 'Then she'll learn. I've got an electric razor. I'll be glad to shave it off!'

Galya and Galya nodded. 'Yes, shave it all off!'

'Then I'll paint her head green and send her into the street,' said Malik's friend.

The mother of the house was slumped over on a kitchen chair.

Liana had never really stopped stealing. She had given it up for a little while. Then things began to disappear again. Fifty roubles here, twenty there, sisters' hair clips, classmates' pens. She had stashed things under her mattress until her hoard was discovered. Again. Later she was nabbed in the school cafeteria, where they sold juice and chocolate.

'Snickers, Liana! Snickers. That's what the money goes on, isn't it?' Hadijat had turned again to Liana, the stone statue.

'I don't have money to buy Snickers,' Hadijat continued, addressing everyone in the kitchen. 'I don't stuff treats into my children; we give you three meals a day. But don't you sometimes get a boiled sweet with your tea?'

Hadijat turned from Liana to me.

'All my life I've tried to teach my children to be proper law-abiding citizens. I've held hundreds of children on my lap over the years; it hasn't always been easy. Remember what the first street boys were like? They were worse than these children. Think of Adam, look at Timur. No, it hasn't been easy. But this, *this* I've never experienced before. Oh yes, a difficult background, a difficult background – we've said that for a year now. Well, I'm tired of your difficult background, Liana! Don't the other children have a difficult background? Have you seen Naid's sores, do you remember the pain he was in when he came? And Naid comes home with the best marks, he hasn't given me a single grey hair. Just think of all the times I've apologised, excused you, defended you, asked forgiveness from your teacher, from the headmaster, from your classmates' parents. How often I've gone to return stolen things. But how much longer? How much longer, Liana?'

Her voice cracked.

Hadijat stood up and rested her arms heavily on the table.

'We have never punished you, Liana. We have always given you another chance. But now, the bread money! Where will this end? What am I going to do?'

New suggestions for punishment were offered, but Hadijat rejected all of them.

'Sending you back to your uncle is out of the question; you know I'll never do that. Sending you to a state orphanage is impossible; they are all closed. Throw you out on the street – I'd never do that either. Wash all the toilets for a month? Do all the housework for a year? Nothing has any effect on you . . .'

'A good thrashing,' said the two Russian women, who were trained in the methods used in Soviet orphanages.

'That doesn't solve anything,' Hadijat said. 'Beating children is useless, it just makes them tougher. If you hit a child once, the seed of hate is planted. Cutting off her hair isn't realistic. She has to go back to school, after all. It would have brought shame on all of us. The same goes for the green paint . . .'

Painting someone's head green was a punishment that the new believers, the Kadyrovtsi, had started to use. Pictures circulated on the Internet and on cell phones. Couples accused of infidelity had their heads shaved and painted green, and had to dance *lezginka* in front of clapping uniformed men while being hit, kicked, jeered at and ridiculed. A woman in one clip had a green cross painted on her head and had to run naked through the streets because she had allegedly had sex with a Russian.

'I will have nothing to do with such things,' said Hadijat.

On the wall behind her shone a glass picture of Mecca. Quotations from the Koran were engraved on it in red, pink and green.

Suddenly she shouted: 'Out! All you children out!'

They flew out like rockets, and the room was quiet.

'I think perhaps she needs a psychologist,' I suggest gently.

Hadijat looks at me intently.

'No psychologists here! Absolutely not! No psychiatrists in my house!'

'I know a child psychologist here in Grozny,' I say, 'who specialises in traumatised children. She is—'

'The psychologist she needs is Malik! She needs a father; she needs discipline, someone who won't allow this. Who would have known what to do.'

Hadijat sinks her head into her hands.

'As if I don't have enough problems? Bills. School bags. Crooks at the mayor's office. I can't think only about Liana, there are so many other children, so many other problems. Many of the children are clever and well behaved, work hard at their lessons and come home with good marks. Even if they struggle, even if they've had traumatic experiences, even if the war has robbed them of their school years. They need my care and concern, too.

But time after time it's Liana, Liana, Liana. I'd thought about trying to get a passport for her in order to send her to Lithuania — that's why we need the documents that are still at her uncle's. But now I don't dare. What if she continued to steal there? Then she would bring shame on all Chechens. People would point at my children and say, "There are those Chechens who steal." The stigma is bad enough here, although I think people can differentiate between her and the other children because we've lived here so long. But in Lithuania, in Lithuania they could come to believe that all Chechens are like that.'

Throughout the confrontation, Timur had stood outside the window looking pale. His eyes had darted from one person to another. Not a word, not a sound had escaped his lips.

There was a time when he had always defended her. Covered for her, excused her, protected her. When she said: 'It's not me, it's just my hands that reach out', he had tried to establish some guidelines for her. He had given his word of honour that she would improve. That she would stop stealing.

But this spring she had stolen twenty roubles from Malika, who hardly owned anything, who scrimped and saved and never spent money on herself, who was the first one up and the last one to bed, who prepared their meals, who had a comforting word for everyone, who covered for them when they were naughty. Malika had put twenty roubles on the window ledge under the bottle for Abu Bakar, a new baby who had come to the children's home after his unmarried teenage mother had fed him beer to make him stop crying. A twenty-rouble note under the baby's bottle, a baby whom only Malika could soothe. When one day she asked Liana to get the bottle, the note disappeared at the same time. Liana finally admitted that she had taken it, and Timur howled: 'You're not my sister any more!' Red-faced, tears streaming down his cheeks, he had turned to everyone standing there and screamed: 'I disown my sister!'

He had run out through the gate and hadn't returned until long after bedtime. Then he was the one to get a scolding. He had angrily tossed his muddy shoes on top of the others', and was reprimanded for that. He went to bed without washing. And got scolded again.

Because he was so rude, so stubborn, and so seldom listened, several of the women had become exasperated with Timur. Why didn't he come to meals with the other children, instead of ten minutes later? And when he didn't turn up at all, what made him think he could just take something out of the refrigerator? With dirty hands, what's more! Why did he think that different rules applied to him than to the other children?

When Liana continued stealing after the big confrontation, Timur stopped talking to her. He completely ignored her, no matter what she said or did. She implored him to take back what he'd said, but she didn't stop stealing. Hadijat told him that it was a great sin for a brother to disown his sister, but he wouldn't listen to anyone and acted as if she didn't exist. His old wolf personality returned. He started to smash things again. He hit the younger children when no one was watching. One day he tore down the pipes that carried water from the roof to the yard, just because the other boys didn't believe him when he said he could do it. The next day he broke into the tool cabinet instead of bothering to look for the key. Then he destroyed the bell outside the gate because he found it too slow. He constantly got into fights at school. Refused to do the jobs he was given. Would not do his lessons. Never went to bed when he should. Stopped observing prayer times.

Then one day he disappeared.

Early one morning he slammed the gate quickly behind him and walked away. He turned off the side road on to one of the main arteries from the city centre. All around him were scaffolding and buildings under construction. Pounding and pulsing. Workers hoisting cranes everywhere. Hanging outside buildings on long ropes. They removed broken windows and put in new ones.

Patched up bullet holes. Covered craters made by rockets. Painted the new buildings in gaudy colours. One lane was closed because they were laying new asphalt. Along it, trees were being planted. Timur felt he was in the way. He wanted to get out. He didn't fit in.

After a while he came to a familiar route. He had walked here so many times before. On his way to the slope by the river. When he caught the stench, his stomach knotted. But he kept on walking. He slid down the festering slope. Down there everything was the same. Nothing to collect, no sign of life except stray dogs. He looked around. Picked up a big rock and weighed it in his hand. He looked over at a pack of dogs and whistled – but no, not now. That was before. He threw the stone as far as he could into the river. Then he stood there and went on throwing stones. The current was strong, so they made no ripples; they just disappeared. Sank to the bottom.

While Grozny rose again along the strip of asphalt up above, the dump was still a forgotten place. The river was as dirty as before, the rubbish was the same. But the current must have taken with it the remains of the hut he had built around the empty pipes, which still lay there. He walked towards the big garbage dump. In the rubble of some ruined buildings he saw blocks of bricks. You didn't get such a good price any longer, because now people wanted to build with new bricks. But still. Some boys were pounding on the wall in order to separate the bricks and remove the mortar. They had hatchets, crowbars, knives. Timur scowled at them. Some were old acquaintances. He was suddenly aware of the nice clothes he was wearing, light blue trainers with dark blue racing stripes, sent from someone abroad. The boy beside him was wearing socks with holes in them, and muddy, adult-size galoshes that flopped about when he walked. He had to keep pulling up his trousers so they wouldn't fall down.

Without thinking, Timur started to knock the cement off some metal reinforcements lying there. He gathered them in a pile. They were heavier than before. He hadn't planned to come down here when he left the home, he had just wanted to get away from the women and screaming children, so he hadn't brought a knife along.

A sharp metal edge cut his palm. A nail went through his shoe. His trousers tore. His hair got oily, his cheeks black. But the pile grew. Quickly. He was better than most of them. *Quick as a squirrel. Slippery as an eel. Lithe as a fox.* The smell of freedom was rusty metal, blackened steel, the contents of an old refrigerator. The pile grew. He kept an eye on it the whole time, watched that none of the others took his scrap metal. There was no trust here. His sweat mixed with iron dust and the filth of the rubbish.

A girl walked by with a school bag.

It stung him a little. He too was a schoolboy now. The first lesson had already started. He should have been at school. But this was where he belonged. He hated the classroom. He hated the teachers. He hated sitting still.

Towards evening a van came and took what they had collected. Timur was left with some roubles. He proudly smoothed out the notes and put them in his pocket. Then he trudged home and sneaked in through the door. The other children were already in bed.

Seda came over to him and gave him a stinging cuff on the ears.

'Where have you been? Just look at you!'

He wriggled out of her grasp.

'Whore!' he shouted.

'What did you say?' Seda hissed.

'Whore! Damned whore!'

'When Mama hears . . .'

Seda was in tears. She stood there speechless. You didn't talk like that at the children's home. But no one could handle Timur any longer. He turned aside, didn't listen, slipped away.

After a week Timur had bought himself a bicycle. An old second-hand one, but a bicycle nonetheless. He cruised around Grozny. Among the buildings under construction and in neighbourhoods that still lay in ruins. Everywhere except in Zavodskoi,

where he risked meeting his uncle. At the same time, he wanted
to meet him, but he had to be prepared. He had to make a plan.

The summer holidays began. The clamour increased. Now all the
children were in the yard at the same time. If the youngest ones
were playing with a ball, Timur might storm in, take it from them
and after a few minutes the ball would be destroyed. Hadijat had
acquired a small plastic paddling pool to help the youngest children cool off. The first day, Timur jumped into it with all his
clothes on. Then he stamped in it so hard that it split and was left
lying there in a wet mass, until it too dried under the burning sun.
If there was something the younger children weren't allowed to
do, Timur would say to them: 'Do it anyway. Take it anyway.'
Everyone was afraid of him, because you never knew what his
mood would be.

Timur was the person who changed most during the time I
lived in the children's home. When I first met him, he did his best
to be an exemplary child. Now he torpedoed that effort. It was as
if he did everything he could to make people dislike him.

One day I sat down next to him on the porch steps.

'Why do you do all these things?' I asked.

He turned to me. His eyes narrowed.

'I'm evil.'

'Evil how?'

'Inside me.'

He pointed.

'Inside me, in my heart, it's full of evil. I'm very evil.'

'But you can choose whether you want to be evil or not, can't
you?'

'No, everything inside me makes me be bad. I'm mean and
wicked.'

'Is there anything you can do to get rid of the badness inside
you?'

Timur grew silent. He regarded me with his green eyes,
beneath dark eyebrows. I looked down into his face. His skin was

smooth and delicate, his lips full and red. But these were the only soft things about him. The rest was bony and angular.

'Yes. There's something I can do,' he said finally.

I looked at him.

'What?'

'There's one thing I can do. One thing I *have* to do. I have to kill him. Only then can I be good.'

'But Timur—'

'I think about it all the time. What I saw. It's always there. I have to kill him. I'm going to look him in the eye. See how afraid he is. How afraid he is of me. Then I'll kill him. That's the only way the disgusting thing inside me will go away. Only then can I be good.'

'What does the disgusting thing feel like?'

Timur thought about it. He was silent for a long time.

'It feels like burning, like fire,' he said finally. 'It burns and it stings. It's as if my heart is burning. It hurts so much, and I don't know how to put out the fire.'

One day Hadijat and I went to 'Factory Town'. Liana did not get permission to go along. Nor did Timur. Hadijat was afraid of what he might do. With the help of the neighbours we found the uncle's wife. The 'wicked aunt', as the two children called her.

She was a trembling leaf of a woman; she wore heavy make-up, a leopardskin-patterned blouse and a dirty, threadbare skirt.

'What do you want?'

Hadijat explained, and the woman in the doorway listened with frightened eyes. She was in her late twenties, thin and pale. Beside her were two small children; she held a baby in her arms. She agreed to talk to us. We walked to the edge of the estate and sat down on a bench next to a busy road so that no one could hear us.

'Are they all right?' she asked in a trembling voice.

Hadijat explained that she needed the children's documents.

'I'm sure you won't believe me, but I wish them all the best.'

The woman began to cry.

'I live in a hell. I don't know what to do.'

She told us about her life with the man she had been married off to, scarcely knowing him, three years earlier. Timur and Liana were already living with him. Most of the time he had sent her home to her parents. He wanted to live alone with the children.

'The children were terrible from the start,' she said. 'Have you ever seen such wicked eyes? Those two are depraved. But they've seen nothing good in life either, poor things. My husband shoved them down on the floor and beat them with a cable. I couldn't do a thing. I'm sure they hate me for that. When we went to the house my husband owns in a nearby village, he put a collar on Timur, like a cow, while he laughed and made fun of him. And here, do you know what Timur did? He put a two-year-old down a deep hole where no one could hear his cries, and let him sit there until nightfall. Such a bad boy. Full of bad blood. He hit the smaller children. Liana did, too. She pinched and bit.'

One day Liana told her about the uncle's abuse. Shortly after that, the police came and got the children.

'My husband went completely mad. I don't dare leave him alone with my girls. He might do the same with them,' she wept.

'How can you live with a man like that?' Hadijat asked.

'My dearest wish in life would be to leave him.'

'Then do it. You've got sufficient grounds. Islam will allow you to leave him. You should also report him to the police. To think that such an animal goes free!'

Hadijat pursed her lips into an indignant knot.

'If I report him, my brother will kill me.'

'What?'

'I asked my brother what I should do. He said that if I reported my husband to the police he would kill me with his own hands. It would be too shameful for the family if a wife reported her husband. "A wife must always stand by her husband, no matter what," my brother said. But, Hadijat, couldn't you report him to the police?' she burst out. 'Please report him, Hadijat!'

'We don't have the strength,' said Hadijat. 'Nor do we have money for a lawyer. And he would take terrible revenge when he got out. It could affect all my children. Besides, if he isn't convicted, if they don't have enough proof, then he would come after us right away. Seeking revenge.'

The women sat in silence. The traffic roared past.

'Can you go away somewhere?' I asked.

'I have to stay here because of the children.'

'Take them with you.'

'He has the right to the children.'

'We will take you if you come, but you must leave the children with your husband,' the brother had said. 'If you bring the children with you, we'll send them back to him,' he had added.

In Chechnya, if there is a divorce, the father keeps the children. If he dies, his family has the right to the fatherless children, even if the mother is alive. The mother and children would then usually live with the father's parents or one of his brothers. If she remarries, she must leave the children with the father's family. Often she never gets to see them again.

'Leaving the children with my husband is out of the question. He hits them if they get in his way, if they irritate him. And then I'm so afraid for my girls . . . But now I must go; he'll be angry . . .'

The woman trembled.

'I will try to find the documents,' she promised.

Back at the children's home, I went to see Liana, who was sitting in a corner, limp as a rag. No one wanted to play with her; no one wanted to talk to her. Her feet lay at a twisted angle, flat against the floor, her arms rested heavily on the rug. She sat like an old woman with her head sunk between her shoulders listening to the conversations around her. Her eyes impassively followed those who were speaking.

She looked up when I arrived, but didn't say anything.

I didn't know what to say, either. Liana examined her fingernails. She had done yet another stupid thing. She had told a girl in

her class about the uncle's abuse. The girl had listened dumbfounded, and Liana had felt that she had finally found a girlfriend
with whom she could share everything. But the next day the girl
had come over to her and said: 'You're not a proper girl any
more', and repeated Liana's confession to the whole class. Then,
just before the summer holidays she was told she had to repeat
class five because she hadn't learned anything.

Her nails were flecked with peeling pearl nail polish. She sat
picking at them, trying to remove the polish by scraping it off.
When Hadijat had searched Liana's shelf for the missing bread
money, she had found the shiny black handbag and opened it. The
pearl nail polish was Hadijat's; the key ring with the monkey on
it was also hers, a birthday present from the younger boys in
Lithuania. Hadijat had angrily emptied the handbag on to the floor
and thrown away the contents.

The only thing left on Liana's shelf was the red dress with the
ruched waist and ruffled skirt. Soon she would grow out of it, and
it would go to someone else.

Two girls walked past the corner without looking at her.

The previous day Adam and Zaur had tied her to a chair and
taken out the scissors to threaten her. Because, once again, she
had stolen something, and now the other children couldn't
stand it any longer. Marha and Aishat, who were one year
younger but would now be in the same class as her, told Hadijat
that they refused to go to school if Liana was there. The others
in her class had started to point at them, too. 'Basayev's children! Maskhadov's children!' they shouted. 'Thieves and
tramps!'

'Besides, she's as stupid as a *kolkhoznitsa* – a peasant woman,'
the two sisters complained. 'Actually, there's no point in her
going to school. She can't get anything into her skull anyway!'

Hadijat got angry.

'If you don't want to go to school because Liana goes there,
then you can just not go!'

The smart little schoolgirls said nothing.

That evening a weary Hadijat said to me:

'Everyone sees her as a lost cause. But I'm not that kind of a mother. I can't just swap a bad Liana for a good Liana!'

Night has fallen. Liana stands up; it's time to go to bed. She wants to come up to my room and show me her exercise book from school, she says. Her steps are heavy. Gone are the floating gait, the elfin dancing. Her head slumps, her back is bent. Liana wants us to sit down on the bench outside the room I share with Hadijat.

A gust of wind tears through the yard. The blue plastic sheet hung up for shade inflates and flaps in the sudden squall.

'I can never forget what happened,' Liana says, and looks at me before her eyes go down to her nails again.

Raindrops drum against the plastic now.

'I hate the night. Nights are so terrible. I have such awful dreams. But in the morning when I wake up, I just want to go back to sleep. Don't want the day to begin. At night I hope that I'll never wake up again. I want to sleep, and I'm afraid to sleep. I pray to God every day that I'll stop stealing. But He doesn't help me. I don't know why. Maybe I don't deserve it.'

The wild apple tree rustles in the neighbour's yard.

Liana isn't very kind. Sometimes she hits out at the smaller children, sometimes she cuddles them. She's not very tidy, not very proper; she's slow, she wriggles her way out of things. In her exercise books she has drawn hearts with a red felt pen where there should have been numbers. A decorated Christmas tree roughly sketched with a ballpoint pen covers the pages where poetry should have been copied out. She opens the book clasped in her hand.

One page has been torn out.

She presses a creased page of lined paper into my hand.

'Can you give this to Mama?'

I nod.

'Read it first. Have I written it correctly?'

I smooth out the page. Wreathed in an ornate border are the words: 'Mama! I am very guilty for what I have done. Please forgive me. You do so very much for me. I love you very much. I am very ashamed. I give you my word that I will never. I have made you very sad. Forgive me! Liana.'

Thank You

I want to thank all those who have shared their life stories with me.

In particular, I want to thank Hadijat and Malik, who made it possible for me to get to know the children in Grozny, in order to understand better what happens when you grow up in the midst of war.

I also want to thank everyone at the Memorial office in Grozny, especially Shamil and Lida, who helped me on my travels.

The two main characters, Hadijat and Malik, have read their own stories, as well as the children's. They have approved everything that deals with them and the children's home.

All the children in the book have been given new names. The adults have chosen whether or not to use their true identities.

Being included in a book like this involves risk. But, as Hadijat said: it is also dangerous to keep silent.

All who are included in the book have themselves chosen to tell their stories. I want to thank them for their extraordinary courage.

Oslo, 17 October 2007
Åsne Seierstad